KELLY

Paris-Nice 1982, the champion Kelly is about to emerge. This stage win over Roger de Vlaeminck at St Etienne was a portent of things to come.

KELLY

A Biography of Sean Kelly

DAVID WALSH

HARRAP
LONDON

For Linda and Mary

First published in Great Britain 1986
by HARRAP Ltd
19-23 Ludgate Hill, London EC4M 7PD

Reprinted 1986

ISBN 0 245-54331-7

Design by Roger King Graphic Studios, Poole
Printed and bound in Great Britain
by Billings, Worcester

Contents

Illustrations

Acknowledgments

Small towns all over Western Europe have had to suffer the stranger coming to their race and winning. Sean Kelly was one of the most formidable strangers. So often has he won that he no longer seems the outsider. To win admiration in strange towns Kelly had to work harder than most of us can imagine. His dedication is the *raison d'être* for this book. Kelly's trust and co-operation were of considerable help to me in putting together the pieces of his life.

I am also indebted to the many people who helped in the exploration of the Kelly-fascination. I hope they enjoyed talking about Kelly as much as I enjoyed listening. A particular debt is owed to Linda Kelly, Nellie and Jack Kelly, Joe Kelly, Dan Grant, Tony Ryan, David Power, John Lackey, Pat McQuaid, Jim McQuaid (sr), Ronny Onghena, Stephen Roche, Jean de Gribaldy, Jean Beaufils, Herman and Elise Nys. Their assistance was of enormous value.

I am also deeply grateful to the *Irish Press Group* and particularly Adhamhnan O'Sullivan (*Sunday Press* Sports Editor) who lit the fuse of enthusiasm by sending me to France six years ago to report on Kelly. They were the pioneering days. My fellow-journalist and friend Sean Flynn (The *Irish Times*) is thanked for his efforts to improve the manuscript. I cannot forget the many cycling journalists encountered all over Europe who were prepared to discuss Kelly at any time. The fruit of those conversations pervades this book. Finally, *L'Equipe*. Its reportage of cycling was of incalculable assistance in tracing the story of Kelly's career.

Prologue

Professional cycling has never been an occupation for the dreamer. The man who organized the first Tour de France in 1903, Henri Desgrange, was an ambitious pragmatist. An organizer who recognized reality. A daily allowance, five francs, was paid to each of the first fifty to finish and so Desgrange got himself sixty volunteers for the inaugural race around France. Over eighty years later things have not changed greatly. The men who perform in the Tour do so because it is their way of life, their means of earning bread and water, of providing shelter. Some turn the pedals better than others, some move well in the mountains, others die when the gradients get steep. But nobody fools around. A man who cannot climb will always suffer in the mountains; those who are unable to sprint never win sprints. Accepting what lies beyond one's capabilities is an integral part of the survival process.

A warm summer's day, July 1984. The thirteen-kilometre Alpe d'Huez climb seemed an eternity to Kelly. At first sitting upright in the saddle, trying to churn a big gear. Then out of the saddle, shifting position, changing gear, hoping that one of the spectators would rush from the roadside and push him all the way to the top. Wanting to scream *Poussez-moi* but not being able to. Thinking this and all the while getting nowhere. Kelly had moved into the red zone and found his body unable to provide an escape route. A number of riders passed him, each one offering a grating reminder of the mounting losses. Up a little further Beat Breu, one of the early leaders, was similarly hurting. Even worse. Barely conscious, he zig-zagged up that horrendous mountain, maintaining motion by pure instinct. Even Kelly passed Breu. Later he would laugh that somebody else had managed to go even slower than he up Alpe d'Huez. The laugh of a man who wasn't amused.

Nine minutes after the Tour de France principals Laurent Fignon and Bernard Hinault had acted out their epic battle on Alpe d'Huez, Sean Kelly crossed the finish line. Nobody recalls seeing him. A few yards past the line Kelly had wheeled around and flowed back down the road towards the team hotel. There wasn't anything to say. At the start of the 151-kilometre race stage from Grenoble to Alpe d'Huez Kelly had been seventh overall and a possibility for Tour glory. Now he had fallen to twelfth. Journalists could form their own conclusions. They did.

That evening it grew cold on the mountain. Kelly and his Skil team were lodged in a hotel in the village. How do champions feel four hours after a crushing defeat? The question touched my curiosity. Enough to seek out the defeated one. The hotel bar was doing a lively trade on this July evening. One of those enjoying a drink was the Skil masseur. Our eyes met and he discreetly supplied information about Kelly's room number. It was five minutes after ten o'clock. For cyclists on the Tour de France it was probably past bedtime and definitely past the hour for entertaining journalists. Walking up the stairs I wondered whether the visit would be appreciated.

Kelly was on the inside bed, sitting up and reading the day's classification sheets. His team-mate Eric Caritoux turned uneasily in the other bed. This was a visit he could do without. Cyclists must sleep. Journalists must find another hour for talking. Caritoux's displeasure was obvious. Kelly didn't appear to mind. What he had felt on the mountain earlier in the day had been utter helplessness. Now he was reading the official confirmation. There was an aura of sadness about him. A Tour de France cyclist reading his own obituary. You looked and asked the obvious question. Did not Alpe d'Huez 1984 convince this athlete that the Tour de France would always lie beyond his reach?

Kelly looked up, at once boyish and vulnerable: 'Yes, I suppose I can never win the Tour.' He said it on the night of 16 July 1984. Cycling is not a sport for the dreamer.

1 A Champion is Born

The bike stood upside down in the garage of Herman and Elise Nys's home at Vilvoorde, near Brussels. Every centimetre of the machine caked in mud. The once shining aluminium now dull, only glinting here and there. Written across the stem leading into the handlebars was the name 'Sean Kelly'. Mud was smeared across the two words. Blotting out a few letters but not wiping away the name. The slime hadn't succeeded in killing the name, just as it hadn't triumphed over the man who had piloted that bike through the filth, the mire, the slop, the hell of Paris-Roubaix. Two days after the race had ended the bike stood upside down in the Nys garage, unwashed. Deliberately so.

Kelly, too, had been caked in the same mud. The slime that might have obliterated. Humans must wash and the after race shower in the velodrome had purged Kelly of the Paris-Roubaix legacy. Back at Brussels the normal Monday routine for Kelly would include restoring the bike to shining health. This Monday came and went but the mud survived. Similarly with Tuesday. It survived because it had carried rider No. 185 to victory in the most important one-day classic cycle race in the world. Carried the first English speaker to victory in this most European of tests. Journalists came to interview Kelly. Some were introduced to the muddied survivor of Sunday's race. They marvelled at how the bike could carry so much dirt and yet move so swiftly. That dull, brown coating of dirt vividly reflected the achievement of the man who had survived. As long as the mud remained there was physical evidence of one's triumph. Kelly was indulging himself.

By Wednesday morning the romance of Roubaix was waning, was being cast into the background by the challenge of the Liege-Bastogne-Liege classic which came four days later. Sure, Paris-Roubaix was big: hadn't Coppi, Bobet, Merckx and Hinault all claimed it in their day? Kelly knew it guaranteed him a place near the top. But sitting down and dwelling upon past achievements held little interest for him. What about the next race? If he could win that, then he would relax. By Wednesday morning that mudied Paris-Roubaix veteran in the garage was a source of irritation. Kelly wondered why he had been so silly. Why had he taken the damned bike home from Roubaix when he could have given it to his mechanic? Now he would have to wash away that dirt himself. He had been a fool. The romantic imposter was being banished; the pragmatist was ready to return.

There was always the danger that Sean Kelly would career through the world of professional cycling and not leave the mark which would adequately record the measure of his ability. He would win many races, earn staggering amounts of money, but only those who had ridden shoulder to shoulder with Kelly would fully appreciate his talents. That was where Kelly stood as winter died and spring brought fresh life to the new year, 1984. George Orwell's year. In Orwell's grim scheme of things this was to be the year of truth for the world. Big Brother would emerge and cast shadows into every corner. The year came and went and Orwell's prophecies remained unfulfilled. For those who maintained an interest in the world of professional cycling the year did produce a Big Brother. He came on a bike, from Carrick-on-Suir, saying little, but exercising a total domination over his world.

The advent of spring is always welcomed by enthusiasts of the bike game. Another cycling season. Starved of the toil and fascination of road racing during the months of

November, December and January, the cycling fraternity
returned to the sport with a particular fervour in 1984.
This February there were special reasons for welcoming
spring and another chapter in the history of the game.
Bernard Hinault, then a four-times winner of the Tour
de France, was re-entering the competitive arena after a
serious knee operation. That operation had forced him
to leave the bike in his shed for the final six months of
the previous season. Related to Hinault's return was the
position of Laurent Fignon. In Hinault's absence,
Fignon, only twenty-two at the time, won the Tour de
France, and 1984 was now going to tell us whether
Fignon had merely been fortunate to fall upon a Tour
without Hinault or whether he was a champion strong
enough to withstand the return of the old master.

There was also the question which hung over the
immediate future of that Irishman, Kelly. After seven
years of trying he had finally won a one-day classic at
the very end of the 1983 season. The common view was
that Kelly always lacked confidence and that his success
in the autumnal Tour of Lombardy would deliver to the
world a changed man. On the night of that first classic
win Jean de Gribaldy, his *directeur sportif*, had said: 'Now
that Sean has got over a major psychological barrier, I
expect him to go on and win many more classics.'

With Kelly it is always difficult to calculate the effects
of victories and defeats. If he had become a more
confident athlete after the first classic success in
Lombardy, the world was not to know. He again win-
tered in Carrick-on-Suir. Maybe there was something in
the fact that he agreed to join his team-mates on a
January skiing holiday, an annual gathering he had
steadfastly avoided all through his professional career.
Hints that he had become a little more assured were
taken from his pre-season training pattern. Normally
January had been the month when the preparation
began in earnest, when daily spins would begin at 30 or

40 miles and have risen to 100 or 110 by the end of the month.

This year it was different. For with the skiing break, bad weather in Ireland and a more relaxed outlook, Kelly had departed for the team's training camp in the south of France with far less fitness than would have been the case in previous seasons. He would complain during the early races, particularly during the eight-day Paris-Nice, that his training schedule had been severely disrupted in January and how he struggled to find his best form. Yet his struggles were relative. They were also premeditated. Throughout the months of January, February and March Kelly had hoped that the change in training pattern would enable him to produce his best form during the month of April. Outside the month of July and the Tour de France April is the most important month in the cycling season, with a series of highly popular one-day classic races.

January had been a month of skiing and missed training spins; he had spent February trying to catch up on lost ground in the south of France and Kelly was racing in earnest during the early days of March. Although a few pounds heavier than his optimum racing weight he still won Paris-Nice. It was Kelly's third consecutive victory in this eight-day event and the performance meant that he had equalled Eddy Merckx's record of winning three-in-a-row. Kelly was getting into good company. On the Wednesday that Kelly won Paris-Nice, 14 March, he travelled back to his team hotel in a car with Jean de Gribaldy. One was as excited as the other, reliving the events of the week like two school chums discussing their latest prank. De Gribaldy and Kelly were almost euphoric. They sensed that if a major victory, as Paris-Nice was, could be achieved with 90 per cent fitness then the immediate future was rich in promise.

After Paris-Nice Kelly and his Skil team left the Côte d'Azure and travelled east to Milan for the Milan-San Remo Classic. This was his first major one-day test of the season. Kelly rode prominently all through but the old caution was still in evidence. When the Italian star Francesco Moser broke away on the Poggio descent five kilometres from the finish, Kelly refused to lead the charge behind him. Others decided that if Sean Kelly wasn't prepared to assume responsibility for the pursuit then Moser would probably stay clear. Over the following three days Kelly's conservatism would be criticized by many, most notably by his team-mate Rene Bittinger and de Gribaldy. Had the Tour of Lombardy altered anything? Winning the mass sprint for second in San Remo provided no compensation. A second place that had been an absolute failure.

Milan-San Remo finishes on the Via Roma — the street has become almost as famous as the race itself. That Saturday afternoon Kelly stood astride his machine on the Via Roma, swore abruptly and bemoaned another lost classic: 'If I had won this I could have gone off on a holiday.' Deep down, he knew that despondency was out of place. His form was still improving but he had a few miles to go before he would be at his very best. He longed for that instinctive feeling of near invincibility but he would continue to wait patiently. Milan-San Remo had fallen on Ireland's most important feast day, St Patrick's Day (17 March), and it would have been appropriate for Kelly to mark the occasion with a victory. Victory in this Italian classic, like the holiday, would have to wait for another time.

On the following day, Sunday 18 March, Kelly left San Remo and returned to the south of France where he trained for a week with his close friend Stephen Roche. Both Linda Kelly and Lydia Roche were invited to the training week although they saw their partners infrequently. Generally only at evening meals. The two bike-men would slip out of the hotel early in the morning, train until mid-afternoon, retire to bed for a few hours sleep and then surface in time for an evening meal. At about

nine-thirty they departed for bed and left their two
ladies to while away the time planning the next day's
shopping expedition. Cycling widows, even when staying
with their husbands on the Riviera.

The week was well spent. Kelly's condition had been
at a point where six days of uninterrupted training
would bring it to the finest pitch. The six days ended on
a Friday. That evening he travelled towards Antibes, a
town on the coast which would host the start of the
Criterium Internationale. This was a race he had won in
1983 and there were indications that he would once
again do well. Run by the organization which puts the
Tour de France on the road, the Criterium Internationale is a two-day, three-stage race. Its format involves
a Saturday stage over a relatively flat course, a mount-
ainous stage on Sunday morning and then a concluding
time trial on that evening. The idea is that each rider is
invited to display the three most important attributes of
the sport: sprinting, climbing and time-trialing. That
weekend Sean Kelly won all three stages; his victory in
the mountain stage had been over two minutes. It
seemed then that Kelly had moved on to a new plain, a
level he never previously attained.

A week later Kelly was taking his place in the Tour de
Flanders, probably the fourth most prestigious one-day
classic. It was 1 April. His preparation over the three
preceding months had been designed to produce an
athlete with brilliant form during this month. The cycling world had watched Kelly closely, understood what
he was trying to do, and he left Saint Niklaas for the
journey through Flanders as most people's likely victor.
Again, he was second. Agonizing and frustrating because in this race Kelly had been strongest. By far. On
the most difficult climb in the race, the cobbled Mur de
Grammont, he had attacked viciously. The race suddenly
was in a confusing swirl, splinters flew everywhere,
only five could follow Kelly. Over the final twenty

kilometres Kelly appeared in control.

The appearance was more apparent than real. Kelly's five companions began to explore counter-attacking opportunities. One of the five, Johan Lammerts of Holland, shot clear immediately after a series of aborted attacks. Kelly had grown weary of trying to orchestrate a one-man performance. He refused to pursue Lammerts. The race was over. Defeat had sprung from the fact that the five riders in the break opted to profit from the favourite's work. The rules of the sport permit such tactics; ethically it is deemed unacceptable. At the finish town in Meerbeke fifty or sixty journalists watched the concluding part of the race in a press tent. When Lammerts got clear about forty of them stood up and indignantly walked away. They were angry with Kelly and Cycling for allowing the best man to lose.

The following morning *L'Equipe*, the French Sports daily, ran a headline which said: 'Kelly Beaten by Five Cheating Wolves.' In Belgium one sportswriter explained Kelly's defeat by asserting that he 'sat on his wallet'. Suggesting that if he had been prepared to buy the services of one or two of the riders in the break then victory would certainly have been his. A good many people felt cheated, not least Kelly himself. With adrenalin still charging through his body he said some uncharacteristically positive things in Meerbeke seconds after the end of the race. He begrudged Lammerts victory, saying it was no way to win a race, that if everybody waited to profit from the riding of others there would be no good racing. Then Kelly delivered the most startling line of all: 'I will get my revenge in Paris-Roubaix.'

A 265-kilometre race, Paris-Roubaix is regarded as the greatest one-day classic of all. Attraction lies in its severity. The second half of the race involves numerous tracts of cobbled roads or pave. The combined distance of the cobbled sections is likely to exceed fifty kilometres. Over such a treacherous route nobody expects to win. The ambitious and talented hope to survive. But Kelly had intimated that he would win, that he would avenge the April Fools Day defeat at the Tour of Flanders. Kelly was asking for trouble. Out of character and fraught with dangerous possibilities, he had deliberately offered his throat to the executioners.

After the Flanders race the Skil team flew to Spain for the five-day Tour du Pays Basque which was to begin the following day. Kelly had not wanted to go, preferring to remain in Belgium and compete in the Ghent-Wevelgem race in mid-week. A second category classic, Ghent-Wevelgem did not interest de Gribaldy who wanted Kelly in Spain: 'While he is there he can prepare for Paris-Roubaix without newspaper men breaking down his door. He can race each day, eat at the normal times and get to bed each night at nine.' Had he been in Brussels the pre-Paris-Roubaix journalistic frenzy would have complicated Kelly's life, would have meant continual media demands. Kelly disagreed but de Gribaldy had a point.

De Gribaldy had told Kelly that he need not win in Spain, that his chief concern was for a regular daily routine before Paris-Roubaix. Such was Kelly's form that avoiding victory was a considerable task. He found himself in the leader's jersey after the first stage and retained it right through the race. He attempted to contrive a situation for one of his team-mates to take possession of the jersey but the plan could never be executed. Almost against his wishes Kelly had won the Tour du Pays Basque. In the process he had won four stages of the race and he granted another to the Spaniard Julian Gorospe when the latter rode positively during a mountain breakaway with Kelly.

He arrived back in Paris on Saturday, the day before Paris-Roubaix. The sequence meant that for Sean Kelly everything depended on this one race, the journey through hell to the velodrome in Roubaix. If Kelly had any doubts about the relevance of this race to his career he

had only to read the *L'Equipe* of that weekend. The
newspaper's colour magazine used a photograph of
Kelly on the front cover and posed the question: 'Will
An Ordinary Champion Become a Super Champion?'
Many had grown weary of Kelly's tantalizing failures in
the classics. If he wanted to be remembered as one of
the great riders of his era he had better win this race.

On the morning of 8 April Sean Kelly was one of the
last riders to show up for the signing-on ceremony in
the giant square at Compiègne, a town about 100 kilometres north of Paris. For one who was about to
undergo the greatest examination of his sporting life,
Kelly was remarkably relaxed. So much so that anyone
who spoke with him remarked upon it. All Kelly would
say was that he needed luck, the luck to avoid bad luck.
This was the race of the hazards, cycling's Grand
National. Crashes, punctures, mechanical problems were
par for this course. The adventure set out from Compiègne; Kelly might have been the favourite but that
didn't prevent him smiling as the giant train of bike-men
wriggled out of town.

Paris-Roubaix patterns don't vary. The first 100 kilometres take place over ordinary roads. No cobbles.
During this part of the race the strong men try to
preserve their energies. Lesser riders are tacitly encouraged to break away and provide some amusement for
the crowds that line the route before the first section of
pave. This year had been no different. First two riders
go clear, then another two; approaching Neuvilly and
the first cobbles their advantage on the pack was twelve
minutes. Nobody behind them fretted. The cobbles
would call a halt to their escapade. Kelly had ridden
Paris-Roubaix often enough to appreciate the importance of being in the front line of the big bunch when
the first section of pave is confronted. Alongside
Stephen Roche he led the pack into Neuvilly and the
first cobbles. The race was about to begin and the

ordinary champion was in position to become a super champion.

The cobbles lie at the heart of the confusion and chaos of Paris-Roubaix. The pieces of pave that had forced journalists to subtitle this classic: 'l'Enfer du Nord' (the Hell of the North). Once on the pave Kelly was absorbed in the struggle. A struggle against the best cyclists in the world and a personal rendezvous with Destiny. He maintained a place close to the head of the pack and at the approach to one of the most frightening sections of pave, Wallers-Arenberg, the original leaders had just a two-minutes advantage. By the time the three kilometres of pave through the forest of Wallers-Arenberg had been crossed the race had taken on an entirely new shape. Wallers had taken a gigantic toll. The brave breakaways that so animated the early part of the race were obliterated. Cyrille Guimard, probably the greatest French *directeur sportif*, would say afterwards: 'At Wallers half of my riders were on their backs and the other half flat on their faces.' Greg LeMond, Laurent Fignon and Marc Madiot numbered amongst Guimard's Renault casualties.

English journalist John Wilcockson has written knowingly of the forest: 'To the men who have survived this far on the road to Roubaix, this forest is the darkest, deepest jungle. One can almost feel the presence of Cerberus, the gate-keeper to the underworld, lurking among the tall, sinister trees, waiting to draw innocent cyclists into his black, boggy clutches.' Entering the forest Kelly and LeMond were near the front. LeMond recalls: 'He was riding within himself while I was going flat out.' Soon after LeMond crashed, Kelly had to swerve into the forest to avoid tumbling and, escaping the dreaded Cerberus, he returned from the trees.

But the unscheduled deviation had been at a cost. Kelly lost his place in the first fifteen riders and two of the strong men, Gregor Braun and Alain Bondue, had attacked. Both were members of the La Redoute team and, given that they would co-operate fully, their breaking clear was an act of immense importance. Leaving Wallers, Kelly was about seventeenth or eighteenth in the line, one-and-a-half minutes behind the two La Redoute riders. There was a little more than 100 kilometres remaining and the pervading question was whether the two leaders had shown their hand too early. A pursuit group of fourteen riders formed, to be joined later by another ten. Kelly was the only member of the Skil team in the twenty-four. He was, as ever, alone. Fighting his own battles. He felt abounding power in his legs, he wanted to go faster and he worried about the effectiveness of the pursuit. Maybe Bondue and Braun would not be recaptured? What then? Moving fluently, the two leaders had already considered that glorious possibility and were in agreement that they would cross the finish line side by side, hands joined aloft. Two winners of the one Paris-Roubaix. History.

Kelly sought advice from de Gribaldy back at the team car. To attack or not to attack? De Gribaldy advised patience, offering the view that Bondue and Braun had been given so much rope they would eventually hang themselves. A few kilometres later Kelly was back seeking approval to cut loose. The team manager continued to utter a cautious message. Kelly was not listening any more. He wanted to find out things about himself, about his rivals. On a flat concrete road, without a cobble in sight, Kelly stamped on the pedals. His sharp acceleration destroying the unity of the group. Where there had been over twenty riders, now there were only eight. That effort pleased, for it suggested that most limbs were tired. Bondue and Braun retained a one-and-a-half minutes advantage but, with fifty kilometres to Roubaix, nobody was quite ready to panic.

Through Kelly's frightened eyes seven companions were far too many. With just five in the Tour of Flanders seven days earlier he had been undone. He had to assault his companions for the second time in the space of six kilometres. On this occasion he chose a jolting, difficult section of pave. Anybody wishing to respond would have to work. There were forty-seven kilometres to Roubaix. His bike covered in mud, his face contorted into a position which allowed his mouth to suck in air, Kelly soon had a clear lead. Jacques Hanegraaf was the rider immediately behind but he was unable to counter. Those who stood on the small ridge at the side of that cobbled track had been fortunate. A father and son stood there, both wearing anoraks, rubber boots and captivated expressions. Dad glanced at Kelly and then whipped his glance back to see who was reacting. The son, a red-haired boy, stood transfixed. His eyes followed the rigid pedal strokes of the one in red and white. In his face the little boy effused a feeling of awe and incomprehension.

Hennie Kuiper tried to pick up the thread of pursuit but couldn't. Then the tall figure of Rudy Rogiers dug deep in search of his last morsels of energy and sprinted away in chase of Kelly. A couple of kilometres later he latched on to the back wheel of the Irishman. Second in the World Amateur Road Race in 1981 Rogiers was a welcome companion for as a non-sprinter he offered no threat. It was two against two: Bondue and Braun against Kelly and Rogiers. The pursuit was controlled but vigorous. Rogiers was willing to help, but Kelly grew impatient with his lack of force and ended up doing most of the pace-making. All the time Kelly kept thinking of how long Braun and Bondue had been out there.

Eight kilometres of pounding on the pedals had halved the deficit to 45 seconds but it took another eighteen kilometres to reel in the tiring leaders. The two pairs joined on a wide stretch of roadway twenty kilometres from Roubaix. Kelly soon accelerated and Braun was shed from the small group. There remained just Bondue and Rogiers. All of France warmed to the efforts of Bondue. It was his birthday and Roubaix was his home town. A perfect story. Life operates on a different wavelength.

Fatique had eaten away at Bondue and on a stretch of mud at a place called La Vache Bleue (the Blue Cow) Alain Bondue fell, losing his chance of victory in the moment it had taken for his back wheel to slither sideways. Braun and Bondue had indeed hung themselves.

Bondue did rise from the mud of The Blue Cow, did pursue and eventually delivered a compelling perform-ance as gallant loser. At the front Kelly was now within sight of the achievement for which he desperately craved. He contemplated leaving Rogiers before the velodrome but resisted the temptation as his fellow-traveller had been good company and, anyway, he couldn't sprint. Into the Roubaix velodrome Kelly tried to be professional, refused to take Rogiers's modest sprinting talent for granted. The Belgian was forced to lead into the stadium, Kelly remained directly in his slip-stream. Half-way around the track Rogiers accelerated; Kelly did not seem to alter his tempo in any way and still stayed exactly one bike-length behind.

With 150 metres to go Kelly steered his bike a little to the right of Rogiers and flew past. With fifty metres to go Kelly led by thirty. Rogiers had endorsed his reputation as a non-sprinter. It was all over for Kelly. The near misses didn't count for so much any more. Eight years as a professional and, at last, vindication. What was it that the newspaper had said? Super-champion.

Since the first days of 1984 Kelly had won thirteen races. More than most professionals win in a career. On the road to Roubaix those successes meant nothing. Then there was but one race to win, allowing one's life to be judged in the Hell of the North. That evening Kelly rambled on contentedly for the journalists. The time for worrying about his career had passed. All in one day. He now had something that couldn't be taken away. The race that Sean Kelly from Curraghduff in County Waterford had to win. The race he did win. His career recollections would now never begin with a regret.

2 Curraghduff

Champions, it is claimed, are born. A statement that is only true in the strictest sense. Find the human who hasn't been born? But the popular notion that champions inherit the seeds of greatness somewhere in the conception process is one that deserves instant dismissal. Sean Kelly didn't enter the world with especially important gifts. Had his home been located near any other rural town and not Carrick-on-Suir then it is certain that he would never have learned to race a bike. He might now be a bricklayer and not a millionaire cyclist. He never had the authoritative presence of the embryonic champion, never spoke with the assurance of one destined to occupy a position in the front line of international sportsmen. And Kelly never, ever, tried to fit himself into the conventional mould of the champion. Ambition was a word that meant nothing. Yet Kelly can't be seen as some bizarre specimen at odds with the norm. His history reiterates the fact that the champion stereotype fails to acknowledge the essential individualism of the few who reach the summit.

But how then does one explain his rise to the pinnacle of world cycling. Rationally. It all happened in a way that nobody could have predicted, much less foreseen. Two years before Kelly became a professional cyclist the idea of earning a living on the bike hadn't caused a momentary ripple on his consciousness. He was going to be a bricklayer, would do some cycling for a time and that was it. If he got to compete in the Olympic Games he would then have achieved something. There hadn't been an Irish

professional cyclist for twelve years and if somebody had
said that the next one would emanate from Carrick, Kelly
would have laughed and said no chance.

The second son of Jack and Nellie Kelly, Sean was
introduced to the world on a farm where only the
essentials mattered. Getting cows milked, collecting eggs,
saving hay, watching over the vegetables, making sure the
sow didn't smother any of her piglets after birth. Jack had
come from a family of small farmers in Jonestown, near
Rathgormack, County Waterford, and only a mile from
where his own farm is located at Curraghduff. Nellie was a
native of Raheen, a townsland near the village of Temple-
orum in County Kilkenny. Nellie's people, the Fitz-
patricks, were also small farmers and her brother, Gerry,
still runs the Fitzpatrick farm at Raheen.

Before marrying Jack in 1950 Nellie had been married
to Martin Power, who died after a stroke. That marriage
bore one son, Martin, who now lives with his wife Helen in
Curraghduff, less than a mile from the Kelly family farm.
Sean and Martin were always close and it is a habit of
Kelly's to refer to his three brothers: Martin, Joe and
Vinny. His reference to Martin is never qualified. Martin
is just Martin, his brother. When Kelly became a professional cyclist he would sometimes stay with Martin and
Helen in their bungalow during his winter breaks. In the
early years he worked for Martin during the off-season to
supplement his earnings as a cyclist.

It is probable that some of Kelly's athleticism came from
his mother's family. Nellie has another brother, Richard,
who lives in Ballygunner, County Waterford. Richard's
son Shay was Irish High Jump champion for a number of
years and has in recent times applied himself to the
Pentathlon. Shay's success in this discipline demonstrates
that his range of talents stretches far beyond the high
jump. As Sean grew up, his first cousin's high jump career
would have been at its peak and would not have gone
unnoticed by the Kellys of Curraghduff.

Four years after their marriage Jack and Nellie Kelly had their first son, Joseph. That was 1954. Two years later the second son arrived. Nellie Kelly delivered Sean on 24 May 1956 at the Belleville Maternity Home in Waterford. Nellie recalls the day as only a mother could: 'It was a Whit Monday, there was horse racing in Tramore and I was worried that my doctor, the late Dr Derivan from John Street in Carrick, was going to miss the races because of Sean's arrival. But when the doctor came back to see me the following day he said it was all okay, he had only missed the first race. I can remember the doctor remarking then that the baby was unusually strong. Even as a new infant he would wriggle out of your hands if you weren't careful.'

The new baby was christened John James, after his father. But, in the great tradition of Irish curiosities, his name was immediately changed to Sean so that he would not be confused with his Dad, the real John James Kelly. Now neither version is known by the names which appear on their birth certificates. The senior one is called Jack and the son Sean. Later in life the casually acquired Christian name 'Sean' would lead to unending awkwardness as continental Europe grappled with the pronounciation and most came up with 'Sian'. Six years after the arrival of Sean, Jack and Nellie Kelly had their third son, Vincent. Three boys, all of whom were destined to serve exacting but rewarding apprenticeships on the farm.

It wasn't a big farm, just forty-eight acres, but enough to support a family of five. 'Subsistence agriculture' might be how the textbooks would categorize life on the Kelly holding in Curraghduff. Most of the family's needs were satisfied from within the farm: milk from the cows, eggs from the hens, vegetables from the garden, meat from the killing of livestock and when the boys were able to walk they were deemed ready for work. Sean reckons he was no more than seven or eight when he did his turn at the milking. At that time he was attending Crehana National

School, about a-mile-and-a-half from his home. He would
go to school each morning with his older brother Joe.

Joe remembers the journey being enacted at speed: 'I
suppose we were like most young fellows at that age —
walking was too dull. Anyway we had to call into the
Carrick-on-Suir Golf Club on the way; there we would
look for lost golf balls. I know we did this for a long time
because we accumulated quite a number of balls. I couldn't
be fully sure but I have a feeling that we then sold the balls
back to somebody in the Golf Club.' Those who have
followed the cycling career of Kelly would not encounter
major difficulties in believing that the seven-year-old Sean
disposed of the balls at a profit.

Sean remembers that run to school because there were
times when he couldn't keep up with his older brother. On
returning home in the evening he would complain to his
parents that Joe wouldn't wait for him on the way to
school. Joe would get a beating and Sean would win a
crude measure of equality. His exploits in later life would
confirm the fact that he was never one to accept defeat
stoically. Life at Crehana National School was probably the
most trying part of Sean Kelly's life. The period when he
was least in control. As Joe recounts: 'He didn't have an
intellectual or academic bent.' Sean is more direct: 'I
wasn't a lover of school. No, I can't say I was. But I always
went, I never mitched.' Official records from those days at
Crehana School endorse Kelly's good attendance. But the
classroom did little for his confidence. Away from the
people he knew and trusted Kelly was intensely shy and
unsure of himself. Feeling that other children in the class
were smarter than he only exacerbated the feelings of self
doubt. Kelly's response was one of almost total silence.
Eight years at Crehana convinced John James Kelly that
he had experienced enough by way of formal education.

The summer after Sean had completed his primary
education at Crehana, discussion raged in the Kelly
household about his future. There were three possibilities:

he could follow Joe to the Christian Brothers School in Carrick, he could go to the Carrick Vocational School or, as was his wish, he could remain at home and work on the farm. Nellie Kelly and Joe thought he should apply himself to a trade and considered that he would do well in the Vocational School. Jack wouldn't have had a strong opinion either way. He liked having Sean around the farm; they had the kind of relationship that transcended the formal boundaries of father-son intercourse.

In the end circumstances intervened and rescued Sean from the tentacles of institutional education. Jack had an ulcer which necessitated a stay in Ardkeen Hospital, Waterford. Somebody had to replace him on the farm. Sean presented himself as the volunteer. By the time Jack was well enough to resume work Sean had missed the first month of the school term. He used this as utter justification for remaining at home. Never, ever, would he be able to make up what had not been learned in that time. Weary from the constant strife, the Kellys relented. At thirteen years of age the classroom education of Sean Kelly was complete.

Jack would have been pleased to have Sean's constant companionship. As a young lad around the place, he liked him. Talk now about the days on the farm and Jack Kelly is at once animated: 'He was a terrible wild young fellow. He nearly killed me a few times. Once we were bringing a load of hay down to the shed from a field up at Killaspie. There was a half acre of hay on the trailer. I said we should tie it but he swore it wouldn't stir. Sure enough, it stirred alright. On the way down it all fell off. I slid off with the load; if I hadn't rolled with it I was in big trouble. I looked at him and said: "Are you still sure it won't stir?" We had some time cleaning up the mess.

'Another day he was teasing the ram, getting him worked up and then when the ram went for him he would hop over the fence. Then back in and again out over the fence when the ram attacked. He called me out and I

didn't know what was going on. When the ram went for
me I wasn't so quick and he got me. I got over it. But Sean
was as tough as any young fellow I ever saw and as hardy
as a goat.' There is a great deal of Jack Kelly in his son.
Both are tough, unemotional men. They take life as they
find it and lose little sleep in the intervals between the
days. Somebody asked Jack about the possibility of Sean
having a bad crash: 'If he meets a bad crash he'll meet it. I
always say let him belt away, good or bad.' An outlook with
which his son would fully concur.

Joe Kelly must accept responsibility for his younger
brother's first adventure with bike-racing. While a student
at the Christian Brothers School, Joe had been captivated
by men who came into the classroom and encouraged the
pupils to join a schoolboy cycling league which had just
started in the town. It was September 1969. Joe cycled to
school each day, three miles each way, and so he suspected
that he might be able to race. The men had said the racing
would take place on ordinary bikes and that there was no
need for anyone to be thinking of getting racing machines.
Soon after joining the league Joe began to win races.

The pattern in the Kelly household had been for Joe to
do something and then for Sean to follow. The fraternal
scheme of things. Being at home on the farm, with most of
his time spent in adult company, Sean viewed the bike-
races as one way of meeting boys of his own age, one way
of getting into the town of Carrick-on-Suir. He, too, had
his own bike. A Raleigh All-Steel. Sean Kelly was fourteen
when he underwent his first competitive examination on a
bike. It was a Tuesday evening, 4 August 1970. The race
started at Kennedy Terrace in Carrickbeg, that part of
Carrick-on-Suir on the Waterford side of the county
boundary. Simplicity directed those who designed the
course. The racers would travel four miles on the Cool-
namucka Road until they came to Millvale Creamery when
they would turn around and pedal the same four miles
home.

Tony Ryan, who founded the Carrick Wheelers Road Club a year earlier, was there the evening Sean Kelly turned up for that first race: 'I didn't know who this lad was. When asked for his name he looked at Joe and said: "I'm his brother." When asked did he do much cycling he replied "a little". He didn't look much so we left him off three minutes ahead of the scratch group. They never got near him. He lost no time on the outward journey and actually gained time on the way back. All knees and elbows but he could still handle a bike.' Over the following years Kelly would go on to win numerous races, many of them since forgotten, but the memory of that first race lingers with a particular sharpness.

'There had been five or six races before I came along. I was the green fellow, the one who didn't know anything. They gave me the maximum handicap. I didn't know how I would go so I belted it from the start. Soon after half-way I saw the twelve or thirteen fellows who were chasing me. Joe was in the group. I didn't know if they had gained on me or not. I didn't give a damn. I just wanted to win the race and that was it. On the way back the car of the organizers, who had waited out at the half-way mark, came past me and I thought to myself the others must be catching up. So I went faster, like I was running from fire. I was scared stiff. It was the first race I rode and I could go home and say I won.'

That performance taught the organizers of the Carrick Wheelers something about Sean Kelly. They had ways of dealing with boys that won on their first night. From then on he was never so generously treated by the handicap system and he became just another aspiring cyclist. Nobody sensed that he had talents above the ordinary. Sean's vivid recollection is of Joe being much better than he. Bikes and racing were largely forgotten about during the winter of 1970-71 and Sean continued to work on the farm. When the sow was getting near her time he would stay up one night, Joe the next, Jack the next. Similarly,

when one of the cows was calving the young Kellys knew
how to assist with the birth. There was no such thing as
being excused from duty.

When things brightened up in the spring of 1971 bikes
again became the centre of the isolated world at Curraghduff. Joe had succeeded in getting his parents to buy him a
racing-bike and the demand from Sean followed quickly.
Jack didn't think much of the pre-occupation with bikes,
lamenting that whenever you wanted the boys 'they
weren't to be found'. Sean's antics amused. He would set
up a line of milk churns and old barrels in the yard and
wriggle in and out between them as fast as he could. Over
a decade later the same swerves and switches would send
shudders through the fearless bodies of the best sprinters
in the Tour de France. The little tricks learned in a yard
with churns and barrels would win many sprints for Kelly
but would also earn him the reputation for being a
dangerous animal. Once, after the ninth stage of the 1980
Tour de France, Jan Raas described Kelly as a 'public
menace'.

1971 was a year when Kelly did a good bit of cycling but
without notable success. He did win some races but mostly
in his home province, Munster. He was fifteen and still
there was no suggestion of a champion. Things began to
happen in 1972. Sean was riding as a Junior and showing
more than average ability. His successes still came mostly
in the Munster region. He would travel in the club minibus
to such faraway places as Youghal, Carrigaline, Fermoy
and Kilmallock. Or sometimes a group of the cyclists
would crowd into Dan Grant's old Corsair and take to the
road. It wasn't the races which attracted young Kelly but
the trips out of town. 'Sometimes our mother would make
us sandwiches; sometimes Joe and I would make them
ourselves. There was great excitement about going off in
the bus or in a car.'

On the first Saturday in July 1972 Kelly was taken to the
Irish Junior Championship at Banbridge in County Down.

This was a test because he would have to beat the best of the Dublin riders whom he had not often competed against. Young riders like Alan McCormack, Oliver McQuaid and John Shortt were all regarded as well above average. Kelly beat them and people began to talk. The boy had something. At sixteen years of age he was Junior Champion of Ireland and would be young enough to defend that title for a further two years. At the end of that year Tipperary's Top Ten Sports Stars for 1972 included Sean Kelly for Cycling. At that time it represented quite an honour.

But to imagine that this adolescent rustic had fallen in love with a frame and two wheels would be stretching reality for the purposes of the story. David Power was a contemporary who regularly rode with Kelly in those days: 'I got the feeling that he wasn't very keen on the game. He lived from day to day, he never planned anything for the future and would often say that he was going to pack up the sport. He was winning trophies, getting publicity and he would say "what the hell, they mean nothing". But I felt that beneath his outward lack of interest in these things, they were important to him. Deep down he wanted recognition.'

For one not blessed with a formidable physique — Kelly was a scrawny youth — the boy from Curraghduff was unusually strong. They tell in Carrick-on-Suir that he could lift an eight-stone bag of cement before he was twelve. There was also about him a pugnacious streak which put all inhibitions to flight once the finish line approached. Kelly, the deeply introverted boy, had found a form of expression that offered him an identity. His sharp instinct soon picked up the message that one could talk through one's legs, express oneself in pedal strokes. On the bike Kelly was freed from the prison of fear and his own self-consciousness: 'I know that in my second year on the bike I didn't win much, but I was riding fairly well. I was never afraid of anybody. I would start off like a bullet

and get bollixed by half-way but I was never afraid. It was
just taking me time to adapt. The big thing was that I had
no fear of any other rider when on the bike.'

3 An Irish Amateur

It was the second week of the Tour of Britain 1976. Jim McQuaid frowned and wondered what he could do. He was manager of the Irish amateur team and had come to suspect that his team's journey to the prestigious British race was destined to yield nothing. Normally such an occurrence would have passed without an eyebrow being raised in Ireland but this year it was different. People expected something; surely one rider in green could deliver one performance on one of the Tour's fourteen days. McQuaid was deemed to have a talented crew at his disposal. Appreciating that the sword of criticism would cut more than the riders, Jim McQuaid sought to salvage something from the last few days of the race. Being a mild-mannered and softly spoken man, Jim had few options when it came to pre-race incitement.

He couldn't scream his desire for success, neither could he subject his riders to the type of verbal assault that would induce a response of one kind or another. Jim worked on different kinds of strategy. On the night before the stage into Stoke-on-Trent the manager gathered his charges around him and outlined his proposal: 'Lads,' he began, 'we have been arsing around in this race for too long. I am prepared to give £20 to the first Irishman to win a stage.' At this time £20 was a princely sum and the spirit of amateurism a worthless currency. The Irish riders were listening. Jim McQuaid had done his bit to motivate them. The Stoke stage ended with a sprint for victory by about fifty riders. Inside the final 100 metres the battle had narrowed down to just two: A man in green, Sean Kelly, fighting against one red and white Pole, Ryzard Szurkowski. Few beat Szurkowski in the sprint. Stoke was a fast, slightly downhill finish. Kelly surged past his rival, who renewed the challenge and Kelly surged again, more desperately this time, to win. He beat Szurkowski by half a wheel.

Seconds later an excited Jim McQuaid was rubbing Kelly down. Something had been rescued. Not only that but Kelly had claimed quite a scalp. McQuaid looked at his rider and suggested that his £20 hadn't got 'much of a run'. Thrilled by the sheer frenzy of the finishing surge, Kelly looked back at the manager: 'Jim, you know I was thinking of that £20 all the way up to the finishing straight.' Kelly was everybody's friend. In beating the Eastern European he had struck a blow for capitalism; on the grand scale and on the personal scale. It was also an appropriate victory on which to end his amateur career in Britain. Immediately after the Tour finished he departed for Velo Club Metz in France. Although he would return to ride the Tour of Ireland later in the season, his amateur career in Britain and Ireland was over.

Kelly's career as an amateur was like the cow's tail: all it lacked was length to reach the moon. On different occasions he rode to the edge of greatness as an amateur. But the suspension which cost him a place in the Olympic Road Race at Montreal removed the prize that might have left the tag of greatness hanging on the neck of his amateur career. Yet in the three years that he traded pedal strokes with amateur racers Kelly left impressive reminders of his strength and class. As well as winning stages of the Tour of Britain in 1975 and 1976 he also won the Tour of Majorca and the Tour of Lombardy, both in 1976. In Ireland he won most of the races worth competing for and his two victories in the Shay Elliot Memorial Race are frequently recalled.

Hints that John James Kelly was blessed with special talent could have been taken from his performance in becoming Junior Champion of Ireland in 1972. A year later he defended his title successfully and he was eligible to try for three Junior Championships in successive years in 1974. Ah, you wonder, but who did he beat to win those races? One of Kelly's contemporaries in Ireland at the time was Alan McCormack who went on to ride the Splendor professional team in Belgium and later became a leading performer on the US Pro Circuit, winning a stage of the Coors Classic in 1985. In those days McCormack was fast, so Kelly had to be very fast to win. McCormack lived in Dublin and raced against Ireland's best all of the time. Kelly operated from Carrick-on-Suir and rarely received the opportunity to compete in the best races.

Kelly's training in those days owed much to a local Carrick-on-Suir man, Tony Ryan. At the time of Kelly's entry into the sport Ryan was an experienced senior rider. Although not a regular competitor on Ireland teams Ryan was never far away from international selection and did represent his country on a number of occasions. He knew Kelly and took a particular interest in his development. Ryan worked as a Rent Collector, an occupation which could be shaped to accommodate his rigid adherence to a training routine on the bike. Seeing the boy's talent, Ryan encouraged Kelly to join him on those sessions and then punished his young protégé on a long and severe spin. At the end of a training ride an exhausted Kelly would tell Ryan that he had to milk the cows as soon as he got home. Ryan would wonder to himself how far Kelly could be pushed before he would cry 'no more'.

But each day he returned for training. Talking with his friend David Power, Kelly seemed not in love with the sport. Cycling was too hard, not worth it. Getting home from training exhausted and then having to work on the farm. He said he would give it up but he was in too deep for that. Somewhere inside there was an urge to explore, to find out how far he could go. His talent was raw, unrefined. What might happen when the lad learned? That was the great imponderable. People were taking an interest. Kelly was sent to a coaching course in England. Dan Grant, a prominent member of the Carrick Wheelers Road Club, had alerted National Team Manager John Lackey to Kelly's promise. Lackey put Kelly on to a Junior Olympic Squad. On first seeing the young Carrick-on-Suir cyclist Lackey was most struck by his rugged style. A year later Lackey had the top English amateur Doug Dailey in Ireland. They went to a race in the south; Kelly happened to be riding and near the village of Urlingford in County Laois Lackey spotted him in the bunch.

He drove his car as close to the rider as was possible and asked Dailey to deliver an assessment. Dailey watched intently for a while and then said: 'You might have something there John but he needs a lot of planing down.' Three years later Dailey stood in Stoke and Kelly beat Szurkowski in the Tour of Britain. He encountered Lackey soon afterwards and conceded that Kelly 'wasn't long in planing himself down'.

All of those who came into contact with the young Kelly liked him. He didn't know how to cause trouble and while others felt the texture of the mattress he was happy to have a roof over his head. Lackey used to say 'give that man a bed of nails, he won't notice'. When others spoke Kelly listened and tried to learn. He wasn't smart but he was prepared to work at finding out how to be. Only when he felt he had something to say did he speak and so he seldom offered opinions. He was the kind of lad that made the team manager's life uncomplicated. He wanted to improve as a bike-rider but the little trophies he picked up on the way meant nothing.

Once, at a meeting of the Carrick Wheelers Road Club, Dan Grant lamented that the club could not buy prizes for its Tinvane Trophy race on the following weekend. There was an acute lack of funds. Although present at the meeting Kelly said nothing. Later that night Grant's house at 11 Treacy Park in Carrick had a visitor. Kelly stood at the front door. In his hand he held a plastic shopping bag. Inside were most of the trophies he had won as a schoolboy and junior. Handing the bag over to Grant he said 'Will these do for Sunday', and left. Grant, a little stunned, accepted. Nobody knew for sure what went on inside Kelly's head. If he spoke, he did so almost exclusively in the monosyllable. Yet it was certain that the world frightened him. He had come from an isolated farm and had left school at just thirteen years of age.

The world presented problems. Like the time he was in England with a team of young Irish riders. As well as winning a few races Kelly crashed heavily and was brought to the nearest hospital for treatment. Christy Kimmage was manager of the team and accompanied Kelly to the hospital. Before attending to his injuries the nurse in the Casualty Unit needed some details. She reeled off the customary questions: name, address, date of birth, and them came the awkward moment. 'Profession?' asked the nurse. Silence. 'Profession?' the nurse repeated. Further silence. Kelly looked inquiringly at Kimmage and then whispered 'What's profession?'. 'Your job,' replied Kimmage. 'Bricklayer,' said Kelly.

Like most teenagers Kelly was attempting to play numerous cards at once. For as well as the bike and catching up on missed schooling, the Curraghduff cyclist was taking the first tentative steps towards a boy/girl relationship. The focus of his vague attentions was Linda Grant, only daughter of Dan Grant, the Carrick Wheelers official. Linda recalls that when her Dad's car was being packed up with bikes and riders to go to a race she was 'the last piece of equipment to be loaded'. Female friends of Linda fell for boys according to their appearance and Linda felt that there were better looking fellows than Sean Kelly around. Yet there was some attraction. Linda noticed that Sean signed his name with his left hand and that he was an okay sort of fellow.

Asking girls for a date demanded certain traces of self-confidence and so Kelly stood before a major obstacle. Formalities can occasionally be dispensed with. Linda retains a memory of the fledgling Casanova exercising his charm: 'He never actually asked me out — just one day we were talking and he said "I'll see you tomorrow night". That was it, I presumed I had a date.' One small step for mankind but a giant leap for Sean Kelly. Linda was sixteen at the time, Kelly a year older. Their relationship didn't exactly flourish from the moment hands touched. Introverted and intensely shy, Sean preferred to let things move along casually. Linda might have wanted something more definite but would have felt that it wasn't her place to lay the ground rules. The relationship was different. Linda likes to remember it as 'drifting'.

Things happened with greater speed in the sporting arena. Twice a Junior Champion (1972 and 1973), Kelly passed up the opportunity to try for a third consecutive Junior title by taking out a senior licence in 1974. His success in the Shay Memorial Race that year created a stir. Kelly was still two months short of his eighteenth birthday and the Elliott race through the Wicklow Mountains is regarded as the most severe one-day race on the Irish calendar. As is the custom in Ireland those displaying any talent are immediately cast into the international arena and Kelly found himself riding the Tour of Scotland and the Tour of Ireland as an eighteen-year-old. That season he recorded ten victories as a senior rider even through he was still eligible to race in junior competition.

Off the bike the successes altered Kelly not a whit. He remained taciturn to a degree that baffled. Yet beneath the silent and sometimes morose exterior there lurked an aggressive and fearless animal. Civilian life provided no outlet for this side of his nature and cycling fulfilled an obvious role. Just how aggressive and fearless Kelly was can be gleaned from his pugnacious performance in the

Liam Toolan race at the beginning of the 1975 season. Late in the race an eight-man break developed and Kelly was one of the eight. From that group three riders escaped and Kelly was left, unamused, at the bus stop. Disgusted to have missed out he tried desperately to regain contact. The other four riders with Kelly refused to offer assistance in the pursuit. As his efforts yielded no great return Kelly grew angry.

One of those with Kelly was the vastly experienced international rider Sean Lally. At that time Lally was thirty-four years of age, sixteen years older than the teenage rival. Lally hadn't enough energy to share the pace-making with Kelly but did have the strength to remain tight on his back wheel. To the continual demands for assistance Lally responded in the negative. Kelly had heard enough and simply drew his arm from the bars and punched Lally. An eighteen-year-old punching a thirty-four-year-old! Lally's recollection is sharp: 'Sean hit me alright and even drew some blood. After the finish a number of people told me to lodge an official complaint and have him suspended but I didn't want that. He was the most promising rider in Ireland. Instead I walked up to him and said "Sean, you know you could have killed me today." I don't know if he felt any remorse but he never said a word in reply.'

Years of competition in the world's most glamorous bike-races have brought a certain control to Kelly's aggression but, even in its refined state, it is not a force that one treats lightly. That he had the pedalling talents to match his hunger for victory was becoming increasingly apparent. Ireland's amateur season has its first major race in Dublin's Phoenix Park, the Jack Woodcock Memorial. In 1975 Kelly beat Kieron McQuaid after the two had broken away. McQuaid had represented Ireland in the 1972 Olympics at Munich and was singularly displeased to lose to an eighteen-year-old. On the long finishing straight Kelly had proved far more astute in executing the final sprint and therein lay the source of McQuaid's anger.

For whatever reason, Kelly retains a clear picture of the after race scene: 'He was very mad. Didn't take it too well. He was furious that I had made him lead out the sprint because the finishing straight in the Phoenix Park is about three-quarters of a mile. "You're the sprinter," he said to me. "You should have led out the sprint." "Fuck off, you're the sprinter." We went on like that for a while. I wasn't worried. I had come a long way in a short time, getting good results, winning big races. I was the King of Carrick, well nearly. A lot of people down there were talking. I enjoyed that.' Carrick-on-Suir's denizens would not be short of conversational matter for the foreseeable future. The Kelly train was only gathering momentum.

Being the monarch of Carrick-on-Suir had, however, its limitations. Beyond, there was a place called the world. June 1975 was the month when Kelly ventured to knock on the world's door. The young man who wanted to be recognized outside his native town found in the Tour of Britain a race to launch his international career. During the first week of the fourteen-day race Kelly found himself in the decisive break on the road to Sheffield. According to Pat McQuaid, Kelly was at that time operating purely on 'brute strength and ignorance', not a bad combination in cycling. His performance on that day into Sheffield astonished his team-mates as much as the rest of the cycling world. A lead group that had originated as a ten-man attack was down to just three nearing Sheffield: Kelly, a Polish rider and Bernt Johansson the Swede.

Johansson, destined to become Olympic champion in Montreal a year later, was riding himself into the yellow jersey and so was consistently forcing the pace at the front of the group. Under orders from team manager Jim McQuaid, Kelly sat quietly at the back and hoped that his presence would go unnoticed. He craved for the chance to sprint at the end. Into the town of Sheffield Kelly was still there; leading was Johansson, then the Pole and Kelly.

Norfolk Park was the location of the finish and the gradual rise to the line from the entrance to the Park made things simple for Kelly. He particularly liked slightly uphill sprints and he easily distanced his two rivals. Johansson was livid that a rider could have the audacity to remain in his slip-stream all through the stage and then produce a sprint for stage glory. Seconds after crossing the line he made his way over to Kelly and sought a confrontation. As Kelly recalls the episode, Johansson grabbed him by the jersey and told him he should not have sprinted. Kelly says he looked at Johansson and told him that 'in Ireland it happens all the time'.

Journalists who interviewed Kelly that day retain a slightly different version. They were endeavouring to illicit background material from the Irish winner (a peculiarly tedious operation at the time) when Johansson barged a passage towards Kelly. As Johansson launched into a tirade about the parasitic cyclist in green, Kelly merely said: 'Fuck off'. It was an English phrase which Bernt immediately understood and the journalists (suitably impressed by Kelly's curt dismissal of the Swede) were allowed to continue their interrogations. That Sheffield stage put Johansson into the race lead and Kelly up to third place. A position that he defended successfully until the final day of the race. Then on the ninety-mile stage to Blackpool Kelly punctured, had mechanical problems and finished minutes down. A respectable third place had become an anonymous twenty-fifth.

Phil Liggett, the cycling journalist who controls the Tour of Britain, encountered Kelly that evening and expected to find a young man ravaged by disappointment. Kelly wasn't much put out. A stage win, third overall for much of the race, a bit of bad luck at the very end; overall, it had been a good experience for him. Liggett was greatly impressed by Kelly's refusal to mourn. Years later others would encounter a similar stoicism in defeat. His placid acceptance of losing performances stems from the

clinical nature of his post-race analyses. Seldom does Kelly
contemplate what might have happened if he had won.
His way is to dissect the defeat in search of the cause, find
it and then remind himself there will be another day. He
knew the 1975 Tour of Britain was just a beginning.

Kelly remained a rugged sight on the bike. If his body
was supposed to be a natural extension of the machine,
then it was a poorly constructed one. As an under-age
cyclist he had used a bike that was far too small for him.
But while the theory states that you make the bike to fit the
body, Kelly then sought to make his body fit the bike. With
an undersized bike, arms could not follow a direct route to
the handlebars just as legs could not sink in a straight line
into the toe clips. Kelly, they used to say, was all knees and
elbows. By 1975 the remedial course was well under way.
Kelly was straightening up or, as Doug Dailey would say,
'he was being planed down'.

If the style on the bike needed refinement so, too, the
person who turned the pedals had to adapt to accommodate the demands of life as a successful sports person. On
the night of the stage win in Sheffield there was a dinner
to honour the day's hero. Irish manager McQuaid sensed
that Kelly would not want to be present. When the
manager broached the subject the response was one of
total refusal. McQuaid politely suggested that Kelly hadn't
a choice. Still adamant that he would not attend, the young
rider said he had travelled without the type of clothes
necessary for such an occasion. Jim McQuaid then asked
his son Oliver, also a team member, to loan Kelly a suit,
shirt, and cufflinks. Although present against his wishes,
Kelly enjoyed the occasion. Pat McQuaid argues that he
returned from that dinner with an altered perspective:
'He saw things there, saw how winners are treated. He
liked the fuss and wanted more of it.'

The world was taking notice of Sean Kelly the cyclist.
Carrick-on-Suir felt it should show its appreciation and the
Town's Urban District Council accorded the nineteen-

year-old a civic reception to honour his Tour of Britain performance. While Kelly had conceived no ambitions for himself, performances on the bike were giving some outline to his future. One of those who noticed during the Tour of Britain was John Morris. A Londoner, Morris had connections with Velo Club Metz in France and considered Kelly to be the type of amateur who would do well with Metz. The President of Metz, Alain Steinhoff, was informed of Kelly's potential. Dutch team manager Jan Kuiper also detected strains of the champion in Kelly during the Tour of Britain and invited Kelly to join his Dutch team in their pre-Olympic training.

Life had become complicated. Apart from cycling opportunities, Kelly had to decide what to do about his bricklaying. Three years of working on his father's farm had satisfied his appetite for farm work and, when fellow-cyclist Martin Wall offered him a start in bricklaying, Kelly accepted immediately. He was sixteen when he began the apprenticeship and now, three years later, cycling was eating into the time he might have been spending in the construction industry. There was also the matter of that 'drifting' relationship with Linda Grant. When faced by diverse possibilities Kelly's natural response is to simply postpone decision-making. He would not accept Kuiper's offer, or Steinhoff's. Neither would he give up bricklaying or allocate more time to it. He would wait and hope that his performances on the bike might shape his future. Decisions would not be made but would follow on automatically from the results of cycling battles.

Kelly returned to ride the Tour of Ireland and claimed three stages and the mountains jersey in the eight-day race. Some time during the Tour Pat McQuaid decided to go to South Africa and compete in the Rapport Tour. In selecting fellow-travellers McQuaid looked first to Kelly. As long-term preparation for the Montreal Olympics the Rapport Tour made sense. Kelly was in complete agreement that the invitation should be pursued. He knew the risks and, when the seven-month suspension was later imposed, it changed nothing. Training schedules were strictly fulfilled and, when he resumed his racing career at the end of April 1976, Kelly was as sharp as ever.

After winning the Tour of the North in Ulster on his return, Kelly travelled to the Tour of Majorca as part of a six-man Irish team. With a strong Danish team and most of the best Spanish amateurs competing, the four-day Tour was quite a race. The Irish and Danish combined to counter the allied forces of Spain. On the final day Kelly escaped with two Spaniards and rode strongly to take the race leader's jersey. Behind, the aptly named Macho was exhorting his countrymen to greater efforts in pursuit of Kelly. When the response failed to satisfy Signor Macho he stopped at the roadside, grabbed a sapling from the hedge, sliced off the twigs with his foot, returned to the bunch and began flailing his weapon at every Spaniard he could reach. Words of admonishment from the race organizers failed to induce Macho to lay down arms.

At the finish the leader's jersey lay in waiting for Kelly and the local police for Macho. The Irishman donned his tunic and Macho was taken away by the police. Although it was his best stage race victory as an amateur, Kelly was more relieved than euphoric after the race concluded. Jim McQuaid was again the manager in Majorca: ' We were damn lucky to get out of there. The Spanish riders and the spectators in Majorca didn't like to lose.' Back in Dublin the Olympic manager, Lackey, followed the Majorca race avidly. At that point in the season he believed he would be taking Kelly to Montreal three months later. Lackey had a system worked out with Dan Grant in Carrick to ferry Kelly from Dublin Airport to Curraghduff. Lackey would collect the rider at the airport and drive to Kilcullen in County Kildare. There he would transfer the valuable cycling merchandise to the waiting Grant.

Having picked up Kelly after the Majorca race, Lackey was extremely anxious to relive every moment of what had been an eventful race. The returned hero proved to be a less than accommodating companion on the journey to Kilcullen. Lackey's curiosity remained unsatisfied: 'All he said of Majorca and the Spaniards was that they were rough bastards over there and you'd have to have your wits about you.' A week later the International Olympic Committee, reviewing the situation relating to cyclists who had raced in South Africa, released the names of sixteen riders whom they would never allow to compete in the Olympic Games. Kelly was one of those to receive the life sentence. He would race for a further five months as an amateur but, spiritually, his idea of amateurism died with that announcement.

Amateurism for Kelly had nothing to do with competing for the love of one's sport; neither was it linked to a refusal to accept monetary reward. (If somebody offered money Kelly's sense of amateurism wasn't offended.) He wanted to retain the amateur tag because it was necessary to get into the Olympic arena. When they said he could never be an Olympian, Sean Kelly, the Irish Amateur, ceased to exist.

4 Ghost-riders in South Africa

Autumn 1975 must have been a happy time in the marital adventures of Elizabeth Taylor and the late Richard Burton. For it was during that season that the couple decided to undertake a second honeymoon. The world's gossip columnists, who followed every movement in the Burton/Taylor roller-coaster, decided this was a big event. When, as a part of their second honeymooning voyage, the two stars arrived into the South African town of Oudtshoorn they were awaited by newspapermen. One of them was John Hartdegen, present to file copy for the *Daily Mail* in England. In the time-honoured journalistic tradition Hartdegen sought out a British angle to the couple's visit to an Ostrich Farm near Oudtshoorn. He thought he had come up with the perfect idea.

At the same time as Burton and Taylor renewed marital bliss in South Africa a bike-race was taking place. On the very day that the honeymooners were in Oudtshoorn this bike-race was arriving into town. Hartdegen had struck lucky. The bike-race, called the Rapport Tour, was an important part of the sporting life of South Africa and it happened that a few British riders were doing extremely well. Hartdegen's idea was to get Taylor and Burton down to the start and photograph them alongside the British cyclists. A reasonable proposition! If you didn't get the story on the Gossip Page you would probably get it on a Sports Page.

Hartdegen decided to seek out Tommy Shardelow, manager of the 'Mum for Men' British team, and set up his clever picture story. But Shardelow said it wasn't possible to have the British riders photographed. Hartdegen wondered why not? His suspicions led him onwards. He insisted on the photograph, even of the British riders on their own. Shardelow spoke with some people. Five young men were delivered before Hartdegen; they wore 'Mum for Men' tracksuit tops and this was the proof that they were the British riders. Hartdegen took the photograph but was convinced that somebody was playing at silly games. In his report for the *Daily Mail* Hartdegen wrote: 'I pointed out to Tommy Shardelow that two of the men I had photographed spoke with pronounced South African accents and that a third was a member of another foreign team.'

Shardelow decided to play things straight. He opted to take Hartdegen into the scheme of things on the Rapport Tour. Firstly the people that had been photographed were not members of the 'Mum for Men' British team; neither were the names listed in the programme for the British riders correct. This was sport in South Africa and the plot grew more complex. Shardelow explained that the riders were competing under fictitious names to avoid being banned from other international events. (South Africa, then and now, is outlawed by the International Cycling Union, and the Rapport Tour is firmly decreed out of bounds by the international authority.)

All of the journalists covering the race knew the score and understood the need for subterfuge. Shardelow hoped that Hartdegen would understand. He pleaded the sportman's case: 'These men are sportsmen, not politicians. They don't give a damn for apartheid. They just want to take part in one of the finest long-distance cycling races in the world today. If that story is printed in London they will be banned and that will be goodbye to their chances of taking part in the next Olympic Games.' Hartdegen refused to understand. He was a journalist and here was a story. To hell with the Honeymoon Couple!

As Shardelow refused to divulge the real names of the
'Mum for Men' riders, Hartdegen thrust himself into a
little piece of investigative journalism. He rang hotels
where the Rapport riders had stayed and inquired about
the names of the athletes who had checked in under the
'Mum for Men' banner. It is a criminal offence in South
Africa to sign into a hotel under a fictitious name and
Hartdegen was sure the hotels would have the correct
names. But the 'Mum for Men' squad had been block-
booked all along the 950-mile route for the Rapport Tour
and Hartdegen was still in darkness. Light eventually
appeared through the tunnel of a zoom lens. If Hartdegen could picture the 'ghost riders', people back at the
London office of the *Daily Mail* could identify them.

At the start of the following day's stage the competitors
lined up at Plettenberg Bay oblivious to the presence of
journalist John Hartdegen with his camera and zoom lens.
Soon the camera was focussed on those riders wearing the
'Mum for Men' jerseys. Those who spotted Hartdegen's
camera turned away, others were captured with reasonable clarity. The photographs were air-freighted to
London. At first nobody at the *Daily Mail* could positively
identify the people in the photographs, and the names
which had been used in the official Rapport Tour
programme (J. Burns, G. Main, D. Nixon, P. Nugent, A.
Owen) meant nothing. The photographs were then shown
to people involved in cycling and it was learned that the
riders, as named in the Rapport race programme, did not
exist. The athletes in the photographs were, however, real
enough. Mum's men were John Curran and Henry
Wilbraham from Scotland; and Pat McQuaid, Kieron
McQuaid and Sean Kelly from Ireland. The *Daily Mail* ran
the story on Thursday 16 October 1975, devoting an
entire page to the tale. Across the top of the page ran the
headline 'Sportsmail Reveals the International Ghost
Riders'. Beneath, in even bigger type, the drama continued: 'The Secret Team Who Masquerade as Britain'.

John Lackey was then Ireland's cycling team manager. The prospect of taking Kelly to the Montreal excited Lackey. On the morning that the *Daily Mail* published its story of the Scottish and Irish cyclists masquerading in South Africa, Lackey received a phone call from Tom O'Shea, a sports journalist with the *Evening Press* in Dublin. O'Shea wanted Lackey to confirm that the cyclists in the *Mail* photographs were the two McQuaids and Kelly. Lackey had not seen the paper, knew nothing of the South African escapade and was utterly bewildered by the story. O'Shea said he would send a boy around to his Dublin business with the photographs. A little later Lackey rang O'Shea: the cyclists in the photographs were Pat and Kieron McQuaid and Sean Kelly. Dublin had the story. Three of Ireland's best amateur cyclists were in deep trouble. For Pat McQuaid and Kelly, who were certain to be on Ireland's Olympic team the following year, the trouble had the potential for catastrophe.

Pat McQuaid considers that he produced some of the best performances of his career during the 1975 Rapport Tour. He won two stages, both bunch sprints, and totally justified the faith which Rapport organizer Raoul de Villiers had demonstrated in bringing three Irish cyclists to his race. Only McQuaid and those on the Rapport Tour of 1975 would ever know of his super form on the roads between Cape Town and Johannesburg. The records show that J. Burns of the 'Mum for Men' won two stages and there is no asterisk explaining that J. Burns was really Pat McQuaid.

One of the stages in the Rapport Tour of 1975 ended in Kimberley, a town famous for its gold and diamond deposits. On that night in Kimberley McQuaid joked with Kelly that they would be sleeping over a wealth of gold and diamond deposits. He wondered would they be able to sleep at all? That night, before retiring to bed, he rang his wife Sharon. She had been staying with her mother in Bristol and had some interesting information for her

husband. The *Daily Mail* had been in touch and had
wanted to know of Pat McQuaid's whereabouts. The
game, so exciting and such an adventure, was suddenly
over and a night's sleep was destined to be troubled not by
rich mineral deposits but by gloomy thoughts of suspension, of missing Montreal: 'I knew how the Irish Cycling
Federation would react,' says McQuaid.

At first there was a seven-month suspension, reduced to
six months on appeal. McQuaid and Kelly appeared to
have been granted a certain leniency for they were back in
competition at the end of April 1976, and had abundant
time to be racing fit for Montreal. But then the International Olympic Committee intervened and imposed a ban
which would prevent Kelly and McQuaid from ever
competing in the Games. For the nineteen-year-old Kelly
the lifetime banishment from Olympic participation was a
punishment certain to induce sombre reflection. Life is a
long term through the eyes of a teenager. Where could an
amateur cyclist go if not the Olympics? Damned South
Africa. Kelly and McQuaid had been unlucky that on the
day they wheeled into Oudtshoorn, Taylor and Burton
were visiting an Ostrich Farm near the town and then even
more unfortunate to encounter a journalist who was far
from being an ostrich.

McQuaid and Kelly had come a long way, originally from
sharply divergent paths, but then they linked up for a
flamboyant period in both their lives. A Dubliner,
McQuaid is the son of a former Irish international cyclist.
Articulate to the point of being downright charming,
McQuaid was already a man of the world at a time when
Kelly was still milking cows at Curraghduff. Six years older
than the Curraghduff rustic, McQuaid came from a family
where the racing-bike was revered. Pat inclined naturally
towards the sporting life and in 1973 he graduated from
Strawberry Hill College in London as an Instructor in
Physical Education.

One of McQuaid's first opportunities to display newly acquired knowledge came from the Carrick Wheelers Road Club who invited him to their club to conduct a coaching weekend. That was in November 1973. On the Saturday night of that weekend he delivered a talk to the cyclists in Tony Kehoe's public house: 'I was going on about physiology and the body's metabolism, things I was deeply interested in at the time, but I was still aware of this little fellow in the corner. People had told me he could fairly ride the bike but all I remember was that for the entire weekend he said nothing.' (Life's penchant for turning things upside down can hardly have been better represented by the quiet little fellow in the corner. Thirteen years later the square where Tony Kehoe's public house rests in Carrick-on-Suir is called 'The Sean Kelly Square'.)

Two years after McQuaid had lectured to Kelly and the Carrick Wheelers on the finer points of physiology, the teacher and pupil were sharing the same green jerseys as Ireland took its place in international competition. Kelly was certain to be impressed by the ease and authority with which McQuaid talked his way through life. McQuaid also earned Kelly's respect for his ability to handle a bike. They were the best in Ireland at the time. Both were seen at their strongest in the 1975 Tour of Ireland when McQuaid claimed the overall prize and Kelly satisfied his particular hunger with three stage wins and the Mountains jersey. Ah, that was a glorious week. Kelly and McQuaid, riding for the Ireland team, sweeping aside the foreign opposition in the Irish Tour. It was also the week which started the train of events that ended with an unscheduled photographic session in Plettenberg Bay.

John Curran, from Ayr in Scotland, rode that Tour of Ireland. The previous winter Curran had ridden the Rapport Tour and picked up a six-month suspension on his return. Although just twenty at the time, his suspension had not caused Curran to change his attitude *vis-a-vis* South Africa. He would return if invited. For others who might have had a notion to ride the Rapport Tour he was the man to whom one might profitably address the questions. McQuaid spoke to John Curran during that Tour of Ireland. The Irishman wanted to compete in the South African race. His reasons were twofold. Firstly he sought to fill some of the blanks which existed between the end of the season in Ireland and the start of the following season: 'Sean and I knew that we would be selected to ride the Olympic Road Race in August of the following year at Montreal. But we also knew that we were going to be without competition from the end of September until the early days of the following March. If we went to the Rapport Tour we would be getting valuable competition and training through the month of October.'

McQuaid is wise enough to acknowledge further reality. He was not fired solely by the desire for Olympic preparation: 'I was an amateur sportsman and I regarded travel as one of the great rewards for all of the personal sacrifices. I wanted to see South Africa for myself, to find out what things were like there. This was the second part of the reason for wanting to go there.' Curran put McQuaid in touch with Raoul de Villiers. Provided that a South African sponsor could be found to accommodate an Irish/Scots team, the trip was on. The riders interested in making up that team were told to keep training and racing through the month of September.

When McQuaid outlined the South African expedition to Kelly he soon had an ally. He also found his younger brother Kieron, who competed in the 1972 Olympics, willing to go. De Villiers had little difficulty finding backers for the team, and in late September the three Irish cyclists collected return Dublin/Johannesburg tickets at Dublin Airport and were on their way. Prior to departure they had observed a discreet silence about the trip. Both families knew. Joe Kelly, Sean's elder brother, considered the venture to be risky. He warned his brother that he would 'never get away with '. The response from Sean was a gesture somewhere between a dismissive shrug of the shoulders and a frown of indifference. Joe got the message.

On the last Sunday of September Kelly left Curraghduff for a race in Enniscorthy, County Wexford. That was the first leg in the marathon trip to Johannesburg. Dan Grant, who would become Kelly's father-in-law seven years later, drove him to the Enniscorthy race. Aware of the greater journey, Grant was pleased to have been involved: 'There was a great secrecy. I had Sean's luggage for South Africa in the boot of my car and it had to be transferred to Jim McQuaid's car. We couldn't do this at the start or the finish of the race as there were so many people around. Eventually we drove some way out of town and transferred the bags on a quiet part of the road.' Dan Grant's vivid and animated recollection of the scene adds substance to the widely held view in Ireland that the native people are happiest when scheming and executing mischievous plans.

The three Irish cycling musketeers first flew to London where they joined up with Curran and Wilbraham. From there they travelled to Paris. On that flight the game was almost ended prematurely for aboard the same aircraft was Scottish cycling official Gerry McDaid. But the Irish and Scots cyclists were seated in different parts of the aircraft and McDaid didn't put two and three together and didn't come up with the Rapport Tour. After Paris they flew to Johannesburg, stopping over in the Congo *en route*. On arrival into Johannesburg the five were met at the Airport by the team's sponsor and his tailor. All five were immediately measured up for blazers and slacks which would arrive the following day. For the next three weeks Sean Kelly would be turning the pedals to promote Mum, a deodorant for Men. Some might see something incongruous in that. The farmer's son from Curraghduff spreading a sweet-smelling message in South Africa. Kelly would merely say that cycling around under the South

African sun in October was a more pleasurable experience than laying blocks on a building site during an Irish winter.

Everything had been fine on the Rapport Tour until the entrance of Burton and Taylor. The weather was hot and McQuaid's form sparkling. One hotel was more luxurious than the next and the team's performance highly satisfactory. As well as McQuaid's two stage wins, Alan Owen (also known as Sean Kelly) was in the top ten overall all through and eventually finished eighth. 'Mum for Men' jerseys were continually at the front of the bunch and the team of Celts from the northern hemisphere had pleased their hosts.

On the night that the bad news was transmitted the three Irishmen were temporarily despondent. They would face a major inquiry on their return, but they sensibly agreed to enjoy their trip until the bell tolled for them to return. Always a convincing talker, McQuaid tried to make Kelly believe that they would not be thrown out of the Olympics: 'I expected that they would be hard on us. Going to South Africa was even then considered a major crime in cycling. But, deep down, I thought we were too good for them (Irish Cycling Federation) to fuck us out.'

When the race ended the 'Mum for Men' brigade expressed an interest in seeing parts of South Africa. The sponsor of their team supplied a Volkswagen Minibus and provided a credit card for the chain of Holiday Inn Hotels in South Africa and another that would get them unlimited petrol for the minibus. Both McQuaids and Kelly have always insisted that they were not paid money to ride in South Africa and were not given cash as they set out on their post-race holiday. Pat McQuaid's denial is categorical: 'We were given return air tickets. The manager of our team, Tommy Shardelow, was told that no matter what we wanted during the race he was to provide it but there were never any payments. Afterwards there was the free accommodation at the Holiday Inn hotels and the Minibus. That was all.' On their return to Ireland McQuaid would actually protest that the trip cost them 'hundreds of pounds'. Given Kelly's track record, before and since, it is asking a great deal to accept that South Africa cost him 'hundreds of pounds'.

All of the journeymen agree that the trip through parts of South Africa was an unforgettable experience. The visits to the Kruger Game Reserve and to Swaziland remain fixed in their memories. So, too, does the reception which awaited them in Ireland. A bit like the reception for the honeymoon couple in reverse! McQuaid had suspected that the governing Irish Cycling Federation would use a big stick. He was correct.

At first the ICF imposed a seven-month suspension. That punishment was not nearly as severe as it sounded for it incorporated four months of the winter when the riders would not be racing. On appeal it was reduced to six months, and the three returned to competition in late April and in plenty of time to be ready for Montreal. Their first engagement was the Tour of the North in Ireland. The Olympic Team Manager John Lackey had considerable difficulty getting into that race for they had not been entered: 'I pleaded with the organizer, John Snodden, to let them in because they needed competition to have them racing fit for the Tour of Britain, and later, Montreal. Snodden laid down two conditions. No expenses for anybody and any rider who won anything would have to stay over on Sunday night for the presentation banquet.

Kelly proved that the six-month suspension had done little to impair his talents. He won the Tour of the North handsomely. Snodden confronted him after the final stage and reminded him that he would now have to stay over for the presentation. Kelly said that he could not, that he had to be back in Carrick-on-Suir for work the following day. Maybe, if somebody offered compensation? A little upset, Snodden took his case to Lackey: 'I told Snodden not to pass any heed to Kelly, he was just trying him out for a few extra pounds. Kelly had every intention of staying but reckoned that if there was more money to be made he might as well try. Tells you something about the kind of lad he was. An out and out professional.'

Lackey was pleased. Kelly had been the rider he most wanted to take to Montreal. Now he was back in competition and just four months away from the Olympic race. A month or so later the file on Sean Kelly, Pat and Kieron McQuaid riding the Rapport Tour was sent to the Federation for International Amateur Cycling. The FIAC was compiling a list of all cyclists it knew to have competed in the Rapport Tour and it forwarded its findings to the International Olympic Committee. As a consequence fifteen riders from seven countries were banned for life from Olympic competition. The IOC delivered its verdict on 29 May 1976.

Sean Kelly would never ride the Olympics. Time and again he would say that missing Monteal was a 'heartbreak'. A curious expression for a man whose way of life, unemotional and hard, suggested that his heart had never acted in anything other than a physical way. Still it wasn't such a 'heartbreak' to induce the victim into complaining or brooding. Rather Kelly took his cycling talents to mainland Europe and began a new life. Later the world would decide that everything had turned out for the best, that the Olympic ban had been a sort of blessing. The old 'if there had not been a ban, he wouldn't have gone to Europe' school of logic. Kelly steadfastly refused to countenance such a facile summary: 'Missing Montreal was', he says,'a heartbreak.'

A decade later he still says it. Then the slight trace of regret is banished from the mind and Kelly reflects that, really, McQuaid walked him into it. That is the view taken by cycling people in Carrick-on-Suir. Big Pat McQuaid leading innocent Sean Kelly to the land of apartheid and precipitating the Olympic ban. Kelly might joke to that effect but he would never seriously hold McQuaid culpable. He was nineteen years of age when he said he would go to the Rapport Tour. Old enough to say yes and old enough to say no. He knew the risks when he collected his air ticket at Dublin Airport

When McQuaid reflects on the Rapport Tour there isn't even a footnote alluding to the disappointment of not competing in Montreal: 'I would say it was the best month of my life. The weather was great, the countryside beautiful, my form was at its best and the time we spent touring the countryside afterwards was superb. It was a great trip.' But then McQuaid may not have been a potential Olympic champion. When he claimed the Sheffield stage of the Tour of Britain in June 1975, Kelly outsprinted Bernt Johansson of Sweden. Fourteen months later, while Kelly raced anonymously at Metz in France, a fourteen-rider break was contesting the finish of the Olympic Road Race in Montreal. Unlike Sheffield, Bernt Johansson won this sprint. Irish people, who thought they knew, said Kelly would have been in that break and would have outsprinted Johansson again.

Six months after returning to South Africa Kelly told John Lackey he had something for him. Lackey wondered what it was. Kelly said it was something small that he had brought back from South Africa for him. Then Kelly presented him with an antelope skin which still adorns John Lackey's living-room in his County Wicklow home. One thing puzzled Lackey. How was it that Kelly had waited so long to give the present? Kelly didn't know what to say, but then muttered: 'I thought you'd be mad with me for going to South Africa and getting caught and I was afraid to give it before now.' There was still much of the boy in the young man.

5 Are You Kelly?

In the summer of 1976 Kelly travelled to the Tour of Britain Milk Race. It was the start of a longer journey. He knew it. His parents sensed it. They had not wanted him to go but were not inclined towards making a fuss. Jack would have shrugged his shoulders, jerked his head upwards and said 'let him belt away'. As mothers generally will, Nellie worried. As he walked out the door the son tried to lessen the impact of his parting: 'Ma, they won't want me on the Continent. I'll be sent home and will be back here much sooner than you think.' A man who had grown up in a stern, rugged boys' world was being as sensitive as he could be. Trying to make things easier. He had just turned twenty and was leaving the safety of the cliff's edge.

The plan was straightforward. After the Milk Race ended Kelly would travel to the Continent and ride with the amateur team V.C. Metz-Woippy. Metz, a city in Eastern France, was to provide Kelly with his first taste of continental life. At the time the amateur cycling club in the city, Velo Club Metz, possessed a broad outlook towards recruitment of cyclists and offered opportunities to riders from such places as Luxembourg, Britain and New Zealand. The British contact was a man called John Morris. A year earlier, during the summer of 1975, Morris had told Metz about Kelly. Alain Steinhoff, president of the Metz club, travelled to the World Championships at Mettet in Belgium that September and intercepted Kelly as he returned to the dressing-rooms after an unsuccessful experience against the world's best. Kelly listened to the propositions, promised to consider them and vowed that he would contact the club sometime during the winter.

Velo Club Metz and Steinhoff heard nothing. Kelly was pre-occupied with the Montreal Olympics preparations and, of course, South Africa. When he might have been penning a few lines to Metz, Sean Kelly was air-bound for Johannesburg. Ironically, South Africa and the Rapport Tour worked to Metz's advantage. The Olympic ban which was imposed the following spring meant an end to the dream of competing in Montreal and Kelly was suddenly looking for a way to fill his summer. Staying in Ireland as an alternative team was being prepared for Montreal was not a possibility that would have amused. The time had come to go. Kelly recalled the interest of V.C. Metz seven months earlier and so wrote a four-line letter to the club. He was never one for superfluous detail. The letter simply asked what Metz could offer.

A reply arrived as quickly as the international postal service would permit. Kelly was offered free lodgings, £25 a week and replacements for equipment damaged during races. Acceptance followed immediately. Kelly wanted to get away. He arrived in Metz in mid-June 1976. Soon he found out that the club had a bonus scheme whereby a rider earned four francs per kilometre for each race won. That arrangement motivated Kelly, for over a five-month period at Metz he won eighteen out of the twenty-five races he started.

Metz knew it had chanced upon a rider with exceptional talents. One who said little, spoke no French but could, nevertheless, propel a bike rapidly. His greatest success at Metz was in the Italian Amateur Classic, the Tour of Lombardy. It was acted out on a wet, miserable Saturday, 2 October. As is typical of the region, the course was undulating and there was much flooding in the valleys. A decade later only fragments of the original picture remain in Kelly's mind: 'I have a memory of looking down at my

chainring going through one flooded valley and trying
to calculate the level of the water. I reckoned it was two
feet deep.' A long professional career had continually
illustrated that Kelly was never bothered by inhospitable
conditions. Never put off by what he calls 'Paddy-
weather'.

In the final twenty of this 190-kilometre amateur
classic the rain eased. At the front there were twenty-
five to thirty riders. Victory would fall to one of the
group. An attack from Dutch rider Henk Lubberding
on the final hill threw the race into tatters. Only those
who were able to follow Lubberding preserved the
chance of winning. Two Italians joined the Dutch cyclist,
then Kelly went: 'I had read about Lubberding, I knew
he was a good one and knew that he had to be
followed.' For Kelly the victory sprint presented no
difficulty. He would wait eight years to win his next
classic. Curiously this turned out to be the professional
edition of the Tour of Lombardy. Then in one of the
final races of the 1985 season Kelly needed to win the
pro Tour of Lombardy again. He did and won the
Pernod Super Prestige Trophy with it. Italy gave more
to Kelly than some of his favourite food.

Success in the amateur Tour of Lombardy impressed
people. There was talk that France's most successful
directeur sportif, Cyrille Guimard, was interested in Kelly
and the word also got round that Jean de Gribaldy also
wanted him. De Gribaldy was then putting together a
French squad for the supremely successful Belgian-
based Flandria team. A team which contained world
champion Freddy Maertens and another highly successful rider Michel Pollentier. Kelly had decided in his own
mind that a professional career, if there was to be one,
could wait. At twenty he felt too young for the rigours
of the professional game and feared that if he tried and
failed he would then have to wait two years before being
regraded as an amateur. Two things are worth recalling

in this context: Sean Kelly never possessed any ambition to be a professional cyclist and he was extremely cautious about the challenge posed by the pro game.

The decision, to be altered three months later, would have been made easier by the fact that the amateur life in Metz was reasonably well paid. When the end of the season sums were totted up at Metz, Kelly returned home £800 richer than he had been at the outset of his journey. It was an amount great enough to render cycling at Metz worthwhile. Kelly told the people in charge at Metz the he would return to them for the 1977 season. They left him with a recommendation that he take French lessons over the winter. Metz had been a successful and homely continental starting-point or, if you like, a magnificent prologue to what would be a marathon and a fascinating stage race.

When Kelly arrived back into Carrick after that first flirtation with continental cycling, his local club ensured that the event did not go unnoticed. Sean had done well at Metz, the town should appreciate his exploits and the Carrick Wheelers Road Club was determined that it would. There was a reception, articles submitted to the local newspapers and a ritual had commenced that would continue each winter for the next decade. For one who showed no overt enthusiasm for recognition Kelly was always available when the spotlight shone. Linda, then his girl-friend, would collect the articles printed about him during his time at Metz and Kelly would browse through them with a curious fervour. Curious because this was the man who said he never cared for publicity.

Kelly's time at Metz had been very fruitful but also very lonely. He didn't speak the language, it had been his first extended period away from home and it had all been very trying. In agreeing to return to Metz, Kelly had silently thought to himself that he would attempt to persuade his fellow Irish international Pat McQuaid to return to the French club with him in the new year. Soon after returning to Carrick that October Kelly contacted McQuaid and asked him would he be interested in going to Metz. McQuaid agreed to go.

In early November Metz flew both to London, sent a representative to meet them there and, with the help of John Morris, agreements were drawn up to cover Kelly and McQuaid in Metz during the 1977 season. Both of the Irish amateurs were housed in an expensive London hotel and a bonus scheme offered them was significantly better than the one which obtained for Kelly in his first season there. Velo Club Metz Woippy knew that this Irish bike-man was not an ordinary specimen. When the offer would come from de Gribaldy a month later one of Kelly's chief concerns was whether he could abandon Metz and leave McQuaid on his own. McQuaid's generosity made it easy for Kelly. He said that he did not really mind; that he could find another to go to Metz with him. In the end Pat's brother Oliver, who had ridden in the Montreal Olympics, replaced Kelly at Metz.

It was on the ninth day of December 1976 that a small aircraft touched down in Dublin. A few hours earlier it had left Dole Airport, near Besançon in eastern France. Three men travelled in the plane. All were French. The pilot was Jean de Gribaldy, his passengers: Noel Converset and Bernard Dagot. Converset, a young amateur cyclist from Besançon, was brought to Ireland by de Gribaldy for the purpose of identifying Sean Kelly and then helping in the recruitment process. Dagot earned his passage because he was a fluent English speaker and thereby equipped to act as an interpreter for de Gribaldy. When not taking his place on bizarre expeditions to Ireland, Monsieur Dagot was Chief Air Traffic Controller at Dole Airport.

De Gribaldy recalls the trip with amusement. An understandable state of affairs given the somewhat unique approach to the matter of rider-recruitment. Once in

Dublin de Gribaldy's problems became apparent. He had to find out where the town of Carrick-on-Suir lay and then find a means of getting there. He decided upon a taxi and then spent sometime haggling about the price. De Gribaldy has always been a dour negotiator and there was never any likelihood that a taxi-driver from Dublin would make his fortune on the strength of this trip to Carrick. The taxi-driver appeased, the three Frenchmen departed for the distant Norman settlement of Carrick-on-Suir.

On arrival into the town they were directed to the Kelly family farm at Curraghduff, three miles out on the County Waterford side of the town. The lane to the Kelly home is rocky and narrow and the taxi-driver must have wondered about the effects to his vehicle. Jack and Nellie Kelly recall the arrival of the Dublin taxi into their yard for it wasn't the kind of event that a Curraghduff farmer expected. Sean wasn't at home. At the time he was working for his stepbrother Martin Power who had a farm machinery business. That afternoon Sean had driven a tractor to the village of Mahon Bridge and was to collect another tractor there and tow it back to Curraghduff. If Monsieur de Gribaldy cared to drive out the Dungarvan road he would probably meet Sean on his way back.

And so it was back up the lane, but instead of turning right towards Carrick the taxi swung left in the direction of Dungarvan. De Gribaldy smiles contentedly as his mind flicks back over the search: 'No matter what it took I wanted to meet this Sean Kelly. I was determined to get my man.' A few miles out on the Dungarvan Road the occupants of the taxi observed a tractor travelling towards them. The taxi slowed but continued on past the tractor. A hundred yards past de Gribaldy told his driver to turn around and drive slowly back to the tractor. Converset was now about to play his part. In the neat little party that had come from Besançon, each had a role.

Noel Converset fixed his eyes upon the driver of the tractor, shook his head deliberately and told de Gribaldy

that this boy was not the Sean Kelly he had ridden against
on the Continent. Kelly was being both cute and cautious
for he recognized Converset instantly but said nothing.
Noel Converset's performance did not humour de
Gribaldy who thought that this wiry-looking farmer's son
had to be Kelly. De Gribaldy told Dagot to ask the driver of
the tractor if his name happened to be Sean Kelly: 'Yes, I
am Sean Kelly,' came the timid reply. Through Dagot, de
Gribaldy explained why he had come. They talked for a
while on the road before Kelly said they could go back to
his stepbrother's house and talk there.

At Martin Power's bungalow they spoke for over an
hour. De Gribaldy found Kelly an extremely cautious
individual, the deep-rooted caution that can be so much a
part of rural life. When de Gribaldy left the room for a few
minutes Converset busily engaged Kelly in talk about the
pro game, how Kelly would do so well, how much money
he would make. Enthusiasm can sometimes be founded
upon peculiar motives. Kelly saw through Converset: 'He
wanted me to sign, for his sake. Before leaving Besançon
"de Gri" had told Converset that if he could persuade me
to sign then he, too, would get a contract. While I had
decided to have at least one more amateur year,
Converset's dream in life was to be a pro. It couldn't
happen soon enough for him.'

Jean de Gribaldy is very much of the old school. It is
doubtful if there are any other graduates still operating
from the world which produced him. Very much against
de Gribaldy's principles would be the notion of handsome
payment for a first-year professional. Rather de Gribaldy
prefers to offer the legal minimum, sometimes not even
that, and then pay the rider according to performance. A
salary structure that would be adjusted upwards after each
victory. In this way those new professionals who fail to win
races are encouraged back to normal life because the
monetary return from professional cycling is so inadequate. Kelly was being offered an annual salary of £4,000

and the prospect of more should he deliver. Although quiet and extremely shy, Kelly wasn't about to settle for a salary that he might well have earned in a good year with the amateur club at Metz.

De Gribaldy pressed for immediate agreement. It is very much a part of Kelly's nature to wait, to defer decision-making, to play for time, and so he told his French suitor that he would contact him a week later. In the interim Kelly sought advice from every possible source. Two of his closest associates, Pat McQuaid and John Lackey, received phone-calls, asking what they thought he should do. McQuaid said that the offer should be increased and then accepted. Lackey sharply recalls his assessment of the offer: 'I told him that while he had ridden brilliantly at Metz there was no guarantee that he would be nearly as successful if he went back again. This was the chance to be a professional and I told him to take it.' A week or so later Kelly rang Besançon, the salary was negotiated upwards to £6,000 and Sean Kelly agreed to ride as a professional for the Flandria team in 1977.

Kelly had never been starry-eyed about professional cycling. Nobody ever remembers him dreaming aloud about the joys of life as a pro. When de Gribaldy offered reasonable money and the prospect of a rewarding livelihood, Kelly then decided that he wanted to be a professional cyclist. The decision was steeped in pragmatism. As a cyclist he reckoned he had certain talents but his self-belief failed dismally to reflect the extent of his ability. He did, however, understand the consequences of signing himself into a professional team.

At once his association with the bike had taken on an entirely new colour. No longer could he look upon his involvement as a means of having fun and earning a little money. It was now his way of life. Progress would depend upon the rapidity with which he could turn pedals. If he failed as a professional they would not allow him to ride as an amateur for two years. Sobering reality. Bereft of

Converset's infatuation with the glamour of the professional circuit, Kelly was very much aware of what he
had to do: 'As soon as I signed I knew that my life had
changed. I had to to everything differently. Training,
eating, resting and early nights all became very important
things. I was determined to lead the life of the serious
professional. I wanted to give this everything I had.'

Signing for Flandria meant an end to what had been a
very fruitful, if brief, relationship with V.C. Metz. As it
had been agreed that Kelly would renew his amateur
career at the club in 1977, the news that he had signed
himself into the professional league came as a surprise.
Club president Alain Steinhoff responded in a manner
which hinted that the Irish boy, Sean Kelly, was seen as
something more than a piece of interesting cycling talent.
Steinhoff's final message to Kelly came in the form of a
written note. It said: 'In a professional team, especially in
the Flandria team, Life will not be good every day. But you
are courageous and strong. Continue to be the person that
we have known, uncomplicated and polite. And I am
certain that you will progress and make a success of the
life. Once again, good luck.' Kelly had been just five
months at Metz; he never spoke any French and had
become famous amongst the riders there as 'Sprint-Prime'.

The curious nickname again pinpoints the essence of
Kelly's professionalism. 'Prime' is the term for the intermediate sprints which are designed to animate a long road
race. Generally the winner of a prime receives a cash prize
and Kelly's team-mates at Metz were valuable in identifying the location of the primes during the race. The
Irishman would sense something when the pace increased
early on in a long race; he would shout 'Sprint-Prime?' at
one of his team-mates and would be told that there was
one in the next village. His hunger to contest each sprint
meant that he was forever shouting 'Sprint-Prime?' The
expression/question became synonymous with Kelly — the
lad hadn't left Curraghduff for a continental holiday.

When the last days of 1976 slipped into the new ones of 1977 Kelly was to be found packing his bags for a new life. He would travel light, emotionally and otherwise. If he was to succeed on the Continent he realized he would have to settle into the continental scheme of things. Learn the language, eat the food and drink the wine. Carrick would remain home but no more than that. It would not keep him awake at night, he would not spend his time wondering about the people at home, would not long for those to whom he had grown close. The people at home would have to get on with their lives; he intended to get on with his. Nellie Kelly recalls the time that Sean left to begin his professional career with Flandria: 'We might have been sorry to see him go but there was nothing for him at home; he had to try to make a go of it over there.'

Late in January Sean Kelly flew from Dublin to Geneva. From there he travelled to Besançon, home of Jean de Gribaldy. He would stay in that town during his two years with Flandria, at 18 Place de la Revolution, an apartment which was next to the bike shop owned by de Gribaldy. Always a firm believer in keeping a close eye on his riders, de Gribaldy would have found this an admirable arrangement. There were four other Flandria riders staying in the same apartment: Dominique Sanders, Rene Bittinger, Marcel Tinazzi and Noel Converset. De Gribaldy had honoured his pledge to make Converset a professional if Kelly signed.

For as long as he could remember Converset had wanted to be a professional. Kelly had never consciously nurtured the notion of riding the bike for a living. Now both were in the same house and in the same team, trying to make their way in the bike game. Noel Converset's dream soon collided with Reality. Wanting to be a professional cyclist was a disease of the epidemic variety in France; having the wherewithal to survive as a pro was a much rarer condition. Liberally infected by the first, Converset was singularly devoid of the second. He would remain a professional for but a short time.

Kelly remembers Converset being a strong rider but one whose strength of limb was at odds with his lack of mental foresight: 'Converset had no sense. He was stupid on the road. It didn't matter whether there was a headwind or tailwind, sleet or rain, he would attack. A nutcase. He caused more crashes.' And so John James Kelly went one way, Noel Converset another.

The following eight years would be eventful for Kelly, mostly successful but with many disappointments. Any review of his time as a professional would place much emphasis on the December day in 1976 that Jean de Gribaldy glided his own aircraft into Dublin. He would be a constant influence in the rider's life. Always close, always offering advice, and many of Kelly's views on the sport reflect what he has learned from de Gribaldy.

Professional cycling can often seem a world in which great contradictions rage. On one side the glamour, the wealth and admirable athletic discipline. Pitched against these positive forces are the cowboy aspects of professional cycling. The great abuses: riders being coerced into racing beyond the boundaries of what constitutes healthy competition, riders being underpaid, not being paid at all, the abuse of drugs, the casual exploitation of the top riders.

In an obvious way that trip to Carrick-on-Suir by Jean de Gribaldy was a precise reflection of the great contradiction. That de Gribaldy should arrive in his own aircraft, hire a taxi for the 110-mile journey to Carrick and then proceed to outline his propositions on the side of a country road is something that might only have occurred in cycling. Kelly, on his way home from Mahon Bridge on a tractor, being offered an annual salary of £4,000 by a man who had flown from France especially to confront him, took more than a little explaining. Sean Kelly might have been a quiet, shy country boy but nobody would have branded him naïve.

He would have considered the cost of flying from

Besançon, the taxi-fare from Dublin to Carrick, and
decided that £4,000 was not enough. When he rang de
Gribaldy they talked money, the contract was negotiated
upwards to £6,000 and acceptance followed. There was
more to being a professional than winning races. Kelly had
got off to a good start.

6 Flandria

Cycling in Ireland is not a major sport. There are approximately 2,000 racing-cyclists in the country; which is a way of stating that only the committed few and their next of kin compete. Sustained excellence at the highest level by Kelly and Stephen Roche has greatly increased the Irish public's awareness, but the numbers participating remain relatively small. In the pre-1980s the sport was little more than a minor curiosity in the tapestry of Irish life. Occasionally the sports pages concerned themselves with cycling but only when there was an explosion of public ill-feeling between the three associations which governed the sport. There was also the distinctly Irish Ras Tailteann, a nine-day stage race which struck at the romantic cord in Celtic hearts. It began in 1953 as a predominantly national tour and has continued uninterrupted, ever since.

Professional cycling was a phenomenon about which Irish people knew very little. Even those who formed the hard-core cycling fraternity could only draw upon knowledge acquired in specialist magazines. Before Kelly, you could have counted the Irish cyclists who had ridden as professionals in Europe on one hand and still have had three fingers to play with. There was just Shay Elliott and Peter Crinnion. One an accomplished rider in the pro *peloton*; the other a man who gave it his best shot without making a major impact. Elliott is probably best remembered for his silver-medal performance in the World Championship Road Race at Salo in Italy (1962). As a

team-rider for the great Jacques Anquetil, Elliott enjoyed
a lofty reputation.

Because he was the only Irishman to have achieved
success as a continental professional, Elliott tended to be
seen as an exception. Where in other circumstances
inspiration might have been drawn from his career, those
Irish cyclists who came after Elliott felt intimidated by his
achievement. Fed on a literary diet of Tour de France
heroes and aware of how talented Elliott had been, they
became prisoners of their own fantasies. It seemed better
to aim for the race in the next village. France and its great
professional races were much more than a boat trip away.
Elliott's pro career ended in the mid-sixties. His life on the
bike had been testimony to one man's ability; it didn't
mean Ireland could produce good bike-riders.

Ten years after Elliott's retirement Ireland's best amateurs dreamed of the Olympics, the Tour of Britain and
the race in the next village. Sean Kelly might have felt that
he had the means to propel his bike rapidly — he knew he
could win races but he did not dare to think of becoming a
pro. That would be heresy, akin to elevating oneself to the
level of an Elliott. Pat McQuaid shared rooms with Kelly
when they rode together as amateurs on Ireland teams.
When McQuaid won the 1975 and 1976 Tours of Ireland,
Kelly excelled as a team-rider. When Kelly did well in the
1975 Tour of Britain and won the Tour of Majorca in
1976, McQuaid was at his side. McQuaid knew Kelly better
than most: appreciated the cycling talent and understood
the person. He didn't envisage Kelly making it into the
pro game. Succeeding as a professional was utterly
beyond the range of possibilities: 'Nobody had done it for
so long. To us the gap between what the pros did in
Europe and what we did in Ireland seemed so great. So
vast.'

On 30 January 1977 Sean Kelly checked into Dublin
Airport for a flight to Geneva in Switzerland. His life as a
professional cyclist was about to begin. Kelly would arrive

into the Swiss city, be picked up there and driven to
Besançon in eastern France. For the following two years
18 Place de la Revolution in downtown Besançon would be
home. Home was a two-roomed apartment alongside the
retail business of Jean de Gribaldy, the *directeur sportif* at
Kelly's new team, Flandria. From an isolated farm in a
quiet corner of Ireland Kelly had been pitched into the
throbbing centre of a French city. Acute shyness stemmed
his flow of English, total ignorance of the language killed
any possibility of conversing in French, he had no friends
and knew little of what lay in his immediate future.
McQuaid understood: the gap was vast. His apprehen-
sions for Kelly were well founded.

Kelly had signed himself into the Flandria team.
A Belgian company, Flandria manufactured mopeds,
scooters, bicycles and sponsored one of the best cycling
teams in the world. At the beginning of 1977 it had Freddy
Maertens, Michel Pollentier and Marc Demeyer in its
squad. Maertens was then the World Champion, Pollentier
a strong all-rounder and Demeyer a forceful captain of the
road. Guillaume Driessens was *directeur sportif* of the
Flandria team and his pre-race talk tended to assume a
familiar pattern: 'We have the best riders, we are the best
team, now go out and prove it. Show them that we are the
best and that we intend to stay the best.' Results suggested
that Driessen's words were heard. When somebody invites
you to join this team the expectation is that your services
are being required to provide back-up support. It was no
different for Sean Kelly; he was being hired ultimately as a
domestique for Freddy Maertens.

Yet the Flandria set-up did offer Kelly opportunities.
He had been contracted, not by Driessens, but by de
Gribaldy. Flandria wanted a French squad to further its
commercial interests in France. It employed de Gribaldy
to assemble and then direct the new team. A former rider,
de Gribaldy had achieved success as a *directeur sportif* with
such riders as Van Linden, Van Springel and Agostinho.

Later he proved his talent for unearthing cycling ability where nobody else had seen it, and Michel Laurent and Patrick Perret were two of his discoveries. Contained in the Flandria proposition, de Gribaldy saw the means of building up his own team. It was known within the sport that Flandria would be quitting in a few years and de Gribaldy would then be left with the French squad he had assembled. The riders recruited for Flandria's team in France were drawn mostly from the second line of French amateurs and young professionals. De Gribaldy's budget had been limited and there were few potential stars in his crew.

Opportunity presented itself when Kelly rode for the French Flandria team. Without designated leaders de Gribaldy's young hopefuls were encouraged to try for their own victories. To ride for themselves. As the team competed mostly in the smaller French races, different members did do well. Particularly Kelly and the young French rider Rene Bittinger. Good performances meant promotion from de Gribaldy's squad to the team of Driessens and the honour of working in the service of the world champion, Maertens. Kelly's cause was helped by de Gribaldy taking a special interest in him. The *directeur sportif* had recognized Kelly's talent from the outset and, partly because of that bizarre trip to Curraghduff the previous winter, he felt personally responsible for Kelly's development. Their relationship was to be a critical factor in Kelly's gradual improvement as a bike-rider.

At 18 Place de la Revolution Kelly had four fellow-residents; Noel Converset, Marcel Tinazzi, Dominique Sanders and Bittinger. Tinazzi possessed a little English and exchanged the most basic thoughts with the Irishman. Kelly was a long way from home; the loneliness that had been his constant companion at Metz the previous season had come with him to Besançon. For a month Kelly was lost in the Frenchman's world. John Lackey had always said that Kelly, as an amateur, would lie on a bed of nails.

Spiritually, that assertion was being put to the test in Besançon. He suffered from the isolation and struggled desperately to cope with the absence of friends. Salvation was owing to two factors; primarly there was Kelly's mental constitution. The boy who had stayed up during the night to assist at the birth of a calf was quite prepared, as a young man, to live with loneliness.

But there was also the bike. Kelly wasn't a clever talker, he couldn't be deemed physically handsome and he didn't have the advantages of a formal education. Outside of the bike, there wasn't much that Kelly could claim to excel at. His talent was for turning the pedals. He enjoyed the feeling of mastery when he turned them faster than everybody else. If he did it well enough to earn a respectable living then Besançon could be tolerated. The alternative was placing one block on top of another, day in day out, on some nondescript building site near Carrick-on-Suir. For less money and without the thrill of a sprint finish. Jack Kelly's Curraghduff might have offered companionship but the texture of life there was just as severe as the cycling existence in France.

A few days after unpacking his bags in Besançon, Kelly was re-packing them. De Gribaldy was taking his team to the South of France for pre-season training and races. On Monday 7 February 1977 Kelly rode his first race as a professional. It was the opening stage of the six-day Etoile de Bessèges, a 125-kilometre race from Bessèges to Largentiere. The Belgian Andre Dierickx won, Kelly was tenth and the French Sports daily *L'Equipe* impressed. It reported that Dierickx had been on his own at the front when Kelly counter-attacked behind. *L'Equipe* decreed that Kelly was a rider about whom 'we would be speaking again'. Unwittingly, the paper was uttering one gigantic understatement: something akin to Noah peering out of his Ark and suggesting that it 'looked like rain'.

De Gribaldy insists he believed from that very first race in Kelly's potential. He recalls Walter Planckaert, the experienced and successful Belgian, approaching him and asking who was the new pro called Kelly, where did he come from and how old he was. The Flandria *directeur sportif* said he was from Ireland and was just nineteen (de Gribaldy, typically, exaggerated Kelly's youth — he was twenty at the time). Planckaert could not have been more impressed: 'Nineteen, no. This one rides like a twenty-nine year-old.' It was now de Gribaldy's turn to be impressed and he filed away Walter Planckaert's first race evaluation.

Twelve days later Kelly won his first professional race but the triumph escaped the notice of the judge who presided over the finish. There are no records which state that Kelly won the opening stage of the Tour of the Mediterranean yet that slight aberration should not be permitted to cloak reality. At the end of the 85-kilometre race on 19 February a ten-rider group streamed into the Marseille velodrome to contest the finishing sprint. Kelly and Jan Raas, a Dutch rider who would become World Champion two years later, were shoulder to shoulder as they flashed past the line. Raas had, in a gesture of triumph, shot his arm into the air as he crossed the line. The judge, without the benefits of a photo-finish, decided this was proof that he had won. Raas, first; Kelly, second. Kelly was sure he has won; de Gribaldy was utterly convinced. A few years later a photographer who had been at the finish that day met Kelly in the south of France and produced pictorial evidence proving beyond the remotest doubt that the judge had got it wrong.

After the Tour of the Mediterranean the team departed by boat for the Tour of Corsica. On returning from the French island a number of the team drove to Switzerland to compete in the Grand Prix de Lugano. Set in the southern tip of Switzerland, Lugano was a pretty town for a young man to record his first victory as a professional cyclist. Because it was a pro-am handicap race the success didn't mean much to Kelly. He easily outdistanced his five

companions in the six-man break which had controlled the
final part of the race. Kelly doesn't remember feeling
relief to have claimed his first win, much less euphoria.
Success in such a race wasn't something an aspiring star
boasted of. It would only assume a degree of relevance
when the deeds of Kelly's life were being chronicled. This
is probably the first time since the morning after the race (7
March) that the 1977 Grand Prix de Lugano has been
written about.

A month of Kelly's professional career had slipped by
and left the impression that, really, this pro circuit was
nothing like as severe as the lads at home had imagined. In
five of the races he had ridden Kelly had been placed in
the first four. His Lugano victory might have been small
but it was an indication that he could do things in
professional races. So far life on the circuit was a pleasant
competitive experience. That month had, however, little
to do with the reality of serious bike-racing.

Kelly's minor display of prowess over those first few
weeks had been noticed by Driessens and the Flandria
squad in Belgium. Both Kelly and Rene Bittinger were
selected to ride the Paris-Nice race for the Belgian team.
Paris-Nice was the first big stage race of the season. Kelly
was more than a little pleased and immediately accepted
the place; Bittinger found a way to decline the offer. A
month of racing and Kelly had earned promotion to the
best Flandria team. Even if not that precise about the
direction, Kelly reckoned he was going places. As a boy he
had read in the magazines about Paris-Nice. Those photos
of cyclists pedalling through sleet and snow remained in
his mind. Now he would ride this race and as a team-rider
with the World Champion Freddy Maertens. Kelly was the
only one of the French squad on the team. Paris-Nice
began on 10 March — so too did Sean Kelly's education in
the finer points of professional racing. Being a *domestique*
for Maertens wasn't an amusing experience, certainly not
in this particular race. Freddy won the prologue and

Apprentice Carrick Wheelers. The one on extreme right doesn't look like a future champion but it is a thirteen-year-old Sean Kelly

Kelly's first master, Tony Ryan, leads him on a training spin in Carrick, 1971 ▼

Kelly time trials in the jersey of his first professional team, Flandria

In the company of Spaniard Ismael Lejarr· an escape is made on the St Etienne stage · the 1980 Tour

Generally Spaniards don't sprint well. Ism· wasn't an exception

Victory in the seventeenth stage of the 1981 ur de France. Kelly outsprints Jean-ançois Rodriques (partially hidden) and han Van de Velde at Thonon

Overleaf: Riding the Col d'Eze time trial is an exercise in the toleration of pain

Paris-Nice 1982: at the end of the trip to Nice, race *directeur* Jacques Anquetil helps Kelly with the leader's white jersey ▼

lebrating with team-mate Serge Beucherie
g the 1982 Paris-Nice

Sean and Linda – 'marriage is not like the
Tour. If things are going badly you can't
climb off' ▼

▲ Kelly outsprints de Wilde in Pau and gains the bonus seconds to take *le maillot jaune* in the 1983 Tour

Stephen Roche leads the train and Kelly t first classic win in the 1983 Tour of Lombardy ▼

Kelly, centre, had LeMond, left, in his slip-
am during the final part of the race

At the line, LeMond was still in close
attendance. From left: Van der Poel (3rd),
Kelly (1st), LeMond (2nd) and Kuiper (4th) ▼

After each major victory  Irish flag is raised outside home of Herman and Eli
Nys at Vilvoorde, Brusse

In 1984 Kelly and Roche were first and second in Paris-Nice. Friendly rival

defended his leader's white jersey for the following seven days. Kelly, enthusiastic at first, was pushed harder than ever before in his life.

The general pattern was ordained at evening meal each day. Driessens told the team how good they were and how they could and would ride at the front of the *peloton* for the entirety of the following day's stage. By this time Kelly had assembled a few French phrases but the Flandria team spoke Flemish and he was, again, isolated. He could understand the overall drift of Driessens' strategy and he knew that, for him, each team talk meant another murderous day. Early in the next day's stage the Flandria boss on the road, Marc Demeyer, would issue the orders for Kelly: 'You must do this, you must do that, you shouldn't be back here. Come on, let's go up to the front.' In those days cycling permitted team leaders to be towed up hills by their *domestiques*. Freddy Maertens liked to avail of the facility and Kelly was often afforded an insight into the life of the donkey.

Maertens won that Paris-Nice. Driessens could claim that the operation had been an entire success but Kelly's enthusiasm for the life of the team-rider had been savagely undermined. 'Paris-Nice had been a race I wanted to ride but my outlook changed pretty quickly. It was so bloody hard. For three-quarters of the stage you worked for Maertens, then you got dropped and ended up finishing five or six minutes down. By the time you finished, Maertens had already received his bouquet of flowers for winning. Paris-Nice opened my eyes. I would be glad to get back to the French Flandria team where things were easier. I didn't want to ride too often for Freddy.' What the introductory lesson had impressed upon Kelly was that the *domestique's* life wasn't fun, that there had to be something better. He wanted the freedom to ride for himself, but he would wait for a long time before getting it.

Two days after Paris-Nice Kelly rode the classic Milan

San Remo ('When you rode for Freddy in the classics, you
worked for him during the first 150 or 200 kilometres,
after that you climbed off. Your day's work was done.')
and then he went in one direction and Maertens, Pollentier *et al.* in another. Kelly was happy to return to the
collection of modest talents that operated out of Besançon.
He had grown friendly with Christian Muselet, a young
French rider who spoke some English, and over the two
years at Flandria they roomed together when away on
races. Having recovered from the shock of Paris-Nice he
travelled with his French team-mates to the Tour of
Romandy in Switzerland and won the opening stage. Now
this was more like the real thing! More what Kelly wanted
out of his sporting life.

Victory was achieved in the sport's most thrilling
manner: from the scary and frenzied turmoil of the bunch
sprint. With 900 metres to go there was a major crash;
Merckx, Bittinger and others spilled on to the road. Two
hundred metres to go and the supremely fast Patrick
Sercu surged for victory. Kelly had picked the correct
wheel to track. Fifty metres from the line he jumped from
behind Sercu to win, decisively. Having a relatively
anonymous neophyte go flying past you at the end of a
race can be a singularly disconcerting experience. Particularly if you are Patrick Sercu, the champion sprinter from
Belgium. One notes the strains of disbelief in Sercu's post-
race reaction: 'He (Kelly) passed me without any trouble.
There is nothing that I can say. For my part I could not
have gone any faster. After all, nobody can win all of the
time.'

Exactly two weeks later Kelly won the Circuit de l'Indre,
a reasonably important race in France. Made very important for Kelly because he outsprinted Eddy Merckx to
claim the prize. There was a time when a young gun like
Kelly would not dare draw against Merckx, but now the
greatest 'cannibale' of all travelled with thirty-two years in
his legs. Travelled wearily. Kids could make their name

shooting down the ageing star. Kelly savoured his little triumph, deliberately forgetting that he dealt not with the fire of 'le Cannibale' but with his ashes. That evening in Châteauroux Kelly might have spoken to Merckx, if he had had the courage. Merckx might have spoken to Kelly, if the result had been different. They had passed one and other on Sport's ladder — one going up, the other coming down — and had not exchanged a word.

Things were falling into place for Kelly. His French improved, albeit very slowly. Team-mates showed more concern for the 'stranger' as the 'stranger' demonstrated a penchant for winning. Later in that first season Kelly recorded the fourth win of his career: outsprinting Willy Tierlinck of Belgium in a stage of the Etoile des Espoirs. He might have won the Tour of Holland but couldn't recapture the four seconds which Dutch rider Bert Pronk had snatched. First year professional and second in a National Tour, Kelly wasn't exactly screaming his dissatisfaction. That first year had gone well. A reputation had been established, the Irish one could sprint. Not in the Maertens league of super finishers but then who was in that league? (In 1977 Freddy had won the Tour of Spain and thirteen stages on the way.)

Kelly's recognition had emanated from the force he could generate at the very end of a race. There was something good in that and something dangerous. Any respect, whatever its basis, added to the rider's value and furthered his self-esteem, which for Kelly was a factor of enormous significance. Danger existed in the categorization. Accepting that one has a sprinting talent can carry a tacit acceptance that one can do nothing else. Kelly had come to the continent of Europe with a suitcase full of apprehension: 'Ma, they won't want me over there, I'll be back sooner than you think.' Who had been Ireland's last successful pro? Who had been Ireland's only successful pro? How long ago had he performed?

Offered a tag which carried a certain authority, Kelly

immediately said yes. He would wear it willingly. That this tag labelled the owner as a sprinter and nothing more made not a whit of difference to Kelly. He now had something that he could hide behind.

7 Freddy, Michel *et al*

Flandria wasn't just any old successful team. Kelly found himself matching pedal strokes with the best and a few of the best happened to be his own team-mates. Most of all there was Freddy. World Champion in 1976 and later in 1981, certainly one of the best sprinters the sport has known. What kind of beast could go to the Tour of Spain, win the overall prize and thirteen stages? Freddy Maertens, 1977 Vintage. Phew! Flandria had a mega-star. The spotlight of World Cycling focused almost exclusively on Maertens in 1976 and 1977. His athletic frame cast a giant shadow and those around him were engulfed. Michel Pollentier, his Flandria team-mate, had to be very good to impress upon the world his claim to be an above average professional racer. Michel was very good. When Freddy and Michel were at their best, winning seemed a mere matter of course. Both achieved spectacular form in 1977, the year of Kelly's arrival.

It began with Maertens's domination of Paris-Nice. Kelly, only a *domestique* for the team leader, struggled to survive. When it ended he returned to his French squad at Besançon while Maertens, Pollentier and the Belgian Flandria team rode the spring classics. Kelly was re-called to service for two of the classics: Fleche Wallonne and Amstel Gold. Freddy claimed Fleche Wallonne. Another notch on his cleats. At the end of the classics the Belgian squad departed for the Tour of Spain; Kelly and the French riders represented Flandria in a series of smaller races in France and Switzerland. While Kelly was

putting together the first few modest pieces in the jigsaw
that will eventually constitute his career, Maertens and
Pollentier were feasting at the best tables.

First there was that Spanish conquest. Michel and the
team working for Freddy, watching him toy with the
opposition. Winning thirteen stages. Riding on the crest of
a tidal wave, the team swept into Italy. Now the Giro
d'Italia. Freddy would be unleashed and the Italians had
better run for cover. Most had indeed hidden as the
peloton sped into Mugello towards the end of the second
week. Freddy had seven stages under his saddle and
appeared likely to take an eighth when an horrific crash
brought him tumbling to the ground. He fractured a wrist
and left a team without its brightest star. Flandria
mourned, even considered calling off the Italian expedition but finally resolved to continue. Sponsors pay the
Piper and sponsors call the Tune. Always continue. Some
publicity is better than no publicity.

With Freddy gone, Marc Demeyer and, especially,
Pollentier blossomed. Cometh the hour, cometh the men.
Demeyer won two stages and Pollentier outclimbed Moser
in the Dolomites to take the pink jersey of race leadership.
Italy, convinced it had been granted a reprieve by
Maertens' ill-fortune, was stunned by Pollentier's authoritative assumption of his master's role. On the final day
race leader Michel reminded the 'tifosi' that his ascension
to leadership was no fluke as he flew to success in a time
trial. That was the Giro. Where to next? Switzerland of
course. Freddy was still out of action so Michel would have
to lead again. This time Michel delivered even more
authentic impersonations of Freddy as he copped four
stages, the yellow jersey and the points jersey. There was
now but one place left for Michel, home. He returned to
Belgium and a week later became National Champion. At
the end of the year Belgium voted Michel its No.1
sportsman for 1977. So that was it: Michel Pollentier,
Chief Lieutenant of the Flandria team, Superstar.

Flandria had built an exceptionally successful team around three men; Maertens, Pollentier and the late Marc Demeyer (he died suddenly in 1982 at the age of thirty-two). Demeyer was a very decent racer, as his victory in the 1976 Paris-Roubaix suggests, but his principal contribution to Flandria lay in his road captaincy. He made a very effective link between the two leaders and their *domestiques*. Marc was a big boy — you did what he said.

The team's success was not, however, without tarnish. Suspicions existed that both Freddy and Michel traded on more than the strength of their legs. After the Tour of Belgium in 1977 six riders were alleged to have had illicit substances in their systems. Three of the six were then the biggest names in Belgian cycling: Merckx, Maertens and Pollentier. A few weeks later Freddy won the Fleche Wallonne, a classic he would later have taken away because of an alleged doping offence. As Freddy swept to his thirteen-stage success in Spain, questions were being asked. Approached by *L'Equipe's* reporter in the town of Igualada in Northern Spain, Freddy's response was disconcertingly cavalier: 'There are no problems in Belgium, everybody is positive.' Michel maintained more discretion and refused to discuss 'these problems'.

Another perspective on how the victims viewed the laboratory findings was provided by the declining star, Merckx: 'I do not believe any more in these controls; it is all becoming ridiculous and hypocritical. I haven't even asked for a second analysis. I am going to make a list of all that is wrong with these controls. As things are nobody could have confidence in them.' For cycling the stakes were high. *L'Equipe* wrote about the Sport's other race. The track pursuit: on one side the Pharmacist, on the other the Laboratory Analyst. New drugs being provided for the cyclists by the former and the laboratory people desperately trying to catch up with the adversary. Accepting the places which Merckx, Maertens and Pollentier

occupied in cycling's chain of being, it was understandable
that their connection with drugs would ignite some sort of
fire. Freddy's casual dismissal had been the only surprising
element in the affair.

Yet, like any self-respecting hurricane, drug controversies blow themselves out. Maertens and Pollentier demonstrated new levels of accomplishment in the Tours of
Spain, Italy and Switzerland. And all dope tests were
negative. Freddy could almost afford to be cavalier. At the
end of 1977, Freddy, Michel and Demeyer could reflect on
an exceptional year. Committed to the Tours of Spain and
Italy they had by-passed the Tour de France, but that
would come in 1978. Everything in 1978 would be for the
Tour. Other things would have pleased the Flandria men
about 1977. For example that new recruit, the quiet one
from Ireland, he was an addition. They would use him
more in 1978.

Quite content to stay out of Maerten's way in 1977, Kelly
enjoyed the less severe routine of the French squad. He
had liked both Freddy and Michel but being a part of their
team was too demanding. It was the two team leaders,
Michel and Freddy, who made the effort to incorporate
Kelly into the general scheme of the team's life. Freddy
had a habit of translating the dinner-table jokes from
Flemish into English for his young *domestique*. Similarly
with Michel, he too spoke some English and used it to
Kelly's advantage. They were not the kind of leaders who
wanted to dominate their *domestiques*. Everybody could be
friends, and if orders had to be issued Freddy spoke
discreetly with Demeyer and maintained his own cordial
relations with the troops.

Kelly saw little of the two big men in the early part of the
1978 season. Mostly he rode with the French team and
actually considered that he might go through the season
without having to ride any of the major stage races with
the Belgian squad. For Freddy and Michel the Tour de
France was the focal point of their year and the campaign

conducted in the first half of the season was mostly preparatory. In his own mind Kelly had planned to give the Tour a miss for another season. Four weeks before the Tour wheels were scheduled to roll, Kelly remained adamant about his non-participation. Then a few of the Belgians that had been considered likely to ride the Tour opted out and the twenty-two-year-old Irishman was invited to take a place. De Gribaldy talked Kelly into acceptance, saying that his comrades, Bittinger, Muselet and Tinazzi were all competing and that Kelly would get through the race without major difficulties. Kelly trusted de Gribaldy's judgement.

De Gribaldy's assessment was utterly vindicated. Kelly worked for Freddy in the sprints and performed diligently in other aspects of team-work. One of his functions entailed the chasing down of breakaways. As a rider or group of riders broke clear Kelly was to attach himself on to the back of the wagon and hope that his presence would discourage the escapers. Why bring Kelly to the finish, on a free ride, and then have him out-sprint you for stage glory? On the sixth stage from Maze to Poitiers two heavies, Gerrie Knetemann and Joseph Bruyere, surged clear inside the final fifteen miles. With the lights flashing at amber, Kelly and Bittinger accelerated; so too did the Swede Sven Nilsson. All got up to Knetemann and Bruyere. The lights went red. The stage was between these five.

Bright and attractive, the yellow jersey danced before Knetemann's eyes. Bruyere considered himself a likely heir once the jersey had dispensed with Knetemann, and into Poitiers the two rode as desperately as they had ever done in their lives. Kelly and Bittinger, present to protect the interests of Freddy and Michel, merely followed wheels. Nilsson's role in the group wasn't easy to define. Had he been blessed with a sprint then he could have passed himself as an opportunist. Defending the position of team leader Joop Zoetemelk would have been his alibi.

Getting close to the finish Kelly concentrated on Bruyere, Bittinger sat tight behind Knetemann, and Nilsson was left to his own, limited, devices.

For Kelly this was an obvious opportunity. Twenty-two years of age, small-time team-rider and suddenly the chance to win a stage of your first Tour de France. A time for keeping one's nerve, an indiscreet move and all was lost. Nilsson did the predictable thing; bolting for home with 500 metres to go. Bruyere reacted first, charging off in pursuit. With his man gone, Kelly felt it time to move. He cut down Nilsson and Bruyere sooner than anticipated and found himself at the front with 200 metres left. A sitting duck for an accomplished marksman like Knetemann. As the line neared Kelly's advantage dwindled. On the line he held on by the width of a spoke. Ten yards beyond the line Knetemann had passed. For the Dutchman there was the titanic compensation of the yellow jersey; time gained racing into Poitiers had enabled him to dispossess team-mate Klaus Peter Thaler.

It had beem frightfully close for Kelly. Fortune had taken his part. The centimetres which divided him and Knetemann at the line lay at the heart of a better life for the young Irishman. His salary would increase; organizers of the criteriums immediately after the Tour would now pay a little to have Kelly in their races. Future employers would need more money to win Kelly's services. And, not unimportantly, the people of Ireland were made aware that they had a cycling ambassador operating in France. Until then Kelly had been an obscure, almost anonymous figure in his native country. Winning a stage of the Tour de France was a deed destined to prise Irish eyes open. The emergence of a star had begun.

For Flandria the Tour was gathering an interesting momentum. On the day before Kelly's Poitiers success Freddy had won in Maze. A day later Freddy would win in Bordeaux. The team's overall strategy depended on Michel performing in the mountains. Freddy didn't climb

well enough to be counted a yellow jersey candidate but
Michel did. And Michel was also a formidable specimen in
the vitally important races against the clock. Michel's
pedigree included victory in the Tours of Italy and
Switzerland and, a few weeks before this Tour began, he
displayed excellent form in winning the Dauphine Libere.
Regarded in France as the number one preparation race
for the Tour, The Dauphine is primarily a test of one's
mountain talents. If Michel could take the yellow in the
Tour, Freddy would certainly take the green, and between
Freddy, Michel, Kelly and Demeyer stage victories would
abound. What a prospect? Sean Kelly stood to be a part of
something special. A small part but a part nevertheless.

On the evening of 16 July Kelly seated himself with the
Flandria team in the restaurant of the Hotel du Castellan
at des Cimes at Alpe d'Huez. Celebration time appeared
near at hand. Kelly took a place alongside Christian
Muselet, his friend and room-mate. It was a little after
eight o'clock. This evening Flandria's warriors were
entitled to an extra glass of wine with their food. Michel,
heroically, had broken clear of the pack on the road to
Alpe d'Huez and then maintained an advantage on the
murderous ascent. He won on his own and assumed
leadership of the race. The prized yellow jersey. The new
award added to Michel's collection for he had already had
the red polka dot of Mountains Leader. Freddy owned the
green. Flandria could smile — the three principal jerseys of
the Tour and all hanging in its wardrobe.

Soon after the meal commenced Kelly noticed journalists coming into the restaurant. They were asking Michel
questions. Thinking to himself that this was a little strange,
Kelly tried to pick up what was happening. Journalists
didn't normally intrude at meal-times. Michel, sitting at the
other end of the table, was being quizzed about what had
happened at dope control? Kelly had heard nothing and
was a good deal more ignorant than the inquiring
journalists. As the questions grew more specific Marc

Demeyer intervened. Standing up to give full expression to his formidable physique, Demeyer told the journalists that if they didn't leave immediately he would throw them out. Not interested in finding out whether Demeyer meant to handle them individually or all at once, the journalists left. Kelly sensed a major problem.

Somebody told that Michel had tried to dupe Dope Control officials by using a plastic tube and rubber bulb apparatus to provide a bogus urine sample. Somebody else said that Michel had been eliminated from the race for his attempted fraud. Others provided conflicting stories. Nobody knew anything for sure. Then came the order for all the Flandria team to report to a room upstairs. Team *directeur* Freddy de Bruyne (he had replaced Driessens earlier in the season) and de Gribaldy presided over the meeting. It was explained that Michel had been found with the bulb and tube contraption in the dope control caravan and that he had been expelled from the race for attempting to commit a fraud. Now the question was whether the team should withdraw from the race and, in this way, voice their protest at the punishment inflicted on Michel. Loyal to his friend, Freddy favoured returning to Belgium.

The prospect of a mass exodus didn't much enthuse Kelly: 'I remember speaking with Muselet in our room and both of us agreeing that, no matter what we felt, other people would make the decision. If it was true that Pollentier was caught with this apparatus, and nobody was denying it, what could we say? Muselet and I had been pleased to have got so far in our first Tour de France and felt that it would be a pity to stop when the hardest part was over. We wanted to continue.' More importantly, Flandria wished to continue. Maertens still had the green jersey and that was worth some publicity. A dream might have fragmented and shattered in the heat of Alpe d'Huez but the sponsor, financially committed, insisted on the employees hanging around to pick up the pieces.

Almost incredibly, Kelly recalls that over the remaining part of the Tour the mood of the team remained positive. Demeyer won at Belfort, Maertens at Soissons. Freddy did retain his green all the way to the Champs Elysees and the team had taken five stages in all: 'You didn't think of Michel half-way through a stage and feel a sense of anti-climax. He was gone and you were still stuck in a race.' Eventually Kelly finished thirty-fourth out of the 110 participants, had won one stage, finished second in another and had ridden well for Freddy. On the day he was second Kelly failed to Hinault in a sprint. A loss which emphasized the limitations of the *domestique's* life. Ten miles from the finish in St Etienne Freddy told Kelly he didn't feel so good: 'Today it is for you to make the final sprint Sean.'

Closer to the finish Freddy revised his strategy. He was feeling a little better and decided that he would take his chance in the sprint after all. Kelly, informed of the new arrangements, suffered his instant demotion quietly. In the long slightly uphill finish at St Etienne Kelly made his way to the front with about 500 metres to go. Freddy should have been in his slip-stream. Kelly presumed he was. Less than 100 metres from the line Hinault appeared from directly behind Kelly. Thinking Hinault to be Maertens, Kelly didn't offer resistance. Near the line Hinault stormed past and Kelly could only cast a horror-stricken glance at his rival. Freddy reigned supreme in the league of big sprinters, but even he suffered an occasional off day, 'un jour sans'. On that day, if you were a free agent, you stood to gain. *Domestiques* tended to go down with the ship and its captain. Kelly noted the difference.

For Freddy and Michel, Alpe d'Huez was the day the music died. Nothing would ever be the same at Flandria. Never again could Freddy be cavalier in his attitude to drugs. Being caught with illicit substances in your system during a minor event like the Tour of Belgium was one form of transgression. Using a rubber bulb, plastic tube

and somebody's else's urine to help take the yellow jersey
in the Tour de France was another. The difference
between shoplifting at the neighbourhood's huckster store
and robbing the Bank of England. Freddy and Michel
shared thirteen years of friendship; they even shared the
same birthday, 13 February (on what other date of the
month could they have been born?). At the end of the
1978 season a parting was deemed advisable. Michel was
going to accept a sizeable offer (estimated at £200,000) to
head the Splendor team, based at Namur in Belgium. He
wanted Kelly to come with him; Freddy wished his Irish
friend to stay at Flandria. Gaining custody of Kelly
produced a tug of war that strained relations between the
two tragic heroes of Flandria.

Years after the Alpe d'Huez episode (one that was
superbly documented by Robin Magowan in his book *Tour
de France: The 75th Anniversary Cycle Race*) Kelly lives with
surprising memories. The sentiment which wasn't apparent then is now felt for Michel: 'He was a sort of crooked
figure on the bike, no style. But he would have taken some
beating in that Tour. In the back of my mind I imagined
that Michel wasn't the type of rider that Felix Levitan, the
Tour director, wanted to win the race. Michel wouldn't
have looked so good in yellow on the Champs Elysees.
What Michel did was wrong, the organizers were entitled
to put him out, but if it had happened with another rider
the reaction might have been different.'

Kelly's not so subtle suggestion is that had it been a
Hinault or another popular French rider the race organizers would have steered a different course. A year earlier
it had been rumoured that a Bernard Thevenet urine
sample was positive in the Tour and that a blatant cover-
up had been effected. All Belgium believed that in the
Tour there were laws for French riders and laws for others
and that the two sets did not correspond. Their Michel
had been a victim. Pollentier was never the same afterwards. Once he had been aggressive and enthusiastic, now

he was a wasted star. In 1980 he did win the Tour of Flanders but that was merely one day off on the journey to cycling anonymity.

In the middle of his last season, when he led the humble Belgian crew Safir, Michel and the team went to Switzerland for the Tour de Suisse. It was the thirteenth day of June 1984, and the location for the prologue was Urdorf, a pleasant suburb east of Zurich. Michel cycled around the start area, trying to keep loose and warm before his four-kilometre effort. As he did, Kelly ambled down the same side road on his bike. They didn't meet much any more. Kelly now led the successful Skil team, was rated the World's No.1 and came to Switzerland on the back of enormous publicity. Michel was now a small man in the *peloton*. Playing out his time without dignity. He looked at Kelly and smiled, an 'I remember you when you were only ...' sort of smile. The warmth in Kelly's smile could not be missed. He called his friend 'Michael', the English version of the name hinting at an affection and familiarity of past days. Kelly too could remember when the circumstances of Michel's life were different. They spoke only briefly. Words could not change anything for Michel.

Similarly, Maerten's career never again reached the heights scaled in 1976, 1977 and 1978. He did make a brief return to the highest level in 1981, winning five stages of the Tour and then claiming the rainbow jersey with an exceptional sprint in Czechoslovakia. Like Michel in the 1980 Tour de Flanders those successes were but a pleasant interruption. Freddy's slide recommenced in 1982. At the time of the 1978 Tour Michel was twenty-seven and Freddy twenty-six; too young to be finished but too weary to continue waging war in the front line. Kelly thinks of Freddy as the most talented bike-man he ever encountered: 'To me he had so much class, getting into the position and then sprinting. There was nobody like Freddy. The classiest bike-man I ever saw.' The latter years in Freddy's life career were even more troubled than

Michel's. Starting races but not finishing. Promising to
start and not showing up. Nobody felt anger. Everybody
felt sadness.

Kelly speaks keenly about the apprenticeship he served
at Flandria. Learning to prepare the sprints for Freddy,
listening to Marc Demeyer assessing situations on the
road, watching Michel's courage in the mountains. What a
school for the neophyte? He doesn't talk about the other
beneficial part of the Flandria curriculum. Observing the
paths pursued by Freddy and Michel and learning
something about what not to do. If you abused the system
then the system was likely to strike back and get you. The
Tour made Michel pay a savage price. Freddy too
suffered. He never enjoyed good health in the final years
of his career.

There was also a financial message for Kelly. Michel and
Freddy earned vast amounts of money. Before both had
finished with the bike, rumours abounded about their
financial ruin. Even allowing for exaggeration, it was clear
that neither was financially secure for life after cycling. A
few months after leaving his bike in the garage Michel was
on the road again, a sales representative for an auto tyre
company. Kelly had the benefit of watching Freddy and
Michel close-up. Earning big money did not in itself make
a man rich. Money had to be earned and then preserved.
Freddy and Michel proved that some skill was also
necessary in the achievement of the second part. When, at
the beginning of 1979, Kelly went to live with Herman and
Elise Nys in Brussels he entered an environment where
thrift was practised and preached. Elise would talk of 'la
folie des grandeurs'. Kelly was listening. Freddy and
Michel had taught their pupil well.

Some time during the month of August 1978 Michel
told Kelly of his plans to join Splendor. Michel encouraged
Kelly to move with him. There were two reasons for saying
yes: increased salary and better winning opportunities.
Through Michel's eyes it was simple. He would lead the

team in stage races and Kelly would be the team's sprinter. Kelly might have been reluctant to part with de Gribaldy but the offer could not be refused. His annual salary was to jump from £12,000 to £20,000 and if he used his new freedom well then he could earn much more. Freddy wanted Kelly to stay and encouraged Flandria to insist that the Irishman fulfil his contractual obligations to the team. (At the end of 1977 Kelly signed a two-year contract with Flandria but because the team changed its subsidiary sponsors at the end of 1978 this contract was declared invalid.) Splendor's *directeur sportif* Robert Lauwers flew to Ireland and confirmed the authenticity of his team's contract with Kelly after talks with the Irish Cycling Federation.

Jean de Gribaldy occupied a place in the back seat as Kelly contemplated and accepted Splendor's offer. Disappointed at losing his protégé, de Gribaldy recognized that Alpe d'Huez had changed things: 'I didn't want Sean to go. Not in my heart. But in my head I knew it was good for him to get away from a team that was dying. A team whose name had been besmirched by drugs. He had learned much at Flandria but would only go down with the team if he stayed. I also thought it was good that he should go to Belgium. Things are bad there. No organization, right from Federation level down to the riders. Sean would suffer because of the Belgian system but it would do him good. Belgium would further his education and he would eventually want to come back to France.'

So Kelly's affair at Flandria was over. One can only surmise at the effects it had on his career, his life. Whatever, it was no ordinary introduction to the world of professional bike-racing. Like a shy, innocent sixteen-year-old whose first romance had been with a thirty-five-year-old lady, Kelly's life after Flandria could never be quite the same.

8 A Belgian Home

When Adolf Hitler set about his war business in the Europe of the late 1930s Herman Nys had turned seventeen. A Belgian, Nys's primary interest in life was sport; cycling, boxing, football. Circumstances can, however, broaden one's endeavours. Nys became involved in the underground movement to resist the spread of Nazi Germany. In Belgium this was the White Army. By the time Europe had been liberated Herman was a regular soldier in the Allied Forces. During his training he spent time in Larne, County Antrim, Northern Ireland and in Hull, England. The experience gave Herman a feel for life beyond the Belgian border.

Wartime life carried its risks and, following a bad motorcycle accident, Herman spent two-and-a-half years in hospital. During that time he received an invitation from the Danish Red Cross to convalesce with other war victims who were recuperating in Denmark. Herman accepted and learned a bit about the Danes. Through the war and subsequent hospitalization Herman tended to his passion for sport. Four years after liberation he married his Belgian girl-friend Elise, and they spent part of their honeymoon at the World Cycling Championships in Copenhagen. That was 1949.

Eight years later the World Championships were staged in Belgium and one member of the competing Danish team remained on in Belgium when the Championships ended. He wanted to compete regularly against the best amateurs in Europe, and Belgium was an obvious location from which to conduct such a campaign. The young Dane was called Eric. He came from a country which didn't have a significant presence in continental cycling and Eric wasn't equipped to alter the situation. Yet he came and tried. Before leaving home for Belgium Eric had been armed with the name of Herman Nys. A man who knew cycling and was certain to offer friendship to an adventurer from Denmark. Herman looked after Eric. Other Danes came and Herman did whatever he could. Preached a little advice, massaged loneliness with encouragement and turned up at the end of a race with a flask of tea. The Danes came to appreciate and like their Belgian friend.

In 1964 Denmark sent a team to the World Championships in Sallanches, France. Herman knew some of those in the official party. They wanted him to come, as their guest but also as a part of the back-up team. Herman talked with Elise and accepted the invitation. On the day following arrival the 100-kilometre team-time trial was taking place at Albertville. Not much enthused by team-time trialing Herman opted to go for a walk around the camping site where he stayed. His eye was turned by a man wearing a green jersey with 'Ireland' written on the back. Herman, remembering Larne in the forties, felt compelled to talk. He began by asking the stranger whom he had come to support. The stranger replied that he had come to Sallanches not as a supporter but as a competitor: 'I will be riding the Amateur Road Race for Ireland on Saturday.' Herman wondered who looked after the Irish competitor? Wondered who had been so thoughtless as to allow a World Championship competitor to sleep in a tent? 'But I came here on my own, I am looking after myself.' It was time for introductions. Herman Nys proffered his name, Liam Horner did likewise. Taken by the indomitable spirit of the Irish cyclist and moved by his own feeling for those from the smaller cycling nations, Herman wanted to help.

He inquired what Liam did with the bike when he was

going to bed at night: 'I put the bike into the tent first and
then I get in myself.' Herman was completely sold. Liam
Horner, one of Ireland's best amateur racers at the time,
had a friend. Having persuaded the Danes to carry Liam
into the Race Headquarters at Sallanches, Herman then
had some explaining to do when the Irish cyclist vomited
in the back seat of the car. Herman did his best. The
friendship with Liam blossomed. From it another relationship developed. Herman Nys and Irish Cycling. In future
years an Irish cyclist lost in Belgium looked up Herman
Nys. His house became a kind of refugee camp for Irish
cyclists.

Kelly's decision to leave Flandria for Splendor at the end
of the 1978 season meant moving from his Besançon
apartment to a new location in Belgium. Two years of
living in Besançon had been good but sharing an apartment with other bike-men had led to some obvious
difficulties. Loneliness remained Kelly's constant companion. His co-residents at 18 Place de la Revolution
could use the apartment as a base, staying a night and
moving on to their parents' homes for a few days. For
Kelly it was a permanent base. When all the others went
home he was left alone. He didn't want to begin a new life
with Splendor in some apartment with riders who might
and might not be around.

During his winter break at the end of the 1978 season
Kelly spoke with his old friend Pat McQuaid and between
them they concluded that Herman Nys should be contacted. McQuaid wrote to Nys and asked whether it would
be possible for Kelly to stay the following season. Herman
and Elise Nys had noticed Kelly winning a stage of the
Tour de France the previous summer and knew him to be
an above-average professional. They agreed to provide a
continental home for the cyclist. Early in the new year
Herman and Elise encountered Splendor's *directeur sportif*
Robert Lauwers and were surprised when Lauwers said
Kelly would be staying with him. Somebody had mis-

understood somebody else. The Nyses said nothing.

Kelly did stay with Lauwers, in a room over a bar. Music blared from a juke box all the time. Kelly survived just three weeks. One day he rang Herman Nys at Vilvoorde, a town north of Brussels, and asked whether there was still a room for him? Herman was tempted to reply that he didn't operate a hotel, but resisted. That evening Sean Kelly arrived at 108 Breemputstraat, Vilvoorde. Six years of his life would be spent under the roof of the Nys home, good years. Passionate cycling enthusiasts, Herman and Elise watched their lodger grow from a reasonable team-rider to the World's No.1. The evolution wasn't straight-forward or easy and all the more satisfying for not being. Kelly became much more than a long-term guest. Gustav Nys, the only child of Herman and Elise, jokes that his father always wanted a son who could be a cycling champion: 'But I grew to be a little big for the bike and was better at basketball. He was disappointed. Then Sean came along.'

At first Kelly was intensely quiet and shy. Elise Nys speaks English well but Kelly needed time before he felt relaxed enough for easy conversation. He spoke mostly with Herman during those first few months. He endeared himself to all by volunteering to go to the supermarket with Elise and helping her with the groceries. Elise would mischievously introduce Kelly as her 'second son'. The Nys family was also impressed by Kelly's fastidiousness in the matters of his bike, shoes, clothing. Everything had to be as near to perfect as possible. Nothing was untended. When you raced, all of your equipment had to be utterly clean and totally functional. But, most of all, Herman Nys liked the dedication of his new tenant.

Each evening at around nine o'clock Kelly left the Nys living-room for bed. Sometimes his departure came during a good television movie or, on another occasion, during an enlivened cycling discussion. A World War Veteran, Herman thought he knew something about people. He wondered about Kelly's early nights. His feeling was that Kelly read in bed, or listened to music. To pacify raging curiosity Herman used to wait fifteen or twenty minutes after his lodger had gone to bed, then creep up the stairs as quietly as possible. Outside Kelly's door he bent down and peeped through the keyhole. He expected to see a light on or hear music playing. But everything was quiet — the lodger lay deep in sleep. Herman went away convinced he had taken in an unusual boy.

Herman and Elise Nys grew close to Kelly. They cared for him as parents care for a son. Elise tried to cook the foods that conformed with Sean's dietary needs and Herman followed his career with unflinching enthusiasm. Herman recognized the cycling talent in Kelly but wondered about the person. Having the physical means was but one part of the overall requirement: 'Sean was being unfairly treated at Splendor,' Herman recalls, 'but he would not stand up to the people who were in charge. Even today, he hasn't the way of a champion. I imagine a champion to be a person who is difficult to live with. Sean was never that. He wouldn't push himself forward in the team. I always thought it was a part of his Irishness.' Elise Nys encountered a similar lack of assurance: 'Sean was never sure of himself. I would say "you must dare to achieve something", but he did not have enough ambition. I still don't believe he is ambitious enough.'

Kelly's needs were few. He didn't socialize in Belgium and his Irish girl-friend was never overburdened with continental mail or long-distance phone calls. Elise recalls that Sean wrote one letter to Linda Grant during his time with them and that manuscript had its origins in persuasion from Madame Nys. 'He was', says Elise, 'like a horse with blinkers on. All he could see in front of him was the next race.' The Belgian couple understood cycling, knew what was necessary if a rider was to succeed and they fully accepted Kelly's single-mindedness. Even admired it.

Kelly spent over six years lodging at 108 Breemput-straat, Vilvoorde. His first three years while racing with Splendor and then three years back with Jean de Gribaldy. With Splendor Kelly realized only a fraction of his talent. Not too many detected a potential champion in the young man who struggled to assert himself in the Splendor team. Herman Nys was one of the few. His belief in Kelly's talent was total. After a race Kelly returned home and explained the reasons for another defeat. Herman listened. Not in the kind, sympathetic way of somebody trying to under-stand but with the deep frustration of a man who believes talent is being wasted. Once Herman went to the Splendor sponsor Armand Marlair and suggested that the team should be re-structured around one rider — Sean Kelly. Marlair heard what Herman said but he wasn't listening.

Herman and Elise Nys provided an important link in Kelly's rise to sporting eminence. They offered a home to a boy badly in need of the familiarity and closeness of family life. They helped with his French and ordered their home to accommodate the presence of a cyclist. In six years of having Kelly in their home Elise remembers just one occasion when she had to speak disapprovingly to her tenant: 'It was just after the 1979 Tour de France. He was going away to ride somewhere and I found a bag of dirty socks in his wardrobe. I said "what a pity about the socks" but Herman immediately said "this boy has just come from the Tour de France, you must not quarrel with him". That was the only time that I ever had to say anything like that to Sean.'

One of Elise Nys's most prized recollections is that for six years she never had to answer the phone and explain to some young Belgian or French girl that Sean was training, or asleep or away. Rene Lombaerts, a sports journalist with the Flemish daily *Het Laatiste Nieuws*, once came to interview Kelly but ended up asking Elise an inordinate number of questions. Elise didn't disappoint the interviewer. Lombaerts wrote a story on Kelly which took its cue from the headline 'Living the Life of a Monk'. An exaggeration? Possibly, on the side of understatement. Linda Kelly never anticipated hearing much from her boyfriend during the racing season. He didn't surprise her. Kelly wanted Linda to be around when the season ended and was otherwise happy to let things drift.

Herman and Elise Nys might be categorized as middle-class Belgians. Owners of a very attractive home with the means to live comfortably. The couple maintain a healthy respect for the value of money and they encouraged Kelly to look after his earnings. They were preaching to the converted. Nevertheless, their words re-inforced his conviction. Greg LeMond and Phil Anderson might have Mercedes and exquisite houses in the Belgian countryside but these were things for which Kelly felt no need. He had ridden as a professional for four years before he permitted himself the luxury of a car.

At the end of the 1981 season Herman, Elise and Kelly went to a market in Vilvoorde. Kelly began looking at some vests. Surprised, Herman asked Kelly what he was about? 'I am going to buy a new vest,' said Kelly. Astonished, Herman replied: 'But you have four of them at home in your room and the team supplies them to you free of charge.' 'I know,' said Kelly, 'but for the entire year I have bought nothing and I just want to buy something.' Herman frowned and smiled to himself. Kelly left the vest on the shelf, the money in his pocket. As Herman and Elise might say: 'La folie des grandeurs.'

9 Racing to *Ziel*

They tell a story about the Splendor days, *circa* 1979. A little tale that invariably stimulates laughter and throws a cloak over bad times. Four months of the season had passed and Splendor's new formation was struggling to achieve even a semblance of respectability. Pollentier, Kelly and their *domestiques* were not delivering. Armand Marlair's investment looked ill-conceived. A lot of money and for what? *Directeur sportif* Robert Lauwers failed to convince the riders that he understood the needs of the professional cyclist. Lauwers had to be replaced. Shortly before the Tour of Switzerland in June Albert de Kimpe was named as Splendor's new *directeur sportif*. He couldn't be with the team for the start of the Swiss Tour but he would join up with it after a few days. He arrived into Zurich Airport, was met by Lauwers and the two travelled to the town which accommodated the race that day.

As they drove away from the airport de Kimpe asked Lauwers which town hosted the race that evening. Lauwers didn't instantly recollect the name. Picking up his race schedule he leafed through the book until he came to the relevant page. Then he said: 'Ah the race finishes in *Ziel* this evening.' De Kimpe hadn't heard of that Swiss town before and told Lauwers as much. Robert insisted that it existed alright. Wasn't it named in the map of that day's stage? Still dubious, de Kimpe said he had never come across any town in Switzerland called *Ziel*. Undaunted, Robert offered undeniable proof: 'Oh I remember driving a coach through that town a few years ago. I used to drive a coach you know.' They motored onwards.

Ziel, of course, is not a Swiss town but the Swiss-German word for '*Fin*'. On the race schedule each day's route is traced from the *Start* to the *Ziel*. Robert Lauwers had a quick glance at the day's map, didn't notice the name of the town, did notice the *Ziel* and jumped to his unique conclusion. Splendor riders heard about the new Swiss town and laughed. What else? The team itself was not working and the natural instinct of the rider tended to highlight the failings of those in control. Cycling's buck-passing. Lauwers, the riders said, knew little about the realities of big-time cycling. Sometime, somewhere, he had picked up the notion that winning bike-races was a straightforward matter. Just jump up on the bike, stamp on the pedals harder than the next guy and, hey presto, you won. One day in Brussels, then in Paris and, finally in *Ziel*.

When Kelly opted to ride with Pollentier and leave Flandria for Splendor, he travelled with lofty aspirations. For two years he had ridden as a *domestique*, one of Freddy Maertens's men. Now, there was the certainty of oppor-tunity. He could be a team leader, at least when the terrain was flat. Splendor also paid better than Flandria. Life promised much. The team which Splendor assembled had possibilities. Pollentier had brought four of his *domestiques* from Flandria and nobody doubted the enthusiasm and commitment of the sponsor, Armand Marlair. As Robert Lauwers might have put it, all that remained was for the riders to get out there and win races.

The team's pre-season training camp was based near Benidorm in Spain. There, they enjoyed ten days of training in perfect conditions. Riders used their own bikes while training and only received the Splendor team bikes in time to compete in their first race, the Grand Prix de Peymeinade in the south of France. Rain fell from the skies as this race went on its way and Splendor's troops were more than a little concerned to discover that the brakes on their bikes failed to operate properly in the wet conditions. Kelly remembers that first race: 'There were about thirty laps of a circuit. On one part there was a descent which meant Splendor riders having to put their feet on the ground to make sure they slowed down. It was a disaster.'

All through the early part of 1979 the team's equipment was appallingly inadequate. As well as deficient brakes, wheels disintegrated when subjected to the cobbled roads of the classics. The team refused an invitation to ride the greatest one-day classic, Paris-Roubaix, because bikes which could not survive on ordinary roads had no place over the cobbles of northern France. Suddenly Kelly's move to Splendor was perceived as unwise. How could a team be so badly organized as to provide its members with inadequate equipment? That was kind of question Kelly would never have asked. He had joined a new team; his idea of settling in entailed months of listening and maintaining an unobtrusive presence within the team group. A champion might have struck the board and screamed his disapproval. Kelly stayed silent.

Victory in the early season Grand Prix de Cannes suggested that Kelly might be on the road to a good season. But that success was misleading, and by the time the Tour of Spain began in April Splendor had suffered serious and consistent losses in its spring classics campaign. Splendor's hope was that things would pick up over the course of a long tour in Spain. Kelly won the first stage by outsprinting Eddy Van Haerens in Seville. But 1979 was determined to be unpleasant. On the second day of the race Kelly came as close to serious injury as he has ever done in a volatile and controversial sprinting career. The finishing straight in Cordoba was wide and slightly downhill. As the pack descended towards the line Fons de Wolf led, Van Haerens was second and Kelly third. Kelly sensed another victory.

About 150 metres further up the straight a policeman

noticed somebody on the wrong side of the barrier and instinctively walked across the road to evict the trespasser. He had his back to the mass of cyclists whose frenzied pounding bore not a trace of fear. In an instant the policeman was in front of them. Dead centre of the road. De Wolf, as leader, was safe. He swerved to the left and got past. Kelly, noticing the misplaced human on the road, left three lengths between himself and Van Haerens. Hoping that gap would leave him a little room for manoeuvre in the event of Van Haerens crashing.

Van Haerens moved to the right but so too did the policeman. Collision. Kelly flew evasively to the left. As he did Van Haerens's bike bounced from the impact of the crash directly into his path. Kelly tried to jump his front wheel over the straying bike. Clever but impossible: 'When I came down I slithered for about twenty-five yards. Everything was spinning, riders going in every direction, all the sounds. Then it was over and all that remained were bodies, a mass of crashed bikes that were stacked five-feet high on the centre of the road and blood. The road was full of blood-stains. I had broken nothing. Still it was a bad one. In terms of frightening crashes this one stands at the top of the list. When I slid along the road flesh was ripped from my arms, knees and backside.'

There were then the days and nights of recovery. Trying to sleep through the pain and discomfort of a wounded body. The heat of southern Spain stoking the fires of soreness. And then having to ride the following day. Stretching on the bike and re-opening the wounds. Nature triumphed and, three days after the crash, Kelly won the bunch sprint for second place into Murche. Another three days and he had won into Benicasim. Learning to live with spills is a part of the life.

The two stage wins changed little. Splendor's mechanical problems remained a factor. Punctures were a daily occurrence and there was a feeling that the team could not be using the best tyres. Jean Jacques Simmler reported for

L'Equipe that the ambiance in the team 'was not a healthy one'. Kelly went for a third stage win on the ninth stage into Saragossa but found himself unable to pass Noel de Jonckheere in the finishing straight. De Jonckheere had left the narrowest gaps for Kelly to come through but the Irishman didn't have the strength. In such situations the laws of sport dictate acceptance of defeat. What laws? Kelly grabbed de Jonckheere's jersey, pulled it and then found himself in front at the line. He told the journalists that the Belgian had 'pushed me into the barriers. If I didn't pull his jersey I would have fallen. It is a scandal.' De Jonkheere and the Race Jury knew better. The result was changed and Kelly demoted to last.

On the next day there was an unpleasant sequel to the affair. The stage ended into Pamplona. Another furious bunch sprint. Chief Commissaire Raymond Trine of Belgium, concerned by the illegalities of the Saragossa sprint, wanted to watch this one close-up. His driver slowed the car in the finishing straight. It motored about fifty metres in front of the bunch. Trine stood up, and through an open roof looked back at Kelly and de Jonckheere acting out another desperate sprint. This time the sprint was fair — hardly a surprise with Trine observing. A few yards beyond the line Trine's car could proceed no further. The police marshalling the finish area had failed to maintain a passageway for cars. Kelly, who had finished second to de Jonkheere, hit the stationary car first. Then his team-mate Pollentier hit it.

'Michel had given me a lead out in the sprint. When I saw the car a few yards past the line I went for the brakes and stuck the bike to the road. But it was too late, I crashed into the rear bumper and went flying out over the handlebars on to the back of the car. I split my ear but that was the only injury. It all happened in an instant but yet I can remember seeing Pollentier as I rolled off the car. He hit the back of the car, flew through the air and bashed his head off the rear window. The window shattered and

Pollentier fell back on to the road. He lay there without
moving, having lost consciousness when his head hit the
window. I was sure he was dead.'

Hindsight infects the scene with strains of slapstick
humour: Michel's balding head drilling a hole in the back
window of the car. But there was nothing funny about the
episode. Kelly told Simmler: 'They (the organizers) are
trying to kill us on this race. For me it is now over. I intend
to return to Brussels tomorrow.' Kelly remained for
another week and was forced to abandon when falling to a
stomach sickness that afflicted many riders. Despite his
two stage wins, Kelly's first Tour of Spain had not been a
pleasurable experience. His retiral with just two days
remaining still stands as the only time he has ever pulled
out of a major Tour.

After Spain the team returned to Belgium and a serious
re-appraisal of its general performance. De Kimpe was to
replace Lauwers as *directeur sportif*. That was the major
outcome. But things had been allowed to slip so much that
a change in leader was not going to turn a dismal season
into a good one. By the time the Tour de France loomed
Splendor found its riders unenthusiastic. New Zealander
Paul Jesson, who had ridden as an amateur for two years
in Belgium, was hired. A month later he was one of
Splendor's ten-rider Tour de France team. With five days
of the 1979 Tour remaining that team had dwindled to
just two, Kelly and Mynheer. The rest had cut their losses
and run back to Belgium. Kelly finished second on the
fourteenth stage, narrowly beaten by his old Flandria
team-mate Marc Demeyer. Flandria had survived the loss
of Kelly and Pollentier. Its riders looked over their
shoulders and smiled at the problems Splendor suffered.
Kelly won nothing on the Tour. The year began with an
equipment crisis and had stumbled along discontentedly
thereafter. At the end of the 1979 season Kelly knew he
was part of a sub-standard organization but not many
teams were offering him an alternative. This was, without

any doubt, the lowest point in his professional career.

The year had introduced Kelly to a young man from St Niklaas in Belgium, Ronny Onghena. A *domestique* on the Splendor team, Onghena was a quiet person. Modestly talented but prepared to fulfil his duties as a team-rider. It seemed to Ronny that Kelly wasn't getting much help from his team-mates and he offered his services exclusively to Kelly. The foreigner was not going to be left entirely unaided. Onghena, a strong rider on the flat, was particularly good at ensuring a comfortable passage for Kelly in the early part of races. He became one of Kelly's closest friends in the *peloton*. Kelly would eventually adopt Ronny as his favoured *domestique* and over the following seasons would demand that his employers also take on Ronny. Kelly had also got to know Jesson, who spoke neither French nor Flemish. During the Tour he tried to help the New Zealander understand what was happening. He knew what it was to feel on the outside, to feel oneself a foreigner.

Given the events of the season in 1979, Splendor's sponsor Armand Marlair was entitled to fold tent and slip quietly out of cycling. He decided to dig deeper and increase the investment. Claude Criquielion, Johan de Muynck and Guido Van Calster were brought into the team. All came with interesting pedigrees and Splendor's team for 1980 was clearly a much stronger combination than the failed collection of individuals in 1979.

The new strength was reflected in a convincing opening to the season. Pollentier interrupted his gradual decline to outsprint Jan Raas and Francesco Moser in the important Tour de Flanders Classic. The team returned to the Tour of Spain far more organized that it had been a year earlier. Kelly finished second in the prologue and then won the opening two stages. He seemed set for a feast. Then on the fifth day he move to claim his third stage win and found a man who was resolved to hit back. In the opening three stages Kelly had outsprinted Klaus Peter Thaler. Enough was enough. Into San Quirce Thaler veered violently to his right as Kelly surged. His hip hit Kelly's handlebars and a man who might have won lay sprawled on the road. After the bunch had screamed past, Kelly picked himself up and limped to the finish line. The girl with the bouquet of flowers was already smiling in Thaler's direction.

Six years on, Kelly's recollection of the crash is matter-of-fact: 'He just did me, plain and simple. There is no such thing as a straight sprinter but Thaler was particularly dangerous. He could handle a bike very well and that allowed him to do things that others would not even try. If his hip had made contact anywhere except the handlebars I might have stayed upright.' Kelly survived Thaler's excesses to win another three stages. His haul of five stage wins and the overall points award pleased him. Splendor had done well. Jesson won his first race as a professional when capturing the difficult mountain stage from Burgos to Santander. In the overall classification Kelly finished fourth, a position he achieved without ever trying to attain it: 'I had gone there to win stages; Criquielion was our man for the overall. If somebody had said I was to try for the yellow jersey I suppose I could have won it, but I was then a sprinter and sprinters weren't meant to win races like the Tour of Spain.'

Things had progressed enormously inside the Splendor team. De Kimpe greatly improved the organization and de Muynck introduced an element of analysis into the team's tactics. Kelly benefited from the experience of de Muynck and remembers him as being a major help to the team: 'For the first time we were talking and thinking about our race tactics.' Splendor used the Alpine Dauphine Libere race as preparation for the 1980 Tour but, for one member of the team, this race ended in tragedy.

The stage victory in the Tour of Spain had been the high point in Paul Jesson's cycling life. His first win as a professional. Back in New Zealand they realized that Paul wasn't wasting his time in Europe. Jesson was extremely quiet. So quiet that, coupled with Kelly, the Irishman seemed loquacious. Now the Tour de France lay in Jesson's immediate future. Riding the Dauphine was a natural stepping-stone. Jesson first stretched for that stone in the seven-kilometre prologue to the Dauphine. The prologue course at Evian began with an ascent, then a descent and finally on to a bigger road and a flat section. Jesson rode fast on the downhill part. Too fast. At the bottom of the descent he lost control and collided with a parked car. He broke a knee. A season had ended suddenly. Jesson spent two days in a nearby hospital and was then transported back to Brussels. Later the damaged leg became gangrenous and was amputated. A career had ended.

In his mid-twenties Paul Jesson was a long way from home. Splendor said they would find a job for him when he finished with the hospital. The job never materialized. Paul had always found the language difficult. He went back to New Zealand. He has returned to Belgium at different times. During the 1984 season he turned up at the Fleche Wallonne Classic. His old friend Kelly had prospered greatly in the years that followed. That morning, in the Belgian town of Huy, Paul wanted to see Kelly. To momentarily recall the days when they rode together, to congratulate Kelly on his outstanding achievements. They met. Kelly felt uneasy. Professional cycling had made one a king and had devastated the other. The dealer of life's cards had never explained motives. Kelly recalls the Jesson story and says: 'Things like that frighten you'.

They may, but the fear is put to flight when the wheels gather a swirling and violent momentum near the finish. Twenty-four hours after the Jesson tragedy, Kelly lost out narrowly to French rider Patrick Friou in a bunch sprint at Macon. A day later Kelly willingly assumed the role of *domestique* and provided a perfect lead out for his team-mate Guido Van Calster. In Spain Van Calster had worked consistently well for Kelly and now the leader was

rewarding his servant's diligence. Van Calster won and
Kelly was second. On the fourth day Kelly won himself,
then Criquielion triumphed. Splendor rejoiced, for Criquielion had also taken the race leader's yellow jersey. Paul
Jesson was on the road to Belgium, *en route* to the loss of a
limb but the Splendor show went on. Not only that but the
performance was apparently undiminished.

The 1980 Tour de France testified to Kelly's strength
and his naïvety. After the Dauphine Libere he had taken
a two weeks break in Carrick-on-Suir. This mid-season
visit to Carrick had become a part of Kelly's year but, on
this occasion, it had come far too close to the Tour de
France. De Muynck saw no logic in the trip and criticized
Kelly, first to his face and then to any pressman who cared
to listen: Kelly's naïvety stretched further. Even though
acknowledged as one of the best sprinters in the *peloton*,
his ambitions for the 1980 Tour did not emcompass the
green jersey of points winner. The omission was bizarre.
Kelly remembers that in those days he rode 'from day to
day and never had the confidence to aim for anything'.
When the points were added up at the end of the Tour
Kelly was second, just forty-one points behind the winner,
Rudy Pevenage.

The 1980 Tour brought two stage wins. Both in the last
four days of the race. After the vacation in Carrick, it had
taken Kelly over two weeks to sharpen up. His second
stage win came in a bunch sprint. Kelly won by about five
lengths, a staggering margin of superiority for one
sprinter over the pack. Interestingly, his other stage win
resulted from untypical adventure. He broke away with the
Spaniard Ismael Lejarreta on the Croix de Chaubouret
climb close to the finish at St Etienne. Lejarreta led up the
hill, Kelly straining to maintain contact. On the descent
Kelly assumed breathtaking control and the Spaniard is
said to have raced downhill in Kelly's slip-stream screaming: 'Kelly, you loco, you loco,'

Despite the lack of focus in Kelly's ambition he was

travelling in the right direction. Geoff Nicholson wrote in the London *Observer* that he was one of the few young riders in the Tour to offer real hope for the future. Could even Nicholson have realized the heights to which Kelly would eventually climb? *L'Equipe's* Jean Marie Leblanc reported that he was of an age (twenty-five) which still held out hope of enormous athletic improvement.

The cycling life was again smiling on Kelly. Teams came looking for him, the money offered escalated. But he liked Splendor's sponsor Marlair, and when Splendor's money matched the others, Kelly re-signed immediately. At the end of 1980 he even treated himself to a new car. Four years as a professional cyclist and he had earned the right to his first form of automated transport. Marlair wanted an even better team and bought the two Planckaerts, Walter and Eddy, for the 1981 season. The younger one, Eddy, came into the team with a big reputation as a sprinter. As a Belgian amateur he had been very success-ful.

Kelly tried to believe that Planckaert's arrival was a good thing. That two sprinters were better than one. He says he got on okay with Eddy. Splendor's team had now taken on an extremely formidable complexion but the strength was at a price. In recruiting Eddy Planckaert the team had added another star to its line-up. Kelly, de Muynck, Criquielion and Planckaert all seemed entitled to support but the pool of *domestiques* was not nearly as impressive as it needed to be. Kelly was assured of Onghena's support but the others tended to offer their services to a Belgian master. Time and again Kelly moaned about a team which was full of Chiefs but devoid of Indians.

The fragility which lay at the heart of Splendor's unity was forcefully exposed in the Fleche Wallonne Classic on 15 April. Kelly was now in his third season with Splendor, in his fifth season as a professional bike-racer. He had yet to win a one-day classic. Ten kilometres remained in the Ardennes Classic when Criquielion detached himself from the leading group. Dutch rider Adri Van Der Poel countered; they were joined by Kelly, Van Calster and Daniel Willems. The quintet established a fifteen seconds lead on the bunch and the odds seemed stacked in Splendor's favour. Three of its riders against Willems and Van der Poel.

Claude Criquielion is one of the few Belgian cyclists from the French-speaking Wallonne region. Fleche Wallone meant a great deal to Criquielion. Criquielion attacked from the group of five with 600 metres to go. He was retrieved by an alert Van der Poel. At the 300-metre post Kelly was tracking Willems. Something was wrong. Kelly should have been in the slip-stream of Van Calster, receiving the benefit of his team-mate's support. But this was a Belgian classic, Guido Van Calster was Belgian and had decided to free-lance for the afternoon. Kelly stayed behind Willems too long and when he eventually moved he found Van der Poel blocking his path. Totally disgusted, Kelly free-wheeled across the line. Willems had won, then Van der Poel, Van Calster and Kelly. Splendor had presented the world with an Everest of incompetence.

Fingers pointed in all directions. Herman Nys watched in horror and held Criquielion most culpable. His attack had been an exercise in selfishness that was bound to fail. Kelly felt Van Calster to be the chief culprit: 'Ninety-nine times out of a hundred I could beat him in the sprint but on this day he tried to win himself. If he had led me out it would have been a straight sprint between Willems and myself.' Ultimately it didn't much matter who had erred. Splendor and Kelly had not delivered. Years later Kelly recounts his time with the team and says that he doesn't have much right to complain: 'Looking back on the records, I didn't win as many races as I should have.' Kelly was being paid about £30,000 a year by Splendor; the salary was based on the presumption that he would win: there was no clause stating under which circumstances defeat would be excused.

Two weeks later Kelly rode the Four Days of Dunkirk
and held the leader's jersey until the concluding time trial.
Raleigh's Bert Oosterbosch ousted him. A month later
Kelly wore the leader's jersey into the final stage of the
Tour of Luxembourg but got into direct confrontation
with three powerful Soviets — Soukourachenkov, Barinov
and Shuun — and was mauled. A two-month period that
might have yielded victories in three major events had
produced nothing. Kelly's lack of authority was a part of
the problem and Albert de Kimpe's failure to impose
discipline within the team was another part. De Kimpe had
two sprinters, Kelly and Eddy Planckaert, but he could
never decide which should get the team's backing on any
one day. With an absence of direction from the top,
disloyalty permeated the ranks. Kelly suffered silently.

During the 1981 Tour de France the feeling existed that
de Kimpe had finally nominated Planckaert as the team's
number one sprinter. Kelly contested the opening sprint
of the race but lost to his former boss Freddy Maertens. As
the race progressed de Muynck sensed that Kelly was not
sufficiently motivated. He goaded Kelly, telling him that
he couldn't win a stage on this Tour, that he (de Muynck)
would hand over a bottle of champagne and 1,000 Belgian
frances (£16) if Kelly should claim a stage. Kelly won at
Thonon les Bains, outsprinting Jean Francois Rodriquez
and Johan Van de Velde after team-mates Criquielion and
Sven Ake Nilsson had helped to create the winning
opportunity. Criquielion, Kelly's room-mate, complained
that with de Muynck's money, Kelly would be able to make
more phone calls to his girl-friend in Ireland and he would
get even less sleep.

Claude Criquielion's reference to Linda suggests that,
even though his cycling career stumbled forward, Kelly's
relationship with his Carrick-on-Suir girl-friend was now
on a more definite path. A year later they married. Years
of drifting ended. Kelly had also resolved to end the
drifting course of his career. Three years at Splendor had

brought more pain than satisfaction. He knew he was a
better rider than he appeared to be at Splendor. De
Gribaldy retained complete confidence in Kelly's ability
and by the middle of 1981 Kelly had determined to return
to his first professional master. De Gribaldy first heard of
Kelly's intentions from Marcel Tinazzi. At the time Tinazzi
rode for de Gribaldy's modest team Sem Puch. During the
1981 Tour Kelly asked Tinazzi to ask de Gribaldy if he was
interested in having his old rider back. It was hardly the
approach of a champion but then Kelly was a long way
from being one.

De Gribaldy's original evaluation had hit the mark.
Belgium could not provide a fruitful home for an
Irishman trying to progress in the cycling world. Kelly
returned to his old *directeur sportif* as undisputed leader of
the Sem France Loire team. De Gribaldy encouraged Kelly
to aim for the biggest prizes and surrounded him with a
team so limited in its talents that the new leader felt a
strong sense of being the only member of the team capable
of even attempting. De Gribaldy displayed much cunning
in finding a way around Kelly's natural lack of confidence.

Although pleased to be jumping off the Splendor train,
Kelly had been helped by the Belgian experience. His
friendship with Claude Criquielion deepened at Splendor
and they became very close. Two of Kelly's greatest classic
wins (Liège-Bastogne-Liège 1984 and the Tour of Lombardy 1985) were owing in a large degree to the help he
received from Criquielion. There was also Ronny Onghena. He proved to Kelly that some *domestiques* could be
loyal. They liked one another well. On the road Ronny
looked after Kelly and afterwards Kelly used his influence
to ensure that Ronny got a good deal. A condition of Kelly
joining Sem France Loire was that Ronny be taken as well.

At the time of Kelly's greatest successes in 1984
newspapers and magazines all over the cycling countries of
Europe delved into his life. In piecing together his past the
Splendor years were mostly dismissed, a blot on the

copybook. The reference usually said something to the effect that he had been unlucky to find himself in a badly-run team. Kelly knows that such a summary errs in divorcing him of responsibility. Things that are clear to some men at twenty were not clear to Kelly until he was twenty-six. For five or six years he had allowed his relationship with Linda Grant to wander on, with no particular end in sight. For three years at Splendor Kelly wasn't sure of where he was going or where he even wanted to go. Cycling greatness was for others. Kelly had turned twenty-five when he cashed in his meagre chips at Splendor. There was still time to begin a new cycling life. Maybe de Gribaldy and his little team could provide the inspiration to embark on a more rewarding journey. Maybe, just maybe....Although a long way from the rider he was to become, Kelly wasn't entirely without hope.

10 Taking off the Mask

For the first five years of his professional career Kelly wore the mask of the sprinter. Or, more precisely, he hid behind it. Le sprinter Irlandais. It was an exciting life. Kelly was assured of winning a certain number of races each season and would earn reasonable amounts of money. His salary as a first year professional with Flandria had been £6,000; twelve months later it was £12,000 and then £18,000. It seemed like a lot of money at the time.

The life pleased Kelly. Sprinters were a special breed in the tapestry of continental cycling - the men who risked all for one victory. No gap was too narrow for them, elbows assumed as much importance as legs, and the common currency was intimidation. Kelly wasn't unsuited by the ground rules. Since his early days as an amateur he had possessed the capacity to produce something extra at the very end of a race and his natural aggression meant that when things got dangerous he was never one to back off.

And so the story ran: Kelly the sprinter, le sprinter Irlandais. The tag was complimentary in as much as it identified him as one of the most rapid finishers in the sport. But the concentration on his sprinting talents fostered the impression that he could do little else. That he couldn't time trial and that he couldn't climb. For five years continental Europe believed Kelly to be purely a sprinter. The rider himself offered no conflicting evidence. The shy, self-conscious son of Curraghduff was content to act out his sprinting part and leave it at that. The sprinter's mask protected him in some way from the world, enabled him to earn his money without having his all-round talents as a bike-man investigated. Insecure and inhibited, Kelly would only answer questions about his favourite subject. Sprinting.

But there was a problem. Sprinters might win an occasional classic, they would often claim stage victories in the major Tours but they rarely won stage races. Kelly had spent five years of his career operating solely as a sprinter and didn't have that much to show for it. Stage wins in the Tour de France, in the Tour of Spain and in a host of lesser races but without ever being in the top position at the end. Kelly's personality provided a home for self-depreciation and self-doubt, and confining one's ambition to sprinting made things simple. Although feeding off only a fraction of his talents, Sean Kelly was not complaining. The boy who never spoke up in the classroom at Crehana National School was alive and still silent on the mainland of Europe.

His place in the cycling order at that time becomes perfectly clear when the 1981 Four Days of Dunkirk race is recalled. Despite its title the Dunkirk race lasts five days and is regarded as a mildly prestigious stage race. Kelly was in his fifth year as a professional and in his third year with the Splendor team. On the second day Kelly won the stage from Aire-sur-la-Lys to San Quentin and claimed the leader's jersey as well. The sprinter as race leader — nobody was getting overly excited.

Michel Seassau wrote a story in *L'Equipe* under the headline 'Kelly Pour Un Interim'. Seassau explained: 'We all know of Kelly's limitations in the test against the clock and one does not anticipate him being at the top after the concluding time trial.' Kelly would have agreed entirely. A day later he spoke with another *L'Equipe* journalist and said: 'I am in very good condition and feel perfectly capable of holding the leader's jersey until the concluding time trial. In this test Oosterbosch and Roche are my superiors.' Having conceded defeat before turning a

pedal, Kelly then acted out the part. Bert Oosterbosch won
the time trial and the race; Kelly went back to being a
sprinter. His courtship of the race leader's jersey had been
nothing more than a brief flirtation.

It had been forgotten that during his amateur days in
Ireland Kelly had shown more diverse talents. In 1975 he
was the Irish National Champion in the fifty-mile time
trial. A non-time trialist, as Kelly was presumed to be,
having somewhere in his pedigree a National title for his
endeavours in the art. Then there was his inability to climb
mountains? In that same year, 1975, Kelly had ridden in
the Irish team in the Tour of Ireland. The fifth stage was a
circuit around the rugged and beautiful Inishowen Penin-
sula in Donegal. It was a very hilly stage with the Gap of
Mamore, one of Ireland's best known climbs, to be
traversed. After thirty of the eighty-five miles Kelly broke
clear with two others, left his companions on a hill soon
afterwards, stayed out in front for the entirety of the trip
and won on his own by three minutes and twenty seconds.

But performing as an all-rounder meant that one had to
accept responsibility, had to live with the added burden
imposed by yellow jerseys, had to go for big prizes and
race furiously each day. Having settled easily into the
sprinter's life, Kelly quite enjoyed it. He liked the idea of
not having to try too hard in the mountains and he
enjoyed being able to coast in the time trials. When the
ambition to do more surfaced, Kelly restrained it. Like
most great transformations the metamorphosis of his
sporting life occurred not because of one single action but
through the interplay of a variety of factors.

Kelly had spent three precious years of his life with
Splendor in Belgium: 1979, 1980 and 1981. The middle
year was successful but the evidence of the other two
suggested that Kelly was no better than an ordinary
sprinter. A respectable member of the *peloton*, no more.
By the first week of May 1981 the divisions that eat away at
the team-work of Splendor had forced Kelly to commit

himself to another sponsor. Kelly told journalists that he
would be leaving Splendor at the end of the season. He
went even further, admitting that he would be joining a
French team. It is unusual for a rider to publicly express
an intention of leaving a team six months before doing so
and even more uncommon that he should have decided
on a new team. Once described by Kelly as the team with
all the Chiefs and no Indians, Splendor was about to lose
the greatest asset it ever had. Kelly wanted to get out.

During his years at Splendor Kelly had remained in
contact with de Gribaldy. If he wanted advice 'de Gri' was
prepared to listen and counsel. After tracing Kelly to a
quiet country road in County Waterford six years earlier
and encouraging him into professional cycling, Jean de
Gribaldy retained a deep interest. Kelly was his protégé.
Away from the competitive arena Kelly had remained shy
and vulnerable. De Gribaldy viewed it as his responsibility
to watch over the development of the boy he brought to
France. Kelly's difficulties at Splendor were spoken of
quite often inside the giant circus of professional cycling.
They said he wasn't hitting it off with the Belgians. That
he and Splendor's other sprinter, Eddy Planckaert, didn't
get on. People understood the problems. Kelly was a
foreigner, Planckaert was Belgian, the team was Belgian.
De Gribaldy sensed it was time to reclaim his boy.

At the end of the previous season, 1981, Jean de
Gribaldy managed a small team. His principal sponsor,
Sem, would not have had the resources of the bigger
teams: Renault, Peugeot or Raleigh. But de Gribaldy did
want Kelly. He sought Kelly as a team leader, not a team
sprinter. He was prepared to find the extra money
required to finance the acquisition. When Kelly studied
the list of riders that de Gribaldy intended employing in
1982, he knew for certain that the offer of team leadership
was totally genuine. There was no other member of the
Sem France-Loire team capable of assuming the role of
leadership. Kelly was being invited to discard the sprinter's

mask. Given his lack of success at Splendor in 1981 and
his trust in de Gribaldy, he accepted the offer without too
much hesitation.

After five years of being nothing more than a sprinter
Kelly was granted the licence to be something else. To be
somebody in world cycling. Although never consumed by
ambition he was interestd in this challenge. Many have
attributed relevance to the splendid performances of new
professional Stephen Roche in 1981, the inference being
that the meteoric rise of Roche made Kelly aware of his
own stagnation at Splendor, Kelly, in his customary off-
hand way, denies this. His dismissal of the notion comes
with the explanation that things are not quite so simple.
Possibly. But Roche's excellence in 1981 had to have had
an influence. Who were they going to love in Ireland?
Back home they were saying Roche had taken over from
Kelly in one season. Kelly, the fighter, would have drawn
both inspiration and motivation from the rise of his
fellow-Irishman.

Realizing that greater responsibilities were being thrust
his way, Kelly prepared with particular diligence for the
opening of the 1982 season. He went to training camp
very fit, and when the early season wheels began to roll in
the south of France the team leader of Sem France-Loire
was ready for his new life. The first important race of the
cycling season takes place towards the end of February,
the Tour du Haut Var. On the day before the race,
Saturday 27 February, L'Equipe said the race signified the
'Vrai Depart' of the season. It listed what it considered
the principal contenders: fifty-seven riders earned a
mention but not Kelly. If the Irish rider had determined
to take his performances on to a higher plane, L'Equipe
had failed to perceive the change in outlook.. Kelly won
the Tour du Haut Var and warned reporters that 'this
success gives me a lot of confidence and suggests to
me that I can have a very good season'. Freed from
Splendor and encouraged to come out from behind the

sprinter's mask, the real Sean Kelly was about to stand up.

For the Sem team leader life was rich in promise. His team would ride the Paris-Nice stage race and that would provide further opportunity for one with a blossoming ambition. It was the spring of 1982 and the spring of Kelly's career.

Kelly had eight team-mates at his side for Paris-Nice. French champion Serge Beucherie, Rene Bittinger, Jean Francois Chaurin, Jock Boyer, Guy Gallopin, Dominique Garde, Ronny Onghena and Marcel Tinazzi. All of them equipped to be *domestiques* but not one with the athletic or psychological wherewithal to lead. They needed Kelly as much as he needed them. De Gribaldy had assembled a team of modest talents but its actual limitations bolstered Kelly's confidence as leader. 'Tour pour Kelly', de Gribaldy was in the habit of saying. There was also an element of Kelly returning home, for when he joined Flandria in 1977 two of his flat-mates at the apartment in Besançon had been Tinazzi and Bittinger. Their lives had pursued different courses over the intervening years but, now, they were all re-assembled in the same camp.

There was a time when Paris-Nice was treated solely as a preparation race for the spring classics and the Milan-San Remo race in particular. The modern edition of Paris-Nice was conceived in 1951 by the painter-poet-cycling journalist Jean Leulliot. Towards the end of the fifties it began to gain in popularity and when Jacques Anquetil and Raymond Poulidor, two great French riders, clashed spectacularly during the sixties, the race had become something much more than a preparation for other battles. Eddy Merckx merely endorsed the standing of the event when claiming the 1969, 1971 and 1972 races.

Jean Leulliot wasn't a man ruled by convention, or even much interested in it. In 1974 he said amateurs could ride his race and a Polish team took part. About a decade later the rest of the world caught up with Leulliot and 'open' races flourished. Innovation was also at the heart of the

1982 Paris-Nice for it was scheduled to start at Luigne in
Belgium. A race called Paris-Nice starting in a Belgian
town! It was Jean Leulliot's last and most magnificent
insult to convention. The organizer of Paris-Nice died a
few weeks before the 1982 version started. His daughter,
Josette, assisted by her sister Jacqueline and her brother
Jean Michel, picked up the thread of organization and
carried on very much in the style of her father.

There were clear indications that Kelly was taking his
new position as team leader seriously on the evening that
Paris-Nice began. At the end of the 5.7-kilometre prologue from Luigne to Mouscron, Kelly was third behind
Oosterbosch and Bondue, two acknowledged specialists in
the art. One of Sem's *domestiques*, Chaurin, won the
opening stage from Chalons to Montereau and claimed
the leader's white jersey. On the fourth day the race grew
difficult. The first seventy kilometres of the 182-kilometre
journey between Vichy and St Etienne involved many
climbs, the most severe of which was the Col de la Charme
(3,675 ft). Chaurin lost fifteen minutes and his temporary
release from the drudgery of the *domestique's* life was
brought to an end.

Kelly remained with the strong men. The predictable
eclipse of Chaurin had left the leader's jersey on his
shoulders and he grasped it authoritatively. In winning
the stage into St Etienne Kelly outsprinted Roger de
Vlaeminck. The margin of victory was about three inches
and Kelly had the audacity and confidence to raise both
hands in the air a metre or so before the line. De
Vlaeminck wasn't much pleased. Not only had Kelly won
the sprint but he displayed customary ruthlessness in the
manoeuvres immediately before the final surge. In jockey-
ing for positions Kelly tangled with Phil Anderson: the
Australian lost ten spokes from his front wheel and
fininshed last of the lead group.

Even though Kelly was clad in the leader's white jersey
there was still a refusal to contemplate the possibility of a

sprinter winning Paris-Nice. Kelly wasn't taken too seriously. This was a race for the all-rounder. At the very end
there would be a mountain time trial. Kelly could neither
time trial or climb and so was deemed to be a non-
contender. Better to look elsewhere. The French decided
that the Peugeot rider Gilbert Duclos Lassalle would win.
Had he not won the race in 1980? Had he not proven his
ability in the Col d'Eze mountain time trial then? The
French rider was only one second behind Kelly in second
place on overall time.

Kelly seized upon the general presumption that he
would fail and tried to further it. After winning into St
Etienne he told the reporters: 'I have known since the
Tour du Haut Var that my form is very good but my
ambitions don't extend to winning Paris-Nice. The mountain time trial on the last day will not favour me.' Only
Stephen Roche saw through Kelly's words. Roche had
been worried by the tactics of his Peugeot *directeur sportif*
Maurice de Muer, who had fully expected that Kelly
would disintegrate on the Col d'Eze. Because he presumed
that Kelly was not a danger de Muer was happy to believe
that Duclos Lassalle would win the race, and felt no need
to try to jump either of his other highly placed riders
(Roche, Phil Anderson or Michel Laurent) over Kelly and
Duclos Lassalle. Always a quick thinker, Roche recognized
the danger: 'We (Peugeot) risk finishing in a nice, neat
group behind Zoetemelk or, why not, Kelly at the end of
the race. Sean Kelly is without doubt, the best rider in the
peloton at the moment and nobody can say for sure what
he can or can not do.' Roche had been the first to publicly
recognize reality.

Kelly's well-being was emphasized with another winning
performance on the fifth stage into La Seyne. He and his
principal challenger Duclos Lassalle had broken away with
Bittinger and the three finished nineteen seconds clear of
the pack. The performance made the French slightly
uneasy, not worried — just a little uneasy. Maybe Kelly

had notions above his station; maybe he would produce a performance on the Col d'Eze. Kelly tried to re-assure everybody. After beating Duclos Lassalle to win in La Seyne Kelly told *L'Equipe*: 'What I said in St Etienne about not being able to win Paris-Nice remains true. Duclos Lassalle and Roche will be my superiors on the Col d'Eze.' *L'Equipe* suspected that Kelly might not be playing things one hundred per cent straight for it headlined the piece: 'This Kelly Who Intrigues'.

After that La Seyne victory there were just two days for Kelly to survive. The second last day involved a spin from La Seyne to Mandelieu. It fell on 17 March, the day upon which Irish people celebrate the feast of their patron Saint Patrick. Rain descended with a vengeance, fog and low cloud combined to make the conditions horrendous and Saint Patrick showed little favour for the Irishman fighting a desperate battle in the south of France. As he had just a one-second advantage over Duclos Lassalle Kelly's position as race leader was precarious. The slightest mishap would dislodge him; the slightest mishap did dislodge him.

All through this eight-day race Kelly and Duclos Lassalle had raced side by side, never separated by more than one second. When one attacked, the other countered. Since the end of the fourth day they had been the principal characters. Victory had decided it would chose one or the other. The confrontation had engaged the attention of France: Gilbert, talkative, friendly, popular, French. Kelly; dour and non-commital, a foreigner. It is the penultimate day and Fate has decided to intervene. One-hundred-and-eighty kilometres lay between La Seyne and Mandelieu. In the final twenty kilometres the formidable Col du Tanneron had to be crossed and then a winding ten-kilometre descent into Mandelieu.

On a clear, dry day the Tanneron descent demands respect. On this wet day, with visibility unsatisfactory, catastrophe beckoned at every corner. A downhill stretch

that was a minefield of disastrous possibilities. Kelly had
reached the summit with Duclos Lassalle, comfortably
defending his leader's jersey. But on the descent turmoil
erupted: Kelly crashed; a few metres later Duclos Lassalle
tumbled and all would depend upon who could salvage
something from the chaos. Duclos Lassalle was back on his
bike sooner than Kelly and finished into Mandelieu five
seconds before his Irish rival. Kelly's one-second advantage had become a four-seconds deficit.

French unease about Kelly's possibilities vanished as the
white jersey passed to Duclos Lassalle. On the final day
there was a morning spin from Mandelieu to Nice and
then the concluding and much anticipated battle against
the clock on the Col d'Eze. The five seconds that Kelly lost
on the drop from the Tanneron to Mandelieu did not
mean that much in terms of time but it provided Duclos
Lassalle with the enormous advantage of starting his time
trial after Kelly. He would get regular time checks on
Kelly's performance and so would know exactly what he
had to do to win. France considered that it had the assured
winner of the 1982 Paris-Nice.

On the night before the final battle Gilbert Duclos
Lassalle was extremely confident: 'I am obviously very
happy with the way things have turned out because Sean
Kelly rode very well today. Even if I was already fairly
confident I believe that starting behind him in the Col
d'Eze test gives me an extra advantage. Provided that I
am not the victim of an accident I don't envisage any
problem.' Kelly, the sprinter, had put up a good show,
had made the race interesting. Now the moment approached when the big prize was being claimed and
Duclos Lassalle wanted the world to know that he meant
business. Happy to avoid predictions, Kelly prepared
quietly for what was to be a day of inestimable
significance.

For eight days Jean Leulliot's race had travelled south
in search of the Sun but encountered nothing — only

pieces of winter that had fallen into spring. Then on the eighth and final day the skies were blue and the sun smiling. The Race to the Sun had justified its name. Kelly surged into Nice on the morning stage and won the sprint for his third stage win. If Duclos Lassalle's confident forecast had amounted to a suggestion that Kelly already had one foot in the grave, the Irishman was still kicking doggedly with the other. Nobody had dared to wonder if Duclos Lassalle's expression of confidence was designed to throw a cloak over other, darker, feelings.

As a climb Col d'Eze represents an interesting challenge. It can not be described as a particularly severe hill for it only rises to 1,680 feet and that is spread over eleven kilometres. However, when this test presents itself as the Final Arbiter to an eight-day stage race then it assumes an entirely new character. As a mountain time trial at the end of Paris-Nice Col d'Eze is a savage test. Kelly was right to be cautious. Duclos Lassalle was foolish to be so confident. During the first half of the event, as the lowly placed riders went through the tired motions of completing a stage race, the leaders warmed up. Although the sun shone Kelly was wrapped up with customary care. He went all the way to the top, monitoring the steepness of each stretch and calculating the correct gear for each incline. In his sixth season as a professional Kelly was frighteningly close to his first major success in a stage race.

It might be an exaggeration to claim that Sean Kelly discovered himself on the Col d'Eze on the afternoon of 18 March 1982. If it is then the degree of hyperbole is slight for in the eleven-kilometre test Kelly produced a performance of power and class. Calling on his enormous strength and using it in combination with the suppleness and skill of a talented athlete, Kelly went up that mountain rapidly. Duclos Lassalle covered the first kilometre of the time trial one second faster than his rival but was trading entirely on raw strength. By half-way he was tiring. All through his career Kelly has ridden time trials cautiously. Starting solidly and trying to increase speed progressively. At the end of the third kilometre Kelly was nine seconds up on Duclos. The advantage had jumped from one camp to the other. Victory was casting seductive glances in Kelly's direction.

At the summit of Col d'Eze Kelly was a staggering forty-four seconds faster than Gilbert Duclos Lassalle. A battle that had raged with compelling intensity for eight days was now concluded with devastating force. Kelly had won the Col d'Eze time trial, fourteen seconds faster than the second placed Alberto Fernandez with Duclos Lassalle a despondent fifth. Kelly had won Paris-Nice and four stages; he had also taken the Points Classification and Sem had won the team award. The new road general of Sem France-Loire had conducted a splendid debut campaign. The summit of Col d'Eze is a barren outpost, not the kind of place that lends itself naturally to the celebratory. The Sem team didn't mind. De Gribaldy took Kelly on his shoulders for the photographers and both spoke positively about the future. Kelly said he might not have won if de Gribaldy had not made him aware of his new possibilities. The admission tells us something.

While the winner and runner-up stood on the podium a minute's silence was observed for the late Jean Leulliot. Kelly and Duclos Lassalle, who had spent eight days exchanging cruel pedal strokes, were now finally together in friendship. One radiating the expression of triumph, the other bearing the burden of defeat. Sad and desolate. Yet both with abounding respect for each other. At first smiling, then joining hands in the air and finally embracing. That was the last moment. Jean Leulliot, poet, painter and cycling journalist, would have understood.

11 A Classic First

Paris-Nice changed everything. For five years Kelly loiter-ed on the fringe of cycling's principal show. Occasionally called up to play a leading role but just as quickly sent back from whence he came. Kelly hadn't figured he was worth a place amongst the elite and, anyway, the second-rate performers earned a reasonable living. Then de Gribaldy came along and claimed Kelly for a second time. Back in Carrick-on-Suir, December 1976, he promised to make Kelly a professional. Six years later he won Kelly's services again and this time he promised to make his Irish racer a great professional. Paris-Nice was the first test. Kelly's triumph reflected well on his master's judgement. A new team and suddenly Kelly copped his greatest prize. What had this cyclist been doing all of his life?

Journalists wanted to speak with Kelly. He practised his French, Flemish and English on them. Sport-stars learn much from the interest displayed by the journalists and Kelly began to feel that he mattered. They wanted to know all the usual things, the things you ask a star. Rarely less than courteous, he maintained a matter-of-fact disposition with all interviewers. Spontaneity played no part. He tried to be respectful. An innate decency protecting him from the dangers of finger-threading as he climbed the ladder. About a decade earlier Kelly's boyhood friend in Carrick-on-Suir, David Power, had detected a desire for recogni-tion in his pal. Now the recognition had arrived and Kelly was ready, with smiling face and limited vocabulary.

One thing about the journalists was their tacit insistence

that you go on winning. They wrote of Kelly's talents and then expected him to vindicate their assessments. After Paris-Nice Kelly needed to remind new admirers that his first major stage race success was indeed a portent of things to come. A week later he rode the two-day Criterium Internationale. After two stages Kelly was out of contention. There remained only the concluding time trial. A year earlier he would have eased through this test. Now the time trial represented opportunity. Kelly won it handsomely. Beating Hinault by over thirty seconds. The French gasped. That effort on Col d'Eze hadn't been a fluke. This man could race. This man was somebody.

Kelly was expected to make his talents count in the April round of spring classics. It never happened. One day the big men wrecked each others chances; on another day Kelly didn't have the strength; on another he didn't have the spiritual bravery and in Paris-Roubaix he was desperately unlucky. Each time he got into a winning position, he crashed or punctured. Jan Raas won the race, Kelly was an unnoticed thirteenth and yet he knew that he had ridden his best race of the season. Classic failures had always been a part of Kelly's life, and after that unsuccessful campaign in the spring of 1982, nobody was too surprised. Kelly, boosted enormously by the Paris-Nice triumph, refused to turn back. There was still the Tour de France and he had resolved to devote all his energies to the quest for the Tour's green jersey of points winner. A year earlier he had ridden the same Tour without any green jersey aspiration.

His final preparatory race for the Tour was the modest Tour de l'Aude. Kelly claimed two stages and impressed his adversaries. English professional Paul Sherwen was asked whom did he think would win the 1982 Tour de France. 'I'm not so sure about the overall but I'm telling you to look out for Sean Kelly in the Tour. He is going for the green jersey and I can't see him being beaten.' Sherwen's prophecy couldn't have been more accurate. Kelly won his first Tour de France green jersey with astonishing authority. His points total more than doubled that of the second placed Bernard Hinault. Kelly's 429 to Hinault's 152. Despite being the dominant sprinter in the race Kelly claimed just one stage, The Pyrenean leg from Fleurance, over the Aubisque, into Pau. It had been the first mountaineous stage in the race and the cycling world wondered what the sprinter Kelly was doing winning a Pyrenean stage in the Tour?

An explanation may be drawn from the conditions which existed that day: low temperatures and a dense mist. Another factor was a dismal Kelly performance in the Valance d'Agen time trial on the previous day. He finished thirty-first, almost five-and-a-half minutes down on winner Gerrie Knetemann. The memory of that needed to be wiped away. Kelly had to do a little re-asserting.

On the steep Col du Soular Kelly couldn't hang on to the leaders but wasn't so far back as to be out of the hunt. Joining up with the Italian Mario Beccia, Kelly chased fearlessly on the Soular descent. The pair latched on to the end of the leading train as it tackled the first slopes of the Aubisque. That group comprised eighteen riders, most of them being race favourites. The group's interest was served by all working together and distancing themselves from the 130 stragglers behind. As the leaders arrived into the finish at Pau the advantage was four-and-a-half minutes. Kelly's ability as a rapid finisher made him the likely winner in Pau. A kilometre from the finish Hinault headed the line of leaders, Bernard Vallet was second, Kelly third and Anderson fourth. On the second last corner Hinault swerved to the left, leaving Vallet to come through and lead from Kelly. The finishing straight in Pau is short; Kelly could not have been better placed. He won the sprint easily.

Hinault's manoeuvre so close to the finish attracted attention. Why had he not contested the sprint? He probably wouldn't have beaten Kelly but a place in the top three was more than a possibility. Some suspected that he had reached an agreement of some sort with Kelly. His tactics over the last few kilometres had helped the Irish rider enormously and then, with less than 500 metres to go, Hinault had simply removed himself from the sprint. Those with suspicions considered that the events on the Champs Elysees on the final day offered confirmation that a deal had been done. Hinault set out on that final stage securely attached to the jellow jersey but with the burden of having gone through the Tour without taking a road race stage. The French demand that their winners succeed with style. Hinault's failure to win a road race stage was deemed a notable omission. For the Tour leader it was time to call in that Pau favour. He sprinted brilliantly to win on the Champs Elysees and Kelly happened to get himself into a bad position and crossed the line an anonymous eleventh. Both riders would deny any collusion but the evidence of the two finishes suggests otherwise.

The Tour had been a significant success for Kelly. Never in the history of the race had a rider from the English-speaking world claimed the green jersey. Contracts to ride the post-Tour invitation races followed on automatically from such an achievement. Kelly had built upon the Paris-Nice success at the beginning of the season. He was twenty-six and still progressing.

On the weekend the Tour ended four of Kelly's most enthusiastic supporters travelled to Paris to be present on the Champs Elysees when he arrived. Linda Grant, his fiancée, was one of the group. She and Kelly would marry the following November. The presence of the small group of Kelly supporters in Paris reflected the fact that his successes on the Continent were, at last, winning recognition in Ireland. Two years earlier (1980) a group of about thirty Kelly supporters from Carrick travelled to Sallanches in France for the World Championships. On both occasions the Irish Press Group in Dublin despatched me to report the stories. At that time the Irish newspapers attended to Kelly's achievements in a cursory manner. Irish Press Group Sports Editor Adhamhnan O'Sullivan was one of the few newspaper men to appreciate the quality of Kelly's performance and took what were then brave decisions in sending a reporter to the Continent.

Kelly warmed to the interest shown by his native country. Once in an interview with *L'Equipe's* Jean Marie Leblanc, Kelly was asked about his Irishness. The question drew a definite response: "I may live in Belgium, French may be my daily language but I remain totally Irish. Ireland will always be home.' From another, such a declaration of national identity might be taken with a pinch of lightness. Kelly meant what he said. In those days, 1980-82, he treated every journalistic inquiry from Ireland with a studied courtesy. He wanted people at home to understand what he was attempting and if journalists could transmit the message then they were going to get Kelly's full co-operation. By the end of the 1982 Tour the Irish public, although still confused by the subtleties of stage racing, had come to respect one of its sporting giants.

It happened that the World Championships of that year were held in Goodwood, England. Because of its proximity to Ireland and the relatively undemanding nature of the circuit, Kelly had to bear the burden of considerable expectation at Goodwood. They said he would never get a better chance to win the rainbow jersey. On a warm, very pleasant afternoon in Goodwood he rode like one inspired. The inspiration, alas, emanated from the heart, not the head. Kelly followed all the moves, tried to stay near the front all through and, ultimately, left himself without the sharp acceleration needed for the final sprint. When, with 500 metres to go, the Italian Giuseppi Saronni ripped himself clear of the pack Kelly did not have a response. Then Greg LeMond went and Kelly was the best of the rest. A bronze medal at the Worlds. His best ever World Championship performance. De Gribaldy told him to feel shame — he had ridden like an amateur. A ruthless evaluation but one with which Kelly was forced to concur.

Goodwood also proved that the English cycling public had taken Kelly to its heart. A feeling pervaded that Kelly should win, that he owed it to the world and that the world owed it to him. Defeat, if a bronze medal at the World Championship can be labelled such, did not diminish Kelly in the eyes of his admirers. He fought well. In the press-room afterwards he was, for once, answering questions in his first language. He praised the performance of Stephen Roche: 'If I could halve his medal, then he would have one half.' As Kelly rattled on earnestly about his tactics, the pattern of the race and the finish, a burly Belgian journalist complained that he could not understand English and wanted to ask a question in French. It was an awkward moment. Kelly's control was imposing. Speaking in French and looking directly at the Belgian, he said: 'Okay, ask your question.' The question was delivered timidly. On such occasions Kelly can seem full of authority and decisiveness. These are occasions when his responses are instinctive. When there isn't a need for an immediate decision Kelly can be prevaricating in the extreme.

Since turning professional in 1977 Kelly had always been an above average cyclist. In 1982 he was more than that. His performance in winning Paris-Nice, in claiming the green jersey of the Tour de France and in taking a bronze medal at the World Championships put him on to a higher level. At the end of the Tour the Italian teams came looking for Kelly. As always, they spoke in millions of lire. Kelly had the sense to recognize that success had come with his return to de Gribaldy. Indeed the Sem *directeur sportif* had become a kind of Svengali and Kelly was not about to dissolve the partnership. Still, in his professional way, he did what was best for him. He feigned an interest in his suitors. He articulates the strategy thus: 'What you do is listen to all proposals, then bounce one off another and when you have the highest figure you use it to bargain with the team that interests you most. I might have wanted to stay with de Gribaldy but I had to pretend that I was seriously interested in the other propositions.'

By the end of 1982 Kelly had agreed to ride for de Gribaldy's Sem in 1983. In November 1982 he married Linda Grant. The wedding ceremony and reception passed in the normal way, predictably pleasant. There was, however, one memorable moment. During the course of the after-dinner speeches, the priest who performed the ceremony, Fr Pat Butler, used the Tour de France as a metaphor for marriage. He outlined the different types of terrain and how they made the race straightforward, difficult or very difficult. Marriage, he suggested, travelled over different roads. Sometimes, the going was tough, other times it was less so and occasionally it seemed easy. Just like the various stages of a long bike-race. Kelly was next in line to speak. The guests, even those with only a slight knowledge of the person, expected brevity. Kelly did not disappoint. 'I would just like to thank you all for coming. One thing about Fr Butler's speach. I don't think marriage and the Tour de France are exactly the same. If things are going bad in a bike-race, you can simply climb off.' In a country where divorce is illegal, Kelly knew what he was saying.

At the beginning of the 1983 season Kelly had every right to feel optimistic. He had enjoyed his best ever results the season before and his 1983 programme was more or less identical to that of 1982. Paris-Nice was the first major test, then the classics, and after that the Tour of Switzerland and the Tour de France. De Gribaldy had signed two interesting new riders, Jean Marie Grezet from Switzerland and Steven Rooks from Holland. A year earlier Kelly might have felt his position undermined by their presence but they were now seen as additions. In the race from Paris to Nice Kelly performed with exceptional determination and delivered one of his finest ever performances. The quality derived from the fact that on the first stage he crashed and lost valuable time. The crash, brought about by the careless and highly dangerous riding of Eric Vanderanden, occurred just 150 meters outside of the *flambe rouge*, one kilometre from the finish.

Had the accident occurred inside the *flambe rouge* then Kelly would not have lost any time. Race director Jacques Anquetil sought to bend the rules but rival team managers demanded a strict application of the law. Kelly went tumbling down the classification to ninety-sixth. He conceded defeat publicly, saying that he envisaged nothing more for himself than a few stage victories. The cycling world felt sympathy for Kelly. A crash, that had not been of his making, was set to cost him his chance of overall victory. Kelly worked his way back into contention quietly. Joop Zoetemelk wore the leader's jersey; he did not look beatable. On the morning of the penultimate stage, which included the formidable Col du Tanneron, rain fell from the skies. Mist and low clouds reduced visibility.

Kelly talked with Roche before the start. 'Last night I did not give myself any chance of dislodging Zoetemelk but in this weather I believe there is hope.' Kelly knew Zoetemelk was old, thirty-seven, and no longer had the nerve for hazardous descents on wet roads. The battleground was high up on the Tanneron. Kelly, Grezet and Rooks traded pedal strokes with Zoetemelk and his lieutenant, Michel Laurent. Close to the top, Grezet stamped hard on the pedals and forced Zoetemelk to chase him down. Kelly moved to the exposed left side of the climb and bolted. At the top he was fifty yards clear. It was enough for one prepared to act out the part of kamikaze pilot on the descent. Zoetemelk and the others did not see Kelly again until the finish at Mandelieu. Kelly was asked did he take chances on the descent, was he afraid? 'On a descent like that', he replied, 'you think of winning, not of hospital.'

In scooting clear of Zoetemelk, Kelly had gained the

time necessary to win him the leader's jersey. The rest was an engaging formality. Kelly blasting to a brutal victory in the concluding Col d'Eze time trial. On that mountain test Kelly almost overhauled Zoetemelk who had started two minutes in front of him. His second Paris-Nice had come with three stage wins, the mountains and points jerseys and Sem had claimed the team award. Sean Kelly was not going to go away.

Two days later Kelly rode the Italian Classic, Milan-San Remo, and finished fifth. Another chance to record a first classic success had been lost. Memories of that defeat were obliterated when Kelly produced a super time trial to win the two-day Criterium Internationale. In front of Kelly there was now the vision of ending his long losing sequence in the classics. During April there were six such races and Kelly's form suggested he could win at least one of them. Hope was killed by a simple crash in the unimportant Midi Pyrenees race. The bunch was not travelling fast when Kelly tumbled but he still broke both his thumb and collar bone — the first bones he had ever broken. The thumb needed six weeks for a complete recovery. Kelly remained a man without a classic victory. His failure to win one had become a burden in itself; people spoke about it often. They wondered what was wrong and theories abounded. Kelly, it was judged, didn't have the mentality to win a classic. Unwittingly, Sean Kelly had found himself an albatross.

Kelly's response to injury is one of stoic acceptance. He refuses to eat because, without training, he will put on weight and so he confines himself to the barest necessities. The period of inactivity after the crash worried Kelly. He wondered about his season. His anxiety wasn't helped by the apparent lack of concern by the team and it's *directeur*, Jean de Gribaldy. Kelly *hors de combat*, was forgotten. This anxiety tempted Kelly into cutting corners and, after a crash course in regaining fitness, he returned to racing in early June, just seven weeks after the crash.

He used the minor Tour of Europe as a means of re-introduction and after that went to the Tour of Switzerland. Ostensibly, the Swiss race was for training purposes. But in the early part of that stage race Kelly felt some exciting sensations. 'It was as if the wheels were going around of their own accord. I used to look down at my feet and watch the pedals turning and I didn't seem to be making that much effort. I knew I was going really well.' After a few days and without too much effort Kelly found himself in second place. Two seconds behind the Italian Roberto Visentini. On the difficult stage to Bellinzona Kelly moved clear of Visentini and over the final four days he consolidated his position as race leader.

The Sem team, encouraged by the prospect of an avalanche of Swiss francs, rode splendidly in defence of its leader. For Kelly victory in the Tour of Switzerland was highly important. It underlined his competence as a climber and added to his reputation as a member of the sport's elite. There were many long and arduous climbs in the 1983 Tour of Switzerland and Kelly had survived them. Switzerland's national tour is probably the fourth most competitive stage race in the world. By virtue of that fine Switzerland performance Kelly began the Tour de France, a week later, as a popular choice for the yellow jersey. The newspapers claimed the race hung between he, Joop Zoetemelk and Phil Anderson.

Injury prevented the great Bernard Hinault from taking his place in the 1983 Tour and therein lay the reason for Kelly's place amongst the Tour's front-line candidates. Kelly knew there were dangers. 'I remember being on the plane to Paris for the start and wondering whether I had left my best form in Switzerland. I sensed that I had.' After the injury Kelly had returned to his training schedule with much haste. Rather than build up slowly he immersed himself into a very demanding routine. By the time Switzerland presented itself, Kelly was in peak condition. His best form had come quickly.

Probably too quickly. What had come quickly would go quickly. After a week on the Tour de France, Stephen Roche had seen enough to decide that Kelly was struggling. 'When Sean is going really well he can leave his hands casually on top of the bars all day. Then when he wants to accelerate, he does and you don't even notice him shift position. I could see that during the Tour he was labouring.'

Kelly fought his declining form, substituting determination for pedalling class. By the time the race reached Pau he had battled his way into the yellow jersey. On the following day the Tour headed directly into the Pyrenees and the race's first rendezvous with the mountains. Kelly, clad in yellow, was left ten minutes behind. The mountains took a shocking toll. Anderson, Zoetemelk and Roche, all suffered as Kelly did. In one day the 1983 Tour turned. It was for Laurent Fignon to walk from near anonymity into the living rooms of the French nation. Kelly persevered to finish seventh and dominated the quest for the green jersey. Seventh was his best ever Tour performance but, placed against pre-race expectation, still ranked as a disappointment. His failure to win a stage of the 1983 Tour deepened the sense of having failed.

An exhausting round of criteriums left Kelly typically ill-prepared for the World Championship Road Race. Over a difficult circuit at Altenrhein in Switzerland he rode well to finish seventh. For an athlete with his record, seventh amounted to nowhere. The 1983 season was now into its final phase and Kelly resumed his quest for a classic victory. His ambition focussed on the two principal autumnal classics; the Blois to Chaville and the Tour of Lombardy. In the former Kelly produced what was arguably the least professional performance of his career. When the decisive attack materialized Kelly was at the back of the bunch passing the afternoon in idle chat with his friend Claude Criquielion: 'It was a terrible mistake. About ten kilometres before the break I sensed something was about to happen and I said to Criquielion that we should be getting to the front. He agreed but we didn't bother moving. Suddenly the break had gone and we were left to organize a pursuit. We got the leaders back to 100 metres but we never joined them.' Kelly won the bunch sprint for ninth. Another classic opportunity had slipped by.

There remained but the Tour of Lombardy. Seven years earlier Kelly had triumphed in its amateur equivalent. Few remembered that. Now, Kelly was the one who couldn't win a classic. Wise men nodded knowingly, pointed to their heads, and said it was a matter of mentality. A few days before the Tour of Lombardy de Gribaldy was asked about Kelly's classic failures and offered this explanation: 'He can win when there is no pressure. But in the big races, there is a problem.' A vague assessment but enough to conclude that even de Gribaldy considered Kelly a big-time failure. Kelly could not have travelled to Lombardy with much confidence.

The team had gone to Italy immediately after Blois-Chaville and competed in the Tour of Piemont two days before the Lombardy race. De Gribaldy was to join them on the day before the big classic. A strict disciplinarian, de Gribaldy is notoriously fastidious about food. His belief is that cyclists should eat as little as possible, over-eating being the most common sin. Without de Gribaldy's presence, the Sem riders in Italy indulged themselves: 'We ate much more than we would have got with 'de Gri' around — plenty of beautiful Italian food. We were like boys on a day out from school.'

On the morning of the seventy-seventh Tour of Lombardy 144 riders signed themselves in for examination. The race began in Brescia and, 157 miles later, finished in the lakeside town of Como. Strikingly beautiful, the Lombardy region provides a perfect home for a classic bike-race. Its hills are steep, but not impossible. Only a good all-round cyclist can aspire to success in the Giro di

Lombardia. That morning the skies were grey over the Loggia Square in Brescia and persistent drizzle robbed autumn of its attractions. Kelly, as ever, didn't mind the rain.

Lombardy is one of the few classics which maintains a fast pace from the beginning. It is as if the suffering protagonists are rushing to end their seasons. Daniel Gisiger of Switzerland and the Italian Walter Clivati were particularly keen to get on with it and they broke clear after about fifty miles. They led for the next sixty-five miles. An interesting adventure. After fifty-five miles Gisiger, the stronger of the two, had left Clivati and he led for another ten miles. On the first slopes of the Intelvi climb he was engulfed by the chasing pack. Sited just forty-one miles from the finish it was always probable that the Intelvi would be the first important battleground of the race. And as the giants eyed one and other on the approach to the Intelvi, Gisiger's episode was being ruthlessly terminated. The angler toying with the catch before reeling him in. Gisiger was allowed to have some fun before the *peloton* decided his time was up. Kelly climbed with the Spaniard Marino Lejarreta and Italians Gibi Baronchelli and Silvano Contini at the front of the bunch on the Intelvi. Thirty riders regrouped after the punishing five miles ascent of the mountain. Thirty-six miles to the finish and, already, over 110 riders were out of contention.

A further elimination was effected after the Schignano climb; the lead group was just twenty-five, pursued by twelve riders, then a few lost souls and that was it. According to the race officials, over eighty riders had already abandoned. Kelly's cause depended upon a fast pace being maintained over the final thirty miles of the race. His team-mate Jean Marie Grezet was in generous mood. Working his way to the front, the Swiss upped the speed and, in this way, preserved some kind of order. Such was the pace set by Grezet that few dared to attack and those who did (the most notable being Alfredo Chinetti of Italy) were recaptured by a determined Grezet. With just eight miles to go Grezet paid the price for his heroics.

His energy had been completely drained by the effort and he suddenly lost contact with the eighteen riders who now had this classic between them. After playing his part with great skill and determination Grezet left the rest to Kelly and chance. Immediately after he had fallen away, the Spaniard Pedro Munoz attacked in search of glory. On the difficult climb at the village of San Fermo, Munoz led by ten seconds. Kelly led the pursuit up the climb, keeping Munoz within his sights and the race under control. Then, after the summit, Dutch rider Adri Van der Poel, Hubert Seiz of Switzerland and Dag Eric Pedersen of Norway counter-attacked. Kelly's chances had taken a sharp turn in the wrong direction. He was now a man without a team-mate.

Kelly needed a friend. Stephen Roche assessed the situation quickly and opted to further Ireland's cause in international cycling. For one day he would be Kelly's ally. The rules of cycling forbid riders from opposing teams to work together but the law is, in practice, unenforceable. Roche went to the front of the group and chased down the four leaders. Ostensibly he worked for his Peugeot team-mate Phil Anderson but Roche's real purpose was to help Kelly win his first classic. He wanted to play a part in an important chapter of Kelly's career.

'I rode hard at the front to keep it together. Kelly hadn't asked me to help, he just glanced over in my direction and it was up to me. I wanted to do it for him because we were good friends and I knew he needed to win a classic. But I was also conscious of the fact that if I stayed at the front all the time it would look very bad. So I took occasional breaks but made sure that the situation was under contnrol. After the race my Peugeot manager Roland Berland was angry because I had ridden for Kelly. Berland just didn't understand. Okay I helped Kelly but I wasn't going well enough to win myself. There would be other days when the roles would be reversed. Sean has always been an honest and straight rider, he would repay the debt. I knew that. Berland didn't. We have a saying in cycling that one good turn deserves another. Sean is the type of rider who remembers the help he receives from his friends.'

And so Roche marshalled the group with expert skill over the final eight miles. Franceso Moser was one of the eighteen leaders and his presence ensured the interest of Italy's cycling fraternity. As the eighteen, led by Roche, sped through the streets of Como the volume on Italian televisions was adjusted upwards. In other houses curtains were hastily drawn to cut off shafts of light, husbands called wives from kitchens, mothers fed babies to win their silence. Roche continued to lead through the final kilometre. Just before the final bend into the 300-yard long finishing straight, Dutch cyclist Hennie Kuiper went for victory. Seiz went in pursuit. Then Moser jumped, followed immediately by Van der Poel. It was with a certain horror that Roche watched the triggers being pulled on the turn into the final straight.

'I had worked very hard. It was all for Sean. When Kuiper went past me I expected Sean to follow soon. I mean we were entering the finishing straight. But all these other fellows came by before Kelly. I wondered what he was playing at. Wondered had I been working for nothing. I counted them as they passed, about eight or nine before Kelly went by.'

When he rounded the final bend Kelly had Greg LeMond in his slip-stream. Aware of the American's presence Kelly tried to shake himself free of his rival by going for the most tortuous sprinting route. Weaving through those riders in front of him Kelly had himself in a winning position with one hundred yards to go. LeMond remained close to him. Kuiper's long sprint had beaten most. Moser's effort to overhaul him died. Van der Poel found himself sprinting against his team-mate Kuiper. Tiredness meant that Kuiper swerved to the left, Van der Poel was on the right. Between them Kelly and LeMond charged for the line. Both out of the saddle, lunging instinctively for the white band that stretched across the road.

Less than a foot separated the four riders. Kelly had triumphed by a couple of inches from LeMond, then Van der Poel, Kuiper and Moser. Roche, the gallant auxiliary, finished last of the leading group. Another gallant soldier in Kelly's service, Grezet, lost three minutes and thirty-two seconds in the final eight miles. A testimony to his efforts on Kelly's behalf. The final sprint was fiercely contested. Kelly could so easily have lost. His obsession with getting free of LeMond almost cost him victory. 'I think that if I had sprinted in a straight line I could have won a little more comfortably.'

That Saturday evening Linda Kelly had travelled with Herman and Elise Nys to visit friends in Holland. She watched the closing chapter of the race on television. She saw her husband wriggle up that long straight in Como, recognized the heaving athlete as her Sean. Afraid that he would lose, Linda wondered why he weaved from one side of the road to the other. Finally she saw the four principals flash past the line together. She was sure of only one thing. That was that her husband had lost.

Such is the effect on the eyes of waiting six seasons to win a classic.

12 At the Summit

A wet and cold January afternoon in Dublin. Just two weeks of 1984 have passed but everyone wants to look forward. What was going to happen this year? I had arranged to meet Kelly in the White Horse bar on Burgh Quay. Business interests had him in Dublin and a mid-afternoon chat with a journalist fitted nicely into the schedule. Kelly wanted only coffee; no cream, no milk and no sugar. Even at his most relaxed, Kelly expects the journalist to present questions. He spoke of the effects of bad weather on his training, the contractual problems that Eric Vanderaerden was experiencing, a recent ski-ing holiday in France and his programme of races for the season. About a month previously I had decided to move to Paris for a year and cover an entire season of professional bike-races. Arrangements had been concluded and now it seemed appropriate to mention the plan to Kelly.

On hearing that an Irish journalist would be covering all of his races, Kelly simply nodded his head. Taking in the fact but not commenting on it. His expression softened and seemed to ask was this a wise course? Infected by momentary doubt I looked at Kelly and suggested that if he won a few races in 1984 then the financial affairs of one sports-writer in Paris would be improved. Kelly sensed the worry. A soft and benign expression hardened. In an instant one listened to a different voice. 'You just go on over to Paris, don't worry about me — I'll be winning races alright.' There was nothing more to say on the question of winning races in 1984. Kelly's unquestioned strength of limb was overflowing into his mind. That victory in the autumnal Tour of Lombardy three months earlier had made Kelly a more assured athlete. Two months into the new season Kelly had won fourteen races. Had been as good as his word.

The list of successes included a thrilling third consecutive Paris-Nice triumph. Imagine the scene. Perched high above the city of Nice we waited at the summit of the Col d'Eze for the final act in the eight-day Race to the Sun. Only two riders had a chance. Kelly, the race leader, and Stephen Roche. That morning, *L'Equipe's* front page headline had been 'Le Championnat d'Irlandais.'

The Col d'Eze test is just eleven kilometres but the steeply uphill nature of the course makes it extremely difficult. Kelly had twelve seconds on Roche going into this mountain time trial. Roche, second last rider off, delivered a time that was one minute faster than everybody else. Kelly was, as race leader, the final rider to respond to the timekeeper's *allez*. At half way he was precisely six seconds behind Roche. Defeat was no longer a distant possibility, rather it stalked him on that mountain. Getting very close at around half-way.

Kelly sensed it's presence and dug savagely into his reserves of strength. He described the final two kilometres of the race as the 'longest sprint of my career'. At the finish line journalists were equally divided in their expectations. Many considered that Roche's time would beat Kelly's by the necessary twelve seconds, others preferred to trust in Kelly's sporting cannibalism. The man who kept the time was called Jacques Godot. Seconds were being counted as Kelly came hurtling into the finishing straight, out of the saddle and pounding rhythmically as his shoulders swung to the left and then right. Past the line he crouched over his bike and gulped for oxygen. Unofficial timekeepers swore that Kelly had made it. Nobody was utterly certain. The seconds seemed like minutes. Only one man could deliver the official verdict. We were, like Samuel Beckett's two tramps, 'Waiting for Godot'.

When Monsieur Godot delivered his verdict Kelly had beaten Roche by one second in the Col d'Eze test and had decisively won the race. The other victories arrived with stunning regularity. Paris-Roubaix was easily the best. The continental press struggled to cope with this one-rider domination and came up with 'King Kelly' and *Le Nouveau Cannibale*. Kelly had become public property. He enjoyed the attention. A new World Rankings for cycling listed him No. 1, a position he has retained each month for the last two years. The world and Sean Kelly were getting along really well.

Three days after winning Paris-Roubaix Kelly had shaken himself free of euphoria and was mentally attuned to the challenges of Fleche Wallonne and Liège-Bastogne-Liège. These two classics race over the Ardennes countryside in Belgium. Fleche Wallonne is a respected race but is still seen by some of the big men primarily as a good preparatory exercise for Liège-Bastogne-Liège which comes three days later. In the 1984 Fleche Wallonne all of the pre-race favourites missed the important bus and the race was dominated by a group of jumped-up *domestiques*. Kelly didn't mind. He could afford to pass up a race like Fleche Wallonne. His great Ardennes objective was the Liège-Bastogne-Liège.

On the Friday before Liège-Bastogne-Liège Kelly relaxed at his base in Vilvoorde. He was determined to have a big say in Liège-Bastogne-Liège. At around four o'clock on Friday evening Ronny Onghena, Kelly's close friend and *domestique*, called. They then travelled to the team hotel, a few miles outside Liège. On the journey Kelly and Ronny spoke of little things that seemed so important. Who was going well? Who was likely to win Sunday's race? Two men going about their work, liking what they were doing but not conferring special status upon themselves. Once inside the team hotel an Italian journalist beseeched

Kelly for an interview and Ronny was left alone to watch some television.

I had spent time with Kelly at Vilvoorde that morning and had travelled with him to the team hotel. He asked a couple of his back-up team to drop me back to Liège that night. 'Titi', a young masseur, and Thierry, an even younger mechanic, provided the chauffeur service. They were happy to have an excuse to visit the city and warmed to the idea of a few beers in downtown Liège. At the bar 'Titi' complained that he had not seen his wife or child since the season began two months previously. He counted out the races he was due to work on over the following months: the Tour of Spain, the Tour of Romandy, the Tour of Italy. Almost three months on the road. 'Titi' lived in St Etienne; he wasn't married that long and he knew that for the privilege of rubbing Sean Kelly's legs, he paid a price. 'My child, he is just nine months old. When I last saw him he was crawling. When I next see him he will be walking. I am missing a lot.'

Thierry was from Yfinniac in Brittany. The same town and club as Bernard Hinault. Thierry knew Titi from the days when both worked with the Wolber team. They were acquainted with many of the leaders in the *peloton*. Kelly was their favourite. One suspected that the loyalty to Kelly was based as much on economic reality as human affection. Titi acknowledged this: 'We are human, there is more money for us when Kelly wins. We get a percentage of the prize money. But Kelly is a good *patron*. He treats everybody the same. Other leaders look down on people like us. Not Kelly.' Thierry nodded approval. They spoke of the big race on Sunday. Titi forecast another big Kelly win; Thierry tentatively suggested that the team's Swiss star, Jean Marie Grezet, might ride well. *Peut-être*, said Thierry, not at all convinced that Grezet could deliver in a race as competitive as Liège-Bastogne-Liège.

Thierry and Titi talked cycling over their three beers. They refused to accept that loneliness and drudgery were the features of life on the road. This season had been special. Fourteen wins for Kelly and just two months had passed. They felt a part of that success; Kelly's glory reflected on them. It was easy to romanticize: 'Kelly's muscles are extraordinary. I never knew anybody to have such legs. I am his masseur, you know.' Thierry might have said similar things about the way Kelly wanted his bike before a major race. An escape from the reality of surviving on a wage that was close to the legal minimum and having to watch your son grow up in photographs. When the season ended they would be unemployed and, for three months, claim social welfare payments. At the beginning of the following season they went back into service. The stable boys of professional cycling. The following season Thierry wasn't with de Gribaldy's team. Somebody said he had looked for a twelve-month working contract.

That evening these two servants in the Kelly camp were unconcerned about the quality of their working lives. After the beers they went to a nearby take-away for chips. They walked through Liège's sleazy district as they ate. At each window prostitutes nodded invitingly. Thierry and Titi laughed. They were hardly in a position to buy the ladies chips let alone spend an evening in their company. Contented by their walk and chips, they left for the team hotel at around ten-thirty. Three beers, a take-away and a stimulating walk; Titi and Thierry had just enjoyed a night on the town.

Sunday's race worked out well for these two minor players in cycling's drama. Kelly won again. His third classic success over a six-month period. Nothing for six years and then the Tour de Lombardy, Paris-Roubaix and Liège-Bastogne-Liège, and all in such a confined time-span. Of all the classics he has claimed, Liège-Bastogne-Liège 1984 will be recalled as the most exciting. The story of this classic was bike-racing at its most riveting. It had all begun on the pleasantest of spring mornings.

Kelly tightened the laces of his cycling shoes in his Citroen. There was just ten minutes to wait before the 193 riders began their 246-kilometre race. As her husband fixed his laces, Linda Kelly pressed a sprig of palm tree into the back pocket of his jersey. This was Palm Sunday and Linda was honouring an old habit: 'If Sean races on Palm Sunday I give him a little palm. I don't think it can do any harm.' Greg LeMond turned up at the Place St Lambert and suggested Kelly was the rider that everybody had to beat: 'I think this guy Sean Kelly is the one we have to be afraid of today. He is incredible. Nobody else could sustain the sequence he has achieved this season. He is not just a super rider, he is also a super champion.'

The first two hours of the race were mostly for enjoying the Ardennes landscape. Sparkling sunshine brightened everything as the colourful train sped towards Bastogne on the first part of its journey. On return from that town the steep hills of the Ardennes grew more numerous, the number of leaders dwindled. Kelly had said the race was invariably a process of elimination and was likely to be so on this occasion. On the third last climb, the Mont Theux, forty kilometres from the finish, Laurent Fignon attacked. Phil Anderson sensed a winning move and went in pursuit of the Frenchman. On the descent after the climb Anderson caught Fignon. Behind there was a group of seventeen. On the penultimate La Redoute climb Claude Criquielion counter-attacked in pursuit of the two leaders. Six riders; LeMond, Kelly, Marc Madiot, Steven Rooks, Acacio da Silva and Joop Zoetemelk followed Criquielion. LeMond and Madiot were present to defend the position of team-mate Fignon. Rooks was performing a similar task for Anderson. Of the other four, Criquielion and Kelly were working hardest to retrieve the leaders. Zoetemelk was helping a little and da Silva was merely hoping that something would fall upon his lap.

Fortune had smiled on Kelly by providing Criquielion as a companion in this chasing party. They were good friends and the Belgian was strong enough to be an exceptional ally. Over the final ten kilometres Anderson and Fignon remained between ten and twenty seconds clear of the seven-rider pursuit. The advantage fluctuated constantly. From twenty seconds down to twelve but soon back up to twenty again. Anderson, hindered by an unhelpful Fignon, was delivering an outstanding performance. Madiot tried to disrupt the pursuit by interrupting the rapid rhythm imposed by Kelly and Criquielion. A displeased Kelly bumped him to one side and, sufficiently discouraged, Madiot's resistance was passive thereafter. Four kilometres from the finish it appeared that the two leaders would just hang on. Less than two kilometres from the line they were eaten up. Anderson had been treated cruelly.

As the seven joined up with the two, Madiot attacked. Criquielion countered immediately. Da Silva then tried but he, too, was recaptured. On the second last corner Rooks surged a few lengths clear, frantically trying to find a way around his own sprinting inadequacies. At the final corner he was swallowed up. The final attack came from Fignon. Predictably it was Anderson who cut him down and Kelly was close on the Australian's back wheel. In an instant five of the nine leaders were lined, almost equal, across the road. Kelly called on his last morsels of strength and pounded clear. Anderson, bravely, clung on to second, LeMond third and Rooks fourth. It had all fallen into place for Kelly. Paris-Roubaix and Liège-Bastogne-Liège captured in the same season, within eight glorious days. Sean Kelly had made it.

As the bit players filed through the finish line, Kelly satisfied the needs of journalist and broadcaster. He relived the drama that had enlivened this Sunday in the Ardennes. He tried to be diplomatic about Claude Criquielion's role, suggesting that it was in Criquielion's own interests to form an alliance with him in pursuit of Anderson and Fignon. (A few months later Criquielion offered a more plausible evaluation: 'It was up to me to decide whether I wanted Kelly or Anderson to win. I don't mind admitting that Kelly was my choice. We are similar types — both of us came from small farms and when Sean was at Splendor we became close friends.') Soon Kelly was receiving another bouquet of flowers. The race organizers were delighted that such a big name had won their classic. Eighteen minutes had elapsed since Kelly crossed the line and now the last of those to finish were pedalling towards the end. There were four together.

The last man to cross the line was Ronny Onghena. His eyes searched for faces on the podium. As they fixed on Kelly, the Irishman was stretching his hands into the air in acknowledgment of triumph. A smile lit up Ronny's face. He shouted his congratulations but Kelly never heard. Ronny didn't mind. Not for a second. Feeling good about the world, he shoved off in the direction of his team hotel. He, too, had played a part in this success. Shielding Kelly from the wind in the early part of the race, fetching some *bidons*, being a good *domestique*. Kelly would remember all of this. In future seasons Ronny's strength as a *domestique* diminished but Kelly always provided a home for him in his team. When organizers invited Kelly to their criteriums they found themselves accepting *un autre coureur*. A cyclist they had never heard of but, as a good friend and side-kick, Ronny went with the Kelly package.

Liège-Bastogne-Liège concluded Kelly's total dominance of the first half of the season. He had won fifteen races and his face adorned the front cover of almost every cycling publication at that time. Soon after the Ardennes classic Kelly broke from racing and began his preparation for the Tour de France. His early season successes didn't alter Kelly's perspective on the Tour. It remained a race that he could not be confident of winning. The heat and the big mountains simply did not suit. As in 1983, the Tour of Switzerland was Kelly's principal preparation race. Kelly was a very relaxed cyclist in Switzerland. On the

morning of the opening stage an attractive female radio
reporter approached him in the Zurich suburb of Urdorf.
The lady wanted to interview the World's No.1 cyclist.
Kelly agreed. The lady suggested doing it in German: 'Do
you speak German?' she asked. 'A little,' said Kelly. 'How
much?' asked the girl. Looking into his interviewer's eyes
Kelly uttered the one German phrase he knew: 'I love
you.' The girl blushed and said they would proceed in
English. The interview worked out well.

Switzerland 1984 was mostly for training. Kelly rode
consistently well to finish fourth but never seriously
threatened to involve himself in the quest for the yellow
jersey. A week later he began his seventh Tour de France.
It wasn't a good Tour for him. On the last day he lost the
green jersey to the Belgian Frank Hoste and for the
second consecutive year had failed to win a stage. Kelly
suffered the bitter disappointment of losing the penultimate stage, a fifty-one kilometre time trial by .048 of a
second. He was second on two other stages. Yet it wasn't an
unqualified let-down for, in finishing fifth overall, Kelly
had achieved his best ever Tour placing. Moreover, he
only had one bad day in the mountains although that day
to Alpe d'Huez had been hugely discouraging in terms of
Kelly's overall relationship with the Tour.

On the night the 1984 Tour ended, 22 July, Kelly was in
an unusually talkative mood. He had not finished his meal
at the Sofitel Hotel until after eleven o'clock but, for once,
the lateness of the hour did not send Kelly scampering off
to bed. Alert, animated and wanting to talk, he spoke of
his failure on Alpe d'Huez and ultimately on how he
perceives the cycling press: 'I believe that I would have
been justified in explaining that I got the hunger knock on
Alpe d'Huez. Two days previously had been the rest day;
de Gribaldy gave us very little to eat, sticking by his belief
that before something like a mountain time trial you can
not eat very much. Then on the morning of the test I had
only something very light to eat. That evening fish was our

main course and early the next morning we were into the
Alpe d'Huez stage.

'If you remember I was going well in the early part of
the stage. I was fifth across the Col du Coq and was feeling
pretty good. On the Cote de Laffrey Hinault attacked
very strongly and the race broke up. Still between the
Laffrey and Alpe d'Huez I was in the chasing group
immediately behind Hinault, Herrera, Fignon, Breu and
Arroyo. But I was then beginning to get the feeling that
something was wrong. I could feel myself beginning to
struggle. On the first slopes of Alpe d'Huez I was in big
trouble. The climb was one of my worst ever experiences
on a bike. Maybe my collapse wasn't all due to the hunger
knock but I know it played a part. Still I was not going to
make excuses to any reporter. If there was something
wrong with my preparation then it was up to me and to
find it and make sure it didn't happen again. Finding it
and using it as an excuse is no good to me.

'In general I try to be careful in what I say to reporters.
When asked a question I stop and think for a second
before answering. I always try to anticipate how my answer
is going to be interpreted. If I believe the question to be
dangerous and likely to be used in a controversial way than
I keep the reply as short as possible. The fewer words you
use, the less scope the reporter has for involving you in the
controversy. Put it another way — give him words and he
may hang you with them.'

Four months earlier the same story had been told from a
different viewpoint over lunch on the way to San Remo
during the great Italian classic. A group of Belgian
journalists were interested in asking this Irish reporter
'what kind of guy Kelly really was'. Stefan Van Laere from
Het Volk articulated the collective journalistic assessment of
Kelly: 'Most of us regard him as a closed book. He will
respond to most questions but mostly with a yes or no. He
elaborates on very few. There was one night last winter
when we were both on the same skiing holiday and we got

talking over a few drinks and suddenly he opened up. The book opened. We talked, laughed and joked into the early hours. I thought what a good guy he was. I went to bed that night, very happy. At last, I had cracked Kelly. In future I would have no problem. But, you know, the next morning I met him at breakfast and the book had been closed again. It was if the previous evening had never happened.'

After the 1984 Tour Kelly sped around Europe collecting criterium fees. Again, it seemed that the monetary trail was at the price of a good preparation for the World Championships. Two weeks before going to Barcelona Kelly returned to normal racing and won two stages of the Tour of Limousin, the Grand Prix de Plouay and Paris-Bourges. In spite of the ultra-demanding criterium circuit Kelly's form appeared to be right for the World Championship road race in Barcelona. On the Wednesday before the race Kelly assessed his chances of winning in Barcelona. He appeared very confident. Illness prevented Stephen Roche from competing and Kelly was to be the only rider wearing a green jersey in Spain. He reckoned that he would at least have the support of his friend Criquielion: 'Even though he is riding in the Belgium team, Criquielion will help if he can.'

That evaluation came in Limoges, the day after Kelly's victory in Paris-Bourges. Four days later in Barcelona the heat and humidity of the Montjuich circuit forced Kelly to abandon a little after half-way. In Kelly's forced absence a dark-complexioned man from Wallonne went on to take the rainbow jersey. Claude Criquielion had ridden superbly and had become world champion. Kelly had suffered a bad day. No excuses. So, too, had Fignon, Hinault and Moser. Two days later Kelly began the Tour of Catalonia. He claimed four stages and the overall classification. Everything was back to the point where it had all started — Kelly domination. Thirty-three victories in one season, Kelly won the season-long Super Prestige and Credit

Lyonnais trophies. He claimed both by impressive margins. Kelly was at the summit of his powers and the cycling world knew it. The other stars had their seasons judged against Kelly's and suffered by the comparison.

13 A Sting in the Tale

Friday morning, 12 October 1984. Charles de Gaulle airport, Paris. The Air France flight bound for Milan was scheduled to depart at 10.30. There was just enough time to buy *L'Equipe*. I was on my way to the final classic of the season, the Tour of Lombardy, and the journey could be shortened by the French sports paper. The scene remains fixed in the memory: sitting in the flight departure lounge, flicking through the pages of *L'Equipe*, stopping at the cycling page and then finding one's eye drawn to a short, enclosed paragraph half-way down. What it said was that a rider who had finished in the first three in the Paris-Brussels Classic was rumoured to have failed the dope test. *A rider in the first three*: Kelly had been third in Paris-Brussels. It was he, Eric Vanderaerden or Charly Mottet. Not one of them had ever been linked with drug-taking. Yet, according to rumour it was one of the three.

Normally, the flight over the Alps into Italy is one of the most spectacular in Europe. On this Friday in October it was spent reflecting on a cycling season that was into its final act and in contemplation of a controversy that might possibly erupt. One voice inside me said it was just three sentences in a newspaper, purporting to be nothing other than a rumour and refusing to name *the* name. Kelly had won thirty-two races during the season, had been dope tested countless times and been negative on every occasion. For eight seasons the man had been attending to duties at dope control centres and had always been clear. Nothing seemed to fit. Paris-Brussels is a relatively unimportant classic. Kelly didn't need to win it. On the day he had ridden reasonably well but had finished a weary third in a sprint of four. Close to the finish the muscles in his legs stiffened and he suffered slight attacks of cramp. In the circumstances third place satisfied him. So how then could it be that he had problems at dope control? It couldn't be he. Then another voice inside countered with the reminder that *a rider who finished in the first three* was being accused.

Having checked into a Milan hotel in the early after-noon I walked to the public gardens in the centre of the city. Sited within the gardens is the municipal building which served as headquarters for the Tour of Lombardy. Kelly had to turn up at the race headquarters that afternoon and he could then answer questions relating to Paris-Brussels and that short, mysterious paragraph in *L'Equipe*. Not long afterwards he showed up. As the Skil team car was finding a parking-space I moved closer to get to Kelly before others. Italian journalists had come up with the same plan and were headed towards the car. On meeting Kelly I asked was it he that *L'Equipe* had referred to in its one-paragraph piece about Paris-Brussels. He said it was. At that moment the four other journalists approached Kelly and began asking questions. He interrupted them and said that in this instance he could only answer in one language at a time. He would get round to them when he was finished with me. They diplomatically withdrew and Kelly began his story:

'Last Tuesday week I received a notice which said that my urine sample for Paris-Brussels was positive. I just couldn't believe it. I immediately thought that there had been a mistake and that I would be cleared by the counter-examination of my sample. Through the Irish Cycling Federation and its international secretary, Karl McCarthy, I had an Irish doctor present at the second examination. This morning the news came that the result of the second test was the same as the first. Something is wrong; I did not take anything to ride Paris-Brussels. An error has been made and I will fight this affair until I can get it sorted out.

'In my eight years as a professional bike-racer I have been tested about two hundred times and have always been okay. This season I was tested in every other race and, until now, there was never a problem. Paris-Brussels is not an important classic — after the season I have enjoyed it was not important for me. On the day I was going okay, but got tired in the last few kilometres and was well beaten in the sprint by Vanderaerden and Mottet. There is no way I took anything. If I had is it likely that I would have finished third and therefore ensured I was tested at medical control? I am convinced that the mistake happened because of irregularities at the testing centre that day. The medical control at Paris-Brussels was very badly organized and lots of people were in the room who had no right to be there. When the rider is giving his sample I believe there should be just two people in the room. When I gave mine, there were about seven people there. In all this confusion something must have gone wrong.'

Kelly moved away to recount the same story in French, then Flemish. Unexpressive at the best of times, he had now withdrawn into the safe-house of blank introspection. All the races, all of the victories, all of the glory of the last eight months counted for nothing. He tried to tell himself that Time would heal but that weekend in Milan he suffered. The Belgian Federation had claimed that traces of the drug *Stimul* were found in his urine sample. *Stimul* can be bought in chemist shops in Belgium. It is said to improve concentration and can be beneficial to students preparing for an examination. In the 1970s cyclists had been accused of using the drug. Scottish professional Robert Millar was very reluctant to believe that Kelly had taken *Stimul*: 'I can't imagine that Kelly took this. As a drug it is about ten years out of date and is not something that a rider, who wanted to avail of artificial help, would turn to.'

The story had begun on a mid-week day in September, Wednesday the nineteenth. One-hundred-and-forty-six riders had gathered for the sixty-fourth Paris-Brussels. On a dry and fresh autumnal morning the race moved out of Senlis, a pretty town north of Paris. As the starter told the participants to race, a group of about ten cyclists were chatting away in a shed about 100 metres away from the start line. They saw the cavalcade move out and, without haste, mounted their bikes and set out after it. This was only Paris-Brussels. Three-hundred-and-one kilometres stretched before the racers. Although labelled a classic, Paris-Brussels is not in the same category as a Paris-Roubaix, a Liège-Bastogne-Liège or a Tour of Lombardy. In the public imagination it ranks like a 'B' movie. The riders consider that it is too long and that its route is stunningly boring. That morning in Senlis Paul Sherwen spoke for the world of professional riders when he said: 'This race brings on the end-of-season blues.'

The sixty-fourth Paris-Brussels was enlivened by a young rider called Philippe Saude from the town of Chauny in northern France. After fifty kilometres Saude approached people like Hinault, Stephen Roche and other leaders. He explained that the race passed through his home town thirty kilometres later and that it would be an enormous thrill for him to head the race at that point. Such a concession is rarely granted in a classic but then this was Paris-Brussels and Saude's case did seem special. Two months earlier he had received a letter from his employers, Renault, informing him that there was no contract for him in 1985. A professional for two years with Renault, Saude had been one of Cyrille Guimard's few failures. Philippe Saude bore no grudges; Guimard had been good to him. Just twenty-four and already marked out for cycling's scrap-heap; Hinault and the other leaders said yes to the request from Philippe Saude

— he could lead the race through his home town.
He broke away from the *peloton* twenty-eight kilometres from Chauny. Vigilant *domestiques* were instructed
not to pursue. Through his home town Saude led by
four minutes and twenty seconds. Beautifully balanced on
the bike, Philippe should have begun to relax after
Chauny but opted to do otherwise. The advantage
escalated. Four minutes became seven, it soon grew to nine
and at the first feeding station in St Quentin (114
kilometres) Saude was ten minutes clear. At that feeding
zone he took his yellow *musette* from a team-helper, rifled
through the contents, packed what he wanted into his
pockets and was pedalling furiously again within fifty
metres. He cast his *musette* towards the ditch, it blew back
on to the road and a small, blond-haired boy picked it up.
As the boy waited for the *peloton* to arrive he feasted on
what Saude had discarded. Everything had been consumed by the time the pack came sweeping past.

Saude's advantage continued to grow. At the Franco/
Belge frontier he led by fourteen minutes. Traditionally
the Paris-Brussels Classic begins in earnest at this point
for, with just 110 kilometres remaining, the most difficult
part of the journey has been completed. Fourteen minutes
was a frightening advantage. Suddenly the notion that
Saude could win was being entertained in most imagina-
tions. Nobody was certain that he would tire. But as
attention focused on the young French opportunist, the
signs of fatigue were noted. Shoulders began to droop and
his head shuffled from side to side. Gone was the fluency
of the early part of his escapade. Regular checks from the
race radio confirmed that Saude was losing three minutes
to the pack for each ten kilometres that he travelled. For
Philippe Saude, Paris-Brussels was not going to provide an
escape from cycling oblivion.

He was swallowed up by the bunch in the Belgian town
of Nivelles, forty-six kilometres from the finish. He had
cycled at the front of Paris-Brussels for 205 kilometres. To

those who lined the route during that part of the race he was a hero while the leaders of the *peloton* reminded themselves never to trust this young man again. Many racers tried to escape after Saude's recapture but found the bunch unwilling to tolerate any further adventurers. Arriving into the finishing town of Rhode St Genese, a settlement on the outskirts of Brussels, two laps of an eight mile circuit remained to be completed. The *peloton* was down to sixty-five riders and diminishing all the time. At the beginning of the final lap Eric Vanderaerden attacked, Kelly reacted and so too did the French rider, Charly Mottet. Their lead was quickly up to thirty seconds. Two kilometres from the finish Eric Van Lancker of Belgium shot clear of the bunch and joined the three leaders.

The race was firmly in the control of these four riders. Seven hours on the road and the feeling of cramp in both legs took the zip from Kelly's sprint and he was clearly distanced by both Vanderaerden and Mottet in the race for the principal prizes. Third place was a disappointment, one of those days when the World's No.1 was not at his sharpest. Vanderaerden admired Kelly's performance in defeat: 'When the three of us, Kelly, Mottet and I, were away I could see that Kelly was not going as well as he can but he continued to do his share of the pacemaking. He did not hide behind the fact that he was not going well. He rode like the champion that he is.' That evening a slight drizzle began to fall in Rhode St Genese, and Kelly spoke outside the dope control centre of future plans and past achievements. On the following Sunday he was to take part in the Grand Prix des Nations time trial at Cannes in the south of France. An eighty-nine kilometre test, the Nations counts as the most important time trial on the professional calendar. Kelly looked forward to riding it: 'A year ago I went to the Nations and finished only thirteenth; it was a very bad performance. This year I am going down there not so much to win as to redeem myself for last year's ride.'

He recalled the Tour of Catalonia which he had ridden a week earlier. In the Spanish race Kelly won four stages and the overall award. It had pleased him enormously because on the critical mountain stage he suffered mechanical trouble and, as a consequence, lost nineteen seconds and the race lead. Entering the decisive time trial in the Catalonian race Kelly still had that nineteen seconds to make up on the Spanish star, Pedro Munoz. He won the test by exactly nineteen seconds from Munoz and regained the leaders' jersey by virtue of better stage placings. Then in the final stage Kelly punctured and found himself organizing the most desperate pursuit of Munoz. He regained contact dangerously close to the finish and, after a spectacularly exciting race, Kelly had claimed another victory.

He talked in Rhode St Genese of the huge publicity which the Tour of Catalonia had generated in Spain and how pleased the team sponsor was to have received such exposure in that country. He smiled on recollecting how close he had come to losing out. This writer offered the somewhat cynical view that he was extremely fortunate to survive the Spanish organizers who might easily have tipped the fractions in Munoz's favour after the time trial. Kelly's reply found an even higher level of cynicism: 'I believe that if they wanted anybody to win, it was me. The organizers of Catalonia are very ambitious for their race and would like it included in the events counting for Super Prestige Points. It was better for them that a highly rated foreigner should win than a local Spaniard and so they were not going to bend things to get one of their own fellows to win.' One found oneself taking a step backwards and admiring the man's honesty.

On the following Sunday Kelly dug deep into his reserves of courage and came up with a second place performance in the Grand Prix des Nations time trial. It was his best ever display in the Nations and further increased his lead in the Super Prestige. While Kelly did

not win every race, 1984 was continuing to be a supremely
successful year for him. The FICP World Rankings
confirmed his position as the World No.I each month and
his margin of supremacy over the second placed Laurent
Fignon was a huge 438 points. After the Nations, Kelly
had just two important races to ride: the Blois-Chaville
and Tour of Lombardy classics.

On the Tuesday before Blois-Chaville a letter arrived to
the Nys home in Vilvoorde for Kelly. It contained the
official allegation that Kelly's Paris-Brussels sample had
been positive. At this time the allegation had not been
publicized and Kelly entertained the hope that the
counter-examination would clear him. He wondered what
he could do to lessen the damage. His next race was Blois-
Chaville and he resolved to win that: 'I knew that I had not
taken anything when I finished third in Paris-Brussels and
I wanted to win Blois-Chaville simply to prove that I didn't
need to take anything to win. When a controversy like this
crops up certain people will take your side of the story and
others will not. That is the way with everything. But I
wanted to win Blois-Chaville; I could prove something in
that race.'

Blois-Chaville is France's premier autumn classic.
Changes of location have robbed the race of its identity but
it still remains a prestigious category-one classic.
On Sunday morning 7 October, 140 riders set out on the
journey through the rolling countryside about 100 kilometres south of Paris. The first 140 kilometres of the 239-
kilometre race were over relatively flat terrain and the big
men in the *peloton* conserved their energies. Over the
final 100 kilometres there are nine short but steepish
climbs. On the climb of the Madeleine hill, twenty-five
kilometres from the finish, Claude Criquielion and Gibi
Baronchelli escaped. Their alliance promised much until
Baronchelli crashed on the Madeleine descent, breaking a
collar bone. Alone at the front, Criquielion's prospects
were bleak and fifteen kilometres from the finish he was

swept up by a leading group of about fifty riders.

Kim Andersen and Ludo Peeters counter-attacked just as Criquielion was caught and they poached a lead of sixteen seconds. Kelly felt that everything was still under control. 'Peeters was a member of the Kwantum team and at that time there was a major battle going on between it and its Dutch rival, Panasonic. I knew that with Peeters in the lead, Panasonic would maintain a strong pursuit.' Kelly didn't want any other rider leaving the pack and when the young French star, Philippe Bouvatier, broke away Kelly chased him down immediately. Five kilometres from the finish, the two leaders were defeated as the pack bridged the 300-metre gap which had offered them the prospect of glory.

The final three kilometres through the western suburbs of Paris took the race into narrow streets with sharp bends. An invitation to the kamikaze pilots in the *peloton*. French rider Gilbert Duclos Lassalle was the one to accept as he took the biggest risks and gained a thirty-metre advantage. There was less than a kilometre to go and Lassalle believed he was on the way to a classic win. On one corner he found his path momentarily blocked when a television motorcycle failed to negotiate the bend as fast as he. Turning into the finishing straight Lassalle led but had the Dutch rider Steven Rooks bearing down on him. The finishing straight in Chaville is about 300 metres long and is slightly uphill. This classic had never been a good one for Kelly and in the two previous editions he had trailed in behind the leading group. 'Those performances did give me the chance to study the nature of the finish. I knew precisely what it would be like, that a man could make up a lot of ground inside the final 200 metres.'

Earlier that afternoon the amateur Grand Prix de L'Equipe had finished in Chaville. One of those who rode that race was an Irish cyclist called Paul Kimmage. After changing into ordinary clothes Kimmage took a place at the barriers, about 250 metres from the finish line and quite close to the last corner, and waited for the professionals to come screaming round. Now a continental professional, Kimmage has been a cyclist since he could walk. His amateur record includes a sixth place in the World Championship Road Race. He watched intently as Lassalle and Rooks led the pack into the uphill straight. His eyes searched out Kelly: 'Eventually he went by. I looked at how many were in front of him and reckoned that if he got into the top three he would be doing really well. No matter how far I stretched my imagination, I could not give him the slightest chance of winning. He was much too far back.'

Producing an enormous effort, Kelly danced frantically on the pedals and went past one rider after another. Rooks was the last to resist his surge but fifty metres from the line he, too, was reduced to supporting player. Kelly won with both arms raised and by a clear two lengths. His immediate reaction offers an interesting contrast to Kimmage's reading of the sprint: 'When I produced my effort there was no problem. I felt very strong and never thought I would lose that sprint.'

It was the third classic win of the season for Kelly and the fourth of his career. Twelve months previously he waited to win his first, now he had four. Afterwards he relived the race in the usual matter-of-fact, self-effacing way. Somebody asked why it was that he had never asked his team-mates to work for him during the race: 'There was nothing much for them to do,' said Kelly. 'I was in control of the situation on the road and didn't need their help.' One of those *domestiques* who might have been called to help was Jean Claude Bagot. His respect for the leader was perfectly obvious in Chaville: 'He is a super leader of our team, so easy to get on with and never too exacting. He never has a word of criticism and he is always so relaxed. He looks after us well and I maintain that he can win all the races and on his own at that.'

Even though burdened by the still undisclosed drugs

allegation, Kelly felt a sense of relief in Chaville. He sat in the small caravan which was the dope control centre and looked forward to the last classic of the season, the Tour of Lombardy. His sample after the Chaville victory was negative. In the public eye, that wasn't an issue. *L'Equipe*, realizing that its 'King Kelly' line had been used a little too often, decided that Attila had come from Ireland and was masquerading in the red-and-white-striped jersey of Skil. It was just another classic win. No big deal anymore. Kelly himself knew differently. He could now face the final classic of the season and the possibility of a difficult controversy with more conviction.

During the six days which lay between Blois-Chaville and the Tour of Lombardy, stories began to appear in the Belgian papers about a positive dope test following Paris-Brussels. Kelly was already in Italy, riding the Tour of Piemont and preparing for the Lombardy Classic. Dr Lambert had come from Ireland to be present at the second examination and was staying with Herman and Elise Nys at Vilvoorde. Linda was there as well and, without any doubt, was suffering most of all through this ordeal. It wasn't just the Paris-Brussels controversy: on the same day that the result of the second examination was revealed Linda's aunt, Margaret Ryan, was found dead in her flat. At the same time her father was losing a big part of his job. Through this, the phone rarely stopped ringing at 108 Breemputstraat. Journalists wanting to know at which Italian number Sean could be contacted. Linda simply didn't have a number. One of them rang late at night and demanded to know why Linda didn't have a number for her husband. 'How can you not know?' he remonstrated.

The result of the counter-examination was disclosed on Friday 12 October, the day before the Tour of Lombardy. That night the Skil team stayed in the Leonardo di Vinci hotel in Milan. It was around nine o'clock when I called. Kelly was in his room. He wasn't much enthused by the visit, or at least he didn't appear to be. He sat by his bed, polishing his black Puma cycling shoes, rhythmically pushing the brush back and forth as if to soothe some unseen pain. Ronny Onghena, his great friend, lay on the inside bed. He nodded a greeting as I entered but said nothing during the half-hour of the visit. So often the talkative and humorous side-kick, Ronny couldn't do anything for his friend on this occasion. Kelly repeated his intention to fight the verdict. Even then he doubted if the cycling authorities would reverse the decision but he was going to try. He continued to shine his shoes and comforted himself with the recollection that others had been through the same ordeal: 'Many great cyclists, Merckx for example, have had to cope with this allegation and they survived it. I hope to win tomorrow's race if only to give them something else to think about!'

A day later Kelly didn't win the Tour of Lombardy. His zest for cycling battle had been diminished by the Paris-Brussels affair and when a Peugeot rider lost control of his machine around half-way he crashed directly in front of Kelly. The spill inclined Kelly towards the view that nothing was destined to go his way this weekend. Although he remounted and even returned to the *peloton*, he was no longer thinking about winning. Bernard Hinault claimed a special victory that afternoon. Special because it had come at the end of a long and often very difficult season for the Breton. Afterwards, in the town of Como, Stephen Roche expressed his anger at the allega-tion that Kelly had taken something in Paris-Brussels: 'How can they do this to Sean — he has been easily the best rider in the world this season and they accuse him of taking something in a race like Paris-Brussels. I know Sean well enough to know that it is nonsense.'

After the race the riders changed and showered at the Shingaglia Stadium in Como. Although still down and morose, Kelly was coming round. Traces of animation returned to his face and one sensed the re-emergence of the defiant, resilient Kelly. Walking out of the stadium that Saturday evening he looked forward to an end-of-the-season holiday and getting the controversy further into his past: 'I know I can put this thing behind me. I am a good enough cyclist to do that. I feel terribly sorry for Linda, it has taken so much out of her. Last night we spoke on the phone; she began to cry and I didn't know what to say. There was nothing I felt I could do.'

Soon after changing Kelly and his team-mates left Milan for Paris. On the following day he rode the mildly prestigious *Criterium des As* in the French capital. He won it comfortably. The rehabilitation had already begun. That victory brought the best season of his career to an appropriate conclusion. Thirty-three victories. Soon after he went with Linda and some friends on a two-week Spanish holiday. His case to reverse the Paris-Brussels judgement was first considered by the cycling authorities in Belgium who, predictably, failed to alter their own decision. The case later went to the International Cycling Union (UCI), the body which controls world cycling. It agreed with Kelly's argument that the organization at the dope control centre in Rhode St Genese was so slipshod that a mistake was likely to happen. Accepting this argument, the UCI asked the Belgian Federation to re-open the case. The world body added that it was not empowered to reverse the verdict of the national association. The Belgians, of course, refused to alter their initial judgement and the case ended back in the lap of the UCI. In January 1986, sixteen months after the verdict was delivered, the UCI acknowledged that the initial result could not be altered.

Any investigation of the affair would find it exceedingly difficult to accept that Kelly knowingly took *Stimul* to help his performance in Paris-Brussels. He had enjoyed a superb season and certainly didn't need to win that race. The nature of the drug is also of interest, for as well as Millar's assertion that it was a drug of the 1970s, there are others who insist that it is a substance which will always show up in drug tests. If Kelly had taken *Stimul* why could he not have finished fifth instead of third? Had he been fifth he would not have been tested.

In November Kelly travelled to Paris to receive the Super Prestige award for 1984. *L'Equipe's* Jean Marie Leblanc interviewed him for his newspaper's Saturday magazine. It was a wide-ranging exploration of Kelly's life and values. Leblanc asked about the Paris-Brussels controversy: 'I did not take anything in that race. I believe my record speaks for itself. From the start of the season last February to the end in October I was winning races each month. My form did not fluctuate very much — I was always going pretty well. It is when a cyclist produces exceptional form for two or three months of the season and then disappears that you must begin to question. I am not that sort of rider.'

At the end of 1984 Paris-Brussels was removed from the list of events counting for Super Prestige Points and so its status as a classic race was further reduced. The organizers of the Super Prestige were not impressed by the way the race was run. For the alleged offence Kelly was fined one thousand Swiss francs and given a one-month suspended sentence. If there was another drugs ruling against him in the two years subsequent to September 1984, he would then receive a three-month suspension. But the official punishments were minor in relation to the personal suffering which the episode caused at the time. Linda's recollection remains as the most forceful testimony to its impact: 'I still feel very bad and sad about the whole thing. I know Sean was the victim. Things can never be quite the same. When, in the future, Sean goes to control I will worry. It happened once before; who is to say that it can never happen again?'

14 Nightmares

The Australian rider Phil Anderson has made the interesting observation that cyclists must earn their money twice. First by performing well in the one-day classics and major tours and then on the lucrative criterium circuit. It works in this way: a rider wins a big classic and earns about £1,000 for doing so. That figure will be divided between team-mates and the final return to each is inconsequential. Monetary reward for winning a classic comes in the criteriums, mostly held during the month of August when certain riders are paid a fee for competing. A middle-division rider could increase his criterium fee from £500 to £1,000 should he win a classic. Accepting that he will ride twenty criteriums the £500 increase works out as an extra £10,000 for the year. While that represents a sizeable jump, Anderson's contention that this money has to be earned twice is not without validity.

The criterium circuit, particularly in France where distances are so great, encourages excess. Riders will forget the normal rules in the pursuit of money. Kelly, given his obsession to make the life pay, was always likely to be a front-line warrior in the battle to race just one more criterium. Each year he will say that the criteriums constitute unsatisfactory preparation for the September World Championship Road Race and that he will be doing fewer than previously. There will then be a tussle with his conscience but ultimately he will accept most of the offers available. Why gamble on winning the World title when there is an assured £30,000 to be picked up on the criterium circuit? Kelly's idea of professionalism doesn't stray too far from the mercenary path.

Yet it is a rough and unhealthy existence. Brussels is warm and sunny. It is the first day of August 1984. Far away in Los Angeles the twenty-third Olympiad is progressing. For the cyclists who have recently completed the Tour de France there are the criteriums. At his base in Vilvoorde Kelly is resting up for a day between criteriums. He likes to race in France; they pay him well to come. His presence adds an international dimension to races that will be organized by the smallest village. On the following day he will travel to the village of Chaumiel, a pleasant little settlement in central France. It is about 900 kilometres from Brussels. The posters advertising the Chaumiel race feature the name of *Sean Kelly*.

At around nine o'clock on this Wednesday evening, as Herman and Elise Nys sit down to watch some swimming from Los Angeles, their lodger goes upstairs to his room. There he would shave his legs and pack enough clothes for three days. An hour or so later he returns, ready to depart for Chaumiel. He is travelling with his team-mate and close friend Ronny Onghena, his wife Linda, and me. For a few months I had been asking Kelly about the prospect of sitting in the back seat as he drove to a few criteriums. How else could one write about this part of the life? Kelly agreed totally and went out of his way to encourage the expedition. Over the following three days he was good company but forever conscious that he travelled with a journalist. The man does not shed his professionalism easily.

The following day's race at Chaumiel was scheduled to begin at 2.30 and so Kelly had, characteristically, allowed plenty of time. Chaumiel could not be found on any map. Its absence from the map did, however, make one feel all the more sharply why they wanted Kelly to come to their village from Brussels, why they paid Hinault to travel from

Brittany and why they wanted Fignon to drive from Holland where he had ridden the night before. For at least one day in the year, Thursday 2 August, the world would see that Chaumiel existed.

Ronny Onghena is a professional cyclist from the town of St Niklaas in Flanders, Belgium. He had been a professional with Kelly at Splendor. There they had become friends and when de Gribaldy re-signed Kelly for Sem in 1981 he was in effect buying Onghena as well. Cycling's history is full of stories of unflinching loyalty between team leaders and certain of their *domestiques*. Onghena was devoted to Kelly. He would not want to be a professional in a situation where he could not ride for Kelly but it is equally true that he would not have survived as a professional without Kelly's backing.

The basis to their mutual loyalty was friendship. Kelly liked this off-beat, unassuming cyclist from Belgium. Rarely a winner in his professional career, Onghena lived out his cycling life without illusions. As well as shielding Kelly from the wind, carrying extra bottles for him and generally discharging the duties of the *domestique*, Onghena provided Kelly with an escape from the deadly seriousness of being one of the big riders. Kelly calls Ronny 'Alex', and Onghena becomes 'Onghenack'. They laugh about Life's trivia, recollect past exploits with amusement and Ronny still knows exactly when to be serious. Linda Kelly used to put it like this: 'Ronny is Sean's morale.' When the *domestique* was around Kelly's spirits would rise.

Ronny Onghena would never have been invited to Chaumiel if it were not for Kelly's influence. Onghena would be the only Belgian riding Chaumiel. For the first four hours of driving, Ronny sat behind the wheel. Those were the hours on the autoroute and Kelly would take over on the smaller, more dangerous minor roads. After 860 kilometres it is time to stop. The town is Tulle and the hotel comfortable. Kelly checks the four guests into the

Concentrating on staying upright, Kelly steers a Paris – Roubaix course

Overleaf: Bondue has fallen. Kelly and Rogiers are very much in control

Getting close to home, he shows the way to Rudy Rogiers and Alain Bondue

Clear of Rogiers, Kelly has won the great one-day classic, Paris – Roubaix in 1984

◄ Two days after Paris-Roubaix, Kelly relaxes home. Note the unwashed bike in the foreground

Claude Criquielion leads, Rooks hangs on, Kelly suffers. Without Criquielion's help victory in the 1984 Liège-Bastogne-Liège would not have been possible

The slightly uphill finish to the Blois-
ville race in 1984 suited Kelly

'In Ireland', Kelly said, 'they only do this kind
of thing for you when you are dead ' ▼

Sean Kelly
SQUARE

NAMED TO COMMEMORATE HIS SUCCESS
IN THE WORLD CHAMPIONSHIPS
AND TOUR DE FRANCE 1982

▲ Outside the Kelly home at Curraghduff:
Nellie Kelly, Sean, Vincent Kelly and
Jack Kelly

The unthinkable: Kelly being pipped by V
der Poel for fourth place in Carrick-on-Su
during the Nissan Classic ▼

Kelly signs for a young fan during the 1985 Tour de France

A moment of horror in the 1985 Tour: Hinault has made up the two-minutes deficit on Kelly during the Strasbourg time trial

Kelly sprints, Vanderaerden (left) and Hinault prepare to react

establishment. It is six o'clock in the morning and the receptionist wants to know if the 'S.Kelly' is the real Sean Kelly. At this hour of the morning the receptionist gets no more than a polite yes. There had been eight hours of driving, punctuated by just one stop for diesel and coffee. That had taken place at five minutes past three.

Rapid calculations by Kelly and we are informed that it will be possible to have five-and-a-half hours sleep, six o'clock to 11.30. This message is conveyed with a genuine sense of 'aren't we fortunate?' Going to sleep as the sun rises, driving through the black of night and racing sometime between. At 11.35 Kelly checks that everybody is awake and aware of the hour. Nobody hangs around. At 11.45 the car is leaving Tulle. Half-way between Tulle and Chaumiel there is a stop for some ham, salami, pork, gherkin, bread and mineral water. A little girl approaches with a photograph of Kelly, he signs it and she goes away pleased.

Kelly's politeness in signing the photograph open the door to conversation. Everybody wants to talk cycling. One of the men says he is going to the race in Chaumiel, that he will have bottles of cool mineral water for Kelly on the hill. Temperatures outside are soaring, maybe 90 degrees Fahrenheit. Kelly looks at the man, trying to instil a picture of the face into his mind. Five hours later, as the Chaumiel criterium reached its half-way point, the face was found on the hillside and a large bottle of Vittel was passed from spectator to rider. It provided relief for four other members of the *peloton* as well. France is full of people sensitive to the needs of the cyclist.

At Chaumiel the riders' car park is full of Peugeots, Renaults, Citroens and there is one Mercedes. They are mostly expensive, high-powered vehicles. This criterium is known to be hard, seven laps of a difficult eighteen-kilometre circuit. It would take up to three-and-a-half hours of this Thursday afternoon. Fignon's 1,100-kilometre drive from a Dutch criterium the previous night had taken longer than anticipated and the Tour de France champion causes fleeting consternation and the race to begin five minutes late. Thirty-five riders set out, the course is severe, the distance long and this is not going to be a summer saunter around village streets.

For his three-and-a-half hours work Kelly would receive £2,000. 1984 had been his best ever year: this was now his normal fee for appearing in a French criterium. Fignon and Hinault would receive more, around £3,000 each, but the vast majority of riders would be paid as little as £300 to £500. Each one is paid according to the organizer's estimation of his worth.

Criteriums are competitive and yet not in the sense that a classic or big Tour is. During the first of the seven laps the pace is sedate. The people of Chaumiel are gently re-introduced to professional cycling. Kelly chats with Fignon and Hinault on that first lap, suggesting to them that his team-mate Eric Caritoux would like to win this criterium. Caritoux was born in Carpentras, a town further south, but he would be familiar with the region around Chaumiel and would want to do well in their race. Neither Fignon or Hinault voices an objection, and if Caritoux is good enough to beat all of the other riders in the race they won't interfere. This time one of Kelly's boys is getting an opportunity; the next time it will be one of theirs. There is no big deal — rather it is a part of the reality of the moving circus called the criterium circuit.

Another element in that reality is that if you are being paid to appear, then you appear. That is you get yourself to the front of the *peloton* for a certain length of time and the locals are able to see that you are racing seriously in their criterium. Kelly finds it easy to play the professional game in this instance, believing that for £2,000 he must put on a show. He quietly despises those who come, fool around for half the race, drop out, take their money and run. That is cheating, unprofessional.

The severity of the eighteen-kilometre circuit precipi-

tates continual attacking and counter-attacking. Onghena
gets into the first break of the race. On the steepish hill
Ronny struggles, just managing to stay in touch with the
other four. But on the flat sections he is strong. Soon this
group is caught and there is a lone breakaway, Jacques
Bossis. Kelly is a member of the three-man chasing group.
Earning his fee. Then Caritoux makes his move from the
peloton, joining Kelly and eventually getting clear with
another French rider, Frederic Brun, on the final lap. As
the finish is uphill and Caritoux climbs well, he does his
job convincingly, sprinting away from Brun. Kelly comes
in fifth, pleased that when he surged at the bottom of the
final hill he left his three companions. But this was to be
Eric's day, Eric's win.

It was about six-thirty when the Chaumiel race had
ended. Kelly showers, dresses and returns to his car by
seven-thirty. The thick white envelope containing his
20,000 francs fee is folded over and carried out in his
underpants. At around seven-forty-five the Citroen edges
out of Chaumiel, the post-race traffic still causing near
stagnation in the village. The next destination is Concarneau. A town on the south-west coast of Brittany, it will
take nine hours of driving to reach Concarneau. As we left
Chaumiel behind, one felt bound to ask questions: Had
the crowd which paid to get on to the circuit been big
enough to cover the cost of the race? If not, how would the
deficit be cleared? When Chaumiel had been drained of
the bike enthusiasts how many would be left to carry on
normal life? Kelly, unconcerned, sped away to another
town, another race and more money.

After about an hour's driving, it was time to stop and
have something to eat. The day slipped by with only that
light lunch of ham, salami, pork, etc. In deference to the
presence of his wife and journalist companion Kelly opted
to eat in a slightly up-market restaurant. The intervals
between sitting down, ordering and receiving food were,
in the usual French way, protracted. The unsophisticated

farmer's son from Carrick-on-Suir wasn't much impressed: 'I haven't eaten in a restaurant like this for a long
time and it will be a long time before I am caught in one
again. If you stop at one of the self-service places on the
motorway you can see exactly what you are getting and
have it eaten in half an hour. That means an extra hour's
sleep somewhere further on in the journey.'

Kelly's meal had been straightforward: melon, pork
chops, cheese and black coffee. On the other side of the
table Ronny tackled a dessert arrangement that relied
heavily for its attraction on ice-cream and cream. A
domestique can eat what he wishes during the criteriums;
Kelly remains Kelly for the entirety of the season. By the
time we return to the car, darkness had fallen and
provided a grim reminder of the long night and long road
that lie before us. Night driving is a peculiarly lonely
experience, tiredness being the only companion and it
must be fought all of the time.

The route to Brittany encompassed mostly minor or
subsidiary roads and so Kelly did the driving. A journey
that began at ten-thirty continues until four-thirty in the
morning. Then another tent is pitched at the Hotel Ibis
outside of Rennes. Kelly had been eager to talk during the
journey, wanting something, anything, to divert his mind
from the loneliness of the night. He spoke of the infamous
Tour de France story, when his team-mate Michel Pollentier was expelled from the race while wearing the yellow
jersey. Pollentier's crime had been an attempt to provide a
bogus urine sample at the drugs control centre.

'Ah yes, the early years. Pollentier and the Tour de
France scandal. They would have found it hard to take the
jersey away from Pollentier if he had not lost it in the
medical control room. The organizers could have given
him a second chance but Michel had not the right image
for a Tour de France winner. It was not that he was a
Belgian (as all of Belgium believed) but that he did not
look right on the bike. He was a small, almost crooked man

on a bike, not the kind of figure that Felix Levitan would have wanted in a yellow jersey on the Champs Elysees ...

'When I left Flandria for Splendor in 1979 people said it was because I liked Michel more than Freddy Maertens who was staying on at Flandria. But it wasn't that. It was because Splendor were offering much more money and at Flandria there was a clique which involved Maertens and de Meyer and there were few opportunities for the rest of us to win.' Driving through the night, Kelly had wanted to talk, to fight the black solitude with words. It works for a time, then the words fade and surrender to the darkness.

At around one-thirty in the morning Kelly stopped for refueling — diesel for the car, coffee for the humans. It was suggested to him that no amount of money could make this existence worthwhile. He didn't spend much time contemplating a response: 'What would you do if you were a long-distance lorry driver, having to do this all of your life? We only have to do it for a few weeks each year.' And, the long-distance lorry driver might add, the good bike-men earn more in those few weeks than he does over the entire year. Kelly knows when not to complain.

Arrival time into the Breton town of Rennes was 4.30 in the morning. The Hotel Ibis just outside the town housed four people who would have struggled to know whether, in the words of Tolkien, 'it was today or tomorrow'. Nice rooms, not too expensive, Kelly selects his hotels carefully. At around ten minutes before five Ronny and I are about to sink into sleep when the trip's absolute leader comes with the instructions: 'We sleep until 1.30; that gives us nine hours before the start of the Concarneau race. It should be plenty.' Before slipping back to his room, Kelly goes down to reception to double check the starting-time of the criterium and to check on the precise distance between Rennes and Concarneau. Organization is nothing more than a series of small things well looked after.

As usual the leaving was prompt. At 1.40 the show was on the road and a few minutes later the car had been directed into a self-service restaurant. Kelly was a sight more content in this unpretentious eating house than he had been in the classy restaurant. Standing over the food, examining it, seeing what he was about to eat. Eventually he settled for an assorted salad, rice and meat main course, natural yogurt and finally cheese. Nothing that might arouse the disapproval of the dietitian. Most cyclists will permit themselves occasional treats, Kelly gives the impression of not having to even resist the temptation.

It was about five o'clock in the evening when he became a part of the tourist traffic in Concarneau. Almost five hours before the race. This was the Kelly style. A trip around the circuit brought back memories: 'Last year's Tour was in this town; fellows nearly ended up going into the sea on this bend.' It was an interesting circuit — a big bridge had to be crossed and from that bridge spectators could see the riders wriggling along the harbour edge down below. Juggernauts were used to close the circuit, local organizers waited to collect from spectators and Concarneau was going to have a big sporting night.

Seven-thirty in the evening and Kelly is preparing himself for another show. Pumping up his tubeless tyres, shining his bike with a dry cloth and filling *bidons* with a mixture of mineral water and glucose. On this circuit there are no team-helpers: the champion rider is at once mechanic, *soigneur* and *directeur sportif*. Across the road from Kelly the Renault brigade of Fignon, Vincent Barteau and Pierre Henri Mentheor clean their bikes. Twice Tour de France king, Fignon looked like an oldish boy scout. How can cyclists get self-important notions or court arrogance when an hour before the race they must clean their bikes? Barteau was a particular source of interest to the onlookers. Curiosity value. He had been the one who found himself in the yellow jersey of the Tour de France a month earlier, not at all put out by the fact that a bizarre breakaway lay at the centre of his fame. Barteau wore the golden tunic for eleven days.

Through it all he won many friends. His whole demeanour effused a sense of the unlikely boy having a great time. He had no right to win the Tour but then he never claimed any. His father joined the race a few days before the Alps ended Vincent's engaging performance on centre stage. He said he had come because he thought Vincent, without *le maillot jaune*, would need parental support. You liked Barteau and his father. Now Vincent was making the criteriums. Cashing in the chips he had accumulated at the Tour. Being known entailed problems for Vincent. The previous day at Chaumiel he had lost contact with the leaders. He struggled and struggled but only conceded more ground. Nobody jeered, nobody laughed. There was a common feeling that the unlikely star of the 1984 Tour needed as much encouragement as possible.

Soon after the start of the Concarneau race the skies sent forth thousands of missiles. Riding at night presents its problems; riding on a wet night over a short circuit creates all kinds of unpleasant possibilities. All you need is a lively imagination. Kelly's strategy in the wet has always been to get to the front then 'if you crash at least you have the satisfaction of knowing it was your own fault'. Once at the front Kelly finds himself in a break of four: along with Michel Laurent, Gilbert Duclos Lassalle and his own team-mate Frederic Vichot.

It is good for the spectators, Kelly in the lead group and Fignon alone in pursuit of the four about one minute behind. Blond-haired Laurent is clad in the Tour de France yellow jersey, the bright colour seeming to bestow greatness on the wearer. Towards the end of the race Fignon joined the leaders and the crowd is content. Eventually others join up and the race takes on a new shape as Mentheor, Hubert Linard and Laurent forge clear. Mentheor wins easily.

Certain things remain in the mind from that Breton evening. Who was the portly gent who stood on the barrier near the finish? Each time the race passed he would scream 'Allez Kelly'. If the rain dispersed most people it could not shift this Frenchman who supported his Irish hero. The passion with which he backed Kelly almost frightened. What had Kelly done for him, why the idolatry? Our friend was not dressed in a manner that suggested richness and yet coming near the end he donated 1,000 francs (£100) for a lap sprint. He would merely describe himself as a 'Sean Kelly supporter' to the grateful organizer. Presumably this supporter wished Kelly to win the prize but Kelly never heard the announcement of the donated money, never sprinted for another £100. The Kelly supporter remained to the very end: a sodden face, rain seeping through his clothes and still the 'Allez Kelly' shrieks.

There was also the question of the argument between Fignon and the organizer just before the race started. Kelly refused to confide, although one felt sure that he knew the reason for the conflict. According to most cyclists there are things in professional cycling which should remain undisclosed: Kelly was not about to tell this journalist why Fignon and the organizer argued. Some inquiries and a little deduction suggested that the organizer of the Concarneau criterium wished the Tour de France champion to win his race. Fignon was pleading that such a result might not happen, that some other rider might win. Each criterium organizer would want the Tour winner to triumph in his race but Fignon knew he could only win a few, that others must be given the opportunity to win. That night in Concarneau Fignon had ridden very strongly but his Renault team-mate Mentheor had been rewarded for services rendered in the Tour with this criterium success.

Since Wednesday night, nine-thirty, Kelly had been on the road. Long periods of driving, short periods of sleep, riding the races and hanging around for the money. Now it is Friday night, just a few minutes before midnight and the Concarneau race has ended. Rain falls in unceasing torrents, street lighting capturing the descent of each arrow. Not many wait around for the presentation. Kelly has won the Points Trophy for the race and so a further wait as he is forced to accept another little monument to his cycling talents. He is cold and wet and the photographer from the local newspaper says that he can't fit the banner showing the name of the sponsor into the picture. The riders must wait as the banner is altered. On this night it is impossible to get excited. Nobody even tries.

After showering Kelly returns to the organizer to collect his wages. Another 20,000 francs for the World's No.I. Tax, the agent's fee, diesel, food and hotel expenses must be deducted but the final figure will still be enough to justify the midnight madness. At least through Kelly's eyes. Leaving Concarneau, Friday night has rolled over and become Saturday morning. But who cares about the passing of another day. Kelly and his companions are now bound for Kortenhoef, near Amsterdam. Eleven-hundred kilometres of roadway stretch before the Citroen and its next destination.

An added hazard as Kelly guides the car east is the flow of oncoming traffic. Paris loses a goodly proportion of it population during the month of August, the great holiday month in the country. It appears to us that most are heading for Brittany. Oncoming headlights dazzle at first, then irritate and finally leave Kelly with a sore left eye. Ronny wears a contact lens and is not able to drive at night against such traffic. The following morning Kelly's left eye would be bloodshot and not a pretty sight.

Conversation for the first hour of the journey is lively. Kelly had not been pleased by Ronny's performance in the race and was talking seriously with his friend and teammate. With his contact lens Ronny found the combination of torrential rain and darkness too much. Kelly reminded him that the rain eased off a little and that he shouldn't have pulled out: 'You should have taken it easy for a couple of laps, pulled in on some quiet part of the circuit when the rain was at its worst and then rejoined the race when things improved. Not a sinner would have noticed.' Kelly, the pragmatist, at work again.

Then the conversation flickered and faded as Kelly was abandoned by companions who had all fallen into the arms of sleep. Seven hours of uninterrupted driving had taken us to Brussels and to within 300 kilometres of Kortenhoef. Kelly looked at his watch and decided he could have three hours of sleep. And so, back to Vilvoorde. It was seven-fifteen when he went to bed but this time sleep refused to join him and for once he lay awake. Over-tiredness was the obvious possibility. It had been three days since this cyclist had slept normally.

At eleven o'clock Kelly was scrubbing his bike — medium hot water first, then a hose down with cold water and finally leaving enough time for the bike to dry off in the sunlight. Before going to bed he had asked Linda to wash and polish his cycling shoes, suggesting that she use a hair-dryer to get the Concarneau moisture out of them. The hair-dryer did its job wonderfully well. Before departure time at midday both the machine and cycling shoes, which had suffered horrendous rain in Brittany, were restored to full and shining health.

The drive to Kortenhoef was pleasant. Near the Dutch town the roads were small and pretty. Little bridges across small canals give the houses an aura of romance. Linda had been taken by the setting: 'Wouldn't it be something to have to cross a bridge to get from the road to your house?' Her less romantic partner had wondered how many drunken husbands it would claim in Ireland? 'Not so good for a man unsure of his step on a Saturday night,' Kelly had mused.

Kortenhoef is a small Dutch town. Kelly and Ronny change into racing clothes in a semi-detached house near the start. A year previously they had changed in a house nearby. Dutch criteriums tend to be over a short, flat, fast circuit, with the bunch travelling very rapidly all through. Those who ride criteriums in Holland remark on the excellent organization, but the Dutch races can be far too regular, almost uninteresting, and appear not nearly as severe as their French equivalents.

Kelly has been four days on the road and is tired. He rides the Kortenhoef race without much enthusiasm. His appearances at the front are few and, for once, the professional in Kelly has been subordinated to the demands of an overworked body. The midnight madness is now taking its toll. That Saturday afternoon the guilders were earned easily. It is left to others to provide the entertainment. Dutch rider Leo Van Vliet wins and his countryman Gerrie Knetemann is in second place. Another small statistic that means little. For the big Dutch crowd in Kortenhoef the attraction lay entirely in the spectacle and not in winners and losers.

During the afternoon Anne Anderson (Phil's wife) and Linda had chatted while their husbands went about their business. An outgoing person, Anne complained that Phil had never been allowed to win a Dutch criterium. A common belief then had been that Jan Raas shaped the pattern of the criteriums in Holland. If Raas did not wish you to win a criterium in his country then there was little chance that you would. Phil Anderson, despite being one of the best and most courageous professionals, had never been permitted to win a criterium in Holland. Anne tended to believe that Raas was the reason for Phil's lack of success in these races and offered the view that the former World Champion was a 'jerk'. Kelly had won two criteriums in Holland in the previous two months so his wife didn't have an opinion on Raas, either way.

Kortenhoef ended before five o'clock, Kelly was back in Brussels before nine and dropping his journalistic companion at the Gare du Nord for a nine-fifteen train back to Paris. The Gare du Nord in Brussels is located in one of the city's most sleazy quarters with ladies of the night glaring indiscreetly from giant windows. Helping to remove his passenger's luggage from the boot, Kelly took a sideways glance and said: 'At least if you miss that Paris train you'll not be short of something to do around here.' He smiled but not with the warmth of one at ease. It was the vague expression of a man not naturally inclined towards sentimental farewells.

That evening Sean Kelly climbed into bed at around ten o'clock. Almost three days to the minute since he had departed for Chaumiel. The mercenary's trail has involved 3,500 kilometres, three races and the gross earnings would have been something around £6,000. Hard-earned. Having settled himself under the bedclothes he quickly fell into a deep sleep. It was five o'clock in the evening of the following day when he returned to the land of the living. Refreshed after nineteen hours sleep, Kelly was ready to go again. The next day, Monday, there was an evening criterium in Stuttgart ....

15 Staying at the Top

As an athlete works his way towards the summit, he enjoys a certain protection. He is then just another aspirant, hidden from his adversaries by virtue of his position in the pack. Once he assumes the place at the top he is identified as the target. Others set their sights and aim for him. Hence the idea that getting to the top is one achievement but remaining there is an even more meritorious one. By the end of 1984 Kelly had clearly established his home on the highest rung of cycling's ladder. During the final days of the 1984 season a drugs controversy had arisen. It couldn't take from what had already been accomplished, but there was the question of how Kelly would recover from the ordeal which the controversy had entailed. After a drugs affair some riders lose enthusiasm for the sport and are never again as forceful. So, people wondered about Kelly. 1985 was going to be an important season for him.

At the beginning of the season Kelly was just three months away from his twenty-ninth birthday. Getting close to the time when Nature might begin to diminish his strength. If Kelly fell from the pedestal in 1985 then 1984 could be dismissed as an exceptional year in the career of a very good cyclist. Kelly wanted more than that. By staying at the top he could force the sport's historians to deal at greater length with his contribution. Staying at the top — that was the test. Since the end of 1983 Kelly had been the most consistent professional on the circuit. His victory in the 1983 Tour of Lombardy had been a first classic win and it lifted him to second place overall in that season's Super Prestige Trophy, cycling's unofficial World Championship series. At the beginning of 1984 he was officially adjudged the World's No.I rider by the FICP Rankings and he maintained that position throughout the year. At the end of the season he claimed his first victory in the Super Prestige Trophy and by a gigantic margin.

As had been the case in the three previous seasons, the first important battleground in 1985 was Paris-Nice. Although clearly below best form and still carrying surplus pounds, Kelly won his fourth consecutive Paris-Nice. It was the first time in the history of the event that any cyclist had won four-in-a-row. A year previously Kelly had tied for the record with Eddy Merckx by winning his third successive Paris-Nice. The fourth victory pleased Kelly, for during the race the fickle nature of sporting stardom was very much in evidence. On the flimsiest of evidence Jean de Gribaldy decided that he had a new star in his team and half-way through the race he believed that this latest protégé could win. Kelly, at least for the moment, was left somewhere in the background.

Joel Pelier was just twenty-two at the time. From Valentigney in eastern France, he lived in the same region as Gribaldy. When Pelier won the fourth stage into Bedoin he also claimed the leader's white jersey. Through the first three stages Pelier had ridden well and in taking the leader's jersey he won the admiration of many. He was an aggressive rider. De Gribaldy raved about Pelier's potential. He spoke of a new Hinault. Publicly Kelly expressed satisfaction that Joel had taken the jersey. Privately he felt a little spurned. His feelings were not helped when, on the afternoon after Pelier had taken race leadership, the Skil team trial performance was severely hampered by their new leader. Pelier had not recovered from his morning exertions and because he was race leader the team had to nurse him along, losing valuable time in the process. At the end of the thirty-five kilometre test, they were in second place, just eight seconds slower than Panasonic.

A day later de Gribaldy's hopes for Pelier faded when the 'embryonic Hinault' was cast to one side on the climb of Mont Ventoux. He trailed into the finish, minutes down on the leaders. Kelly didn't need to say anything to de Gribaldy. The old order was restored within the Skil team. Pelier's eclipse left another Skil rider, Frederic Vichot, in the leader's tunic. Vichot, the best descender in the *peloton*, was then, and remains, one of Kelly's most effective *domestiques*. He had but two days to survive and then the biggest prize of his cycling life was his. Vichot contemplated the prospect of this win and was excited by it. He tried not to let it show because there was still the Col d'Eze time trial at the very end and Frederic never was a good rider against the clock. He led second-placed Phil Anderson by just thirty-two seconds and third-placed Kelly by forty-five. The eleven-kilometre Col d'Eze was likely to change everything. Anderson and Kelly were the favourites and in the order.

The dice were rolled against Vichot in the ninety-eight-kilometre morning spin from Mandelieu to Nice on the final day. An audacious breakaway by Renault rider Charly Mottet catapulted him into the race lead at the half-way point on the road to Nice. De Gribaldy was frantic. He told the team to pursue; all hands were ordered to report to the front of the bunch, all except the protected Vichot and Kelly. Mottet maintained an infernal pace; de Gribaldy told Vichot to join in the chase. Kelly could continue to preserve his strength for the concluding Col d'Eze time trial. Cruelly, Frederic Vichot learned that in a race leader's jersey he was still seen as a *domestique*. Vichot never questioned de Gribaldy's order and the Paris-Nice race leader sacrificed his own chances for Kelly.

It worked our for de Gribaldy and Kelly. The Irish rider delivered a strong Col d'Eze performance, losing out by just one second to the winner, Stephen Roche. What was crucial was that Kelly beat Phil Anderson and Vichot decisively. Paris-Nice was his. Kelly felt disappointed for Vichot but found himself agreeing that de Gribaldy only did what was best for the team. It pleased Kelly that the excitement concerning Pelier died before the end of the race. De Gribaldy's 'new Hinault' assessment wasn't uttered again. Kelly had seen off another rival. This time one from within his own team.

As happened in 1984, Paris-Nice fell to a Kelly some way short of his best form. Six days later he rode the Milan-San Remo. His form had not improved much and Kelly rode defensively, content to shadow Eric Vanderaerden through the final act of the race. All of the other strong men in the *peloton* opted to follow Kelly's wheel and the race was left, consequently, to three breakaways: Hennie Kuiper, Teun Van Vliet and Silvano Ricco. Rarely docile at a post-race inquest, Vanderaerden accused Kelly of being totally negative at the end of the race. Unable to deny the charge, Kelly blamed others, saying that they attempted to profit from his marking of Vanderaerden. Kuiper, the winner, had reason to smile. Vanderaerden (fourth) and Kelly (seventh) were arguing again. Losers' tales to fill out the reports.

That Milan-San Remo underlined the problem which was to face Kelly all through 1985. Every move he tried was countered; each time he lifted his posterior from the saddle eyes flashed. Was Kelly about to try something? Better watch out, Kelly is thinking of moving. The price of being No.I. If Kelly couldn't live with the attention he had better move over and allow others into the top position. At first he complained, said that he couldn't do anything with everybody sucking from his wheel. In a short time the protestations faded. He knew he had no right to expect that it would be different. He learned to live with the attention. Performances throughout 1984 meant he had established a commanding lead in the World Rankings and, regardless of results in the first months of the season, he would stay No.I.

Kelly's concentration on Vanderaerden in Milan-San Remo indicated that he didn't feel especially strong. A week later he tried for a third consecutive win in the Criterium Internationale. Having won the first stage and performed satisfactorily in the second, Kelly was perfectly placed to claim the overall award in the concluding time trial. After 400 metres of that test, he punctured. As the air escaped from Kelly's tubular his chance of victory went with it. A minor setback or a portent of things to come? As No.I it is tempting to believe that Fate is looking to make things difficult for you. Kelly is not one to indulge his pessimism and he believed that things would work out. He went to Spain for the Tour du Pays Basque, a race he had dominated a year earlier.

Spain went badly. Two stage wins couldn't compensate for his not doing better in the overall classification. While in Spain Kelly felt ill, a rare condition for a rider whose health has always been one of his chief strengths. He returned to ride the Tour of Flanders. Spain had been warm and dry; Belgium was cold and wet. The change of environment accentuated whatever troubled Kelly's good health. In the days immediately before the Tour of Flanders he felt no strength in his legs. Linda sensed a problem from his morose mood. He rode the Tour of Flanders even though he was not fit enough to do his talents justice. Sensible riders would have said no, waited for the next race and hoped for an improvement. That's not Kelly's way. He went to the Tour of Flanders, rode strongly for about four-and-a-half hours, and then faded from contention. At the end he was nothing, just another struggling failure. The ashes of the former fire.

A year earlier Kelly had exploded into action on the Mur du Grammont near the end of the Tour of Flanders. Now he crawled up that cobbled hill; forcing the pedals around with slow and heavy strokes. To those who watched closely the man who toiled on Grammont was no relation to the Sean Kelly who had dominated on the same

climb a year earlier. Nobody sought an excuse. Kelly
offered none. The champion was not going well. On the
following day he trained and still there was no force. Linda
worried. A day later he returned from training smiling.
Relieved. He had felt something of the old power and he
left that evening in good spirits to join up with the team
for the Ghent-Wevelgem Classic. He rode well to finish
seventh into Wevelgem. Nothing exceptional, but a performance which demonstrated that the worst of his
problem was over. Paris-Roubaix came four days later
and, at least, Kelly had a chance of performing true to his
ability.

He rode desperately in Paris-Roubaix, determined to
win back the esteem lost on the Tour of Flanders. Yet
Kelly couldn't exercise the control that he enjoyed in Paris-
Roubaix a year before. The extra zip of acceleration that
enabled him to destroy his rivals a year ago was now
absent. He traded purely on strength. Sharp competitive
instincts and marvellous bike handling over the cobbles
enabled Kelly to maintain a position near the front. When
Moser, and later Vanderaerden, attacked, Kelly assumed
responsibility for their recapture. The two leaders were
defeated and twenty kilometres from the finish seven
riders had the race between them. Kelly was most people's
favourite. Everything changed in one instant. A motorcycle crashed, Jeff Lieckens tumbled and Marc Madiot
broke clear. The confusion, arising out of the crash,
helped Madiot's getaway.

The French rider was strong. His lead increased all the
way to Roubaix and he won very decisively. Three
kilometres from the finish Madiot's team-mate Bruno
Wojtinek, relatively fresh because he had been able to sit at
the back of the pursuit, ripped himself clear of the others
and grabbed second place. Kelly and Greg LeMond
sprinted for third, a small victory for the Irishman. Third
place in Paris-Roubaix. In the circumstances it was a brave
and skilful performance. Kelly didn't get much credit.

Madiot had eaten the loaf and the crumbs fell to Wojtinek. Kelly, the target at the summit of world cycling, was being hit. Newpapermen went for the straightforward assessment. The 1985 model of Kelly was good but not great. True to his nature, Kelly tried to get on with things. There is always another race, another opportunity. Stopping for inquests in the middle of the spring classics is not the man's style.

Fleche Wallonne came four days later. Soon after half-way Claude Criquielion attacked and got away with three others. Wallonnia is Criquielion country — the race was important to him. Kelly decided against the pursuit. He and Criquielion were friends: 'I wasn't going to chase down Criquielion, even if I was able to. We generally try not to ride against each other and he had helped me in the 1984 Liège-Baston-Liège.' Criquielion rode spectacularly well to win. Kelly, content to use the race for training, finished a modest nineteenth. Three days later the professional circus was in Liège for the second Ardennes Classic, Liège-Bastogne-Liège. Of all the classics, Liège-Bastogne-Liège represents the fairest test of bike-riders. Kelly had won it in 1984 and wanted to do so again.

He went close. Criquielion, Stephen Roche and Moreno Argentin escaped on the La Redoute climb near to the finish. Kelly, Anderson, Fignon, Guido Van Calster and Mario Beccia pursued. They were just twenty seconds behind. Going through the suburbs of Liège, the three escapers appeared certain to be caught by the chasing five. Just 100 metres lay between them. All it needed was for Kelly, Anderson or Fignon to make one violent lunge and the gap would have been closed. Each one waited for the other to move. In that instant of hesitation a classic was lost. Argentin outsprinted Criquielion and Roche. Seven seconds later Kelly beat Fignon for fourth. Third in Paris-Roubaix, fourth in Liège-Bastogne-Liège; Kelly was getting close but never hitting the mark. Good but not great.

His own analysis probably struck the most realistic cord:

'A year ago I rode Liège-Bastogne-Liège and chased two leaders in a group of seven. We caught them about a kilometre from the finish. I won the sprint. This year I chased three leaders in a group of five. We got within 100 metres of them but didn't catch them. If we had, I would have won. What was the difference between the 1984 and the 1985 performances? I was a bit lucky in 1984 and a bit unlucky in 1985. There is one other point worth noting. I was third in Paris-Roubaix, fourth in Liège-Bastogne-Liège and the only rider to finish well up in both. They are different types of tests; few riders do well in both. I did. And I am not supposed to be going well.' At times when the results are not as Kelly wishes, his pragmatism is a source of strength. No histrionics, no despair and no excuses. On the evening of his fourth place in Liège he was content. He was again riding well.

Jean de Gribaldy has never been one to genuflect at the altar of convention. Polite assessments deem him old-fashioned. Others criticize his treatment of his own riders. They race for their money. Eight days a week if de Gribaldy could manage it. Kelly's rugged constitution allows him to survive de Gribaldy's excesses. Others complain that de Gribaldy ridicules the moaners. Eventually they accept or leave for another, more reasonable *directeur sportif*. A story is told concerning Jean Claude Leclerc, who was being asked to ride an inordinate number of races early in 1985. Leclerc protested to de Gribaldy that he needed a holiday. The *directeur sportif* smiled: 'The last time I had a holiday', said the team boss, 'was when riding the 1948 Tour de France.' The joke was that de Gribaldy wasn't joking.

Even by de Gribaldy's eccentric standards, the programme set out for Kelly after Liège-Bastogne-Liège was horrendous. He was expected to ride the three major Tours; Spain, Italy and France. Almost seventy days racing in less than ninety days. Nobody deemed this a good idea but the sponsors insisted. Kelly's team had three principal sponsors: Skil, Kas and Miko. Kas, a Spanish firm, wanted Kelly to ride the Tour of Spain while Skil insisted that he ride the Tour of Italy. And Kelly *had* to ride the Tour de France. The programme had nothing to do with helping Kelly to regain his place at the top but everything to do with generating publicity. Skil, Kas and Miko paid to have Kelly's services and didn't hesitate to exert pressure.

Confronted by the persuasive men from the big corporations, Kelly is weak. Their insistence that he ride the three Tours tempted him to agree to a schedule that was not in his interests. Kelly planned to ease through the Spanish race, pull out before the end and, in this way, concentrate his best efforts on the Tours of Italy and France. Two days after Liège-Bastogne-Liège Kelly rode the prologue to the Tour of Spain. He found himself in immediate bother. The Spanish newspapers copped what he was about and wrote that he would not finish the Vuelta. Kas's boss, Louis Knorr, was displeased. He asked Kelly what was happening. Kelly said the newspapermen were just speculating, didn't know what they were talking about. Of course he intended to finish the Tour of Spain. Explaining his difficulty, Kelly informed his biographer that he would like to 'hang newspapermen, hang them by the balls.' There wasn't even a hint of malice in his simple wish.

And so he had to finish the Tour of Spain. He struggled in the mountains in the early part of the race and so settled for the three stage wins and the blue jersey of points winner. Louis Knorr was happy enough. Since Paris-Roubaix Kelly had suffered pain in one ankle. In Spain there were days when the ankle hurt badly. He vowed to speak with his Belgian doctor, Rene Vankeerberghen, immediately after the Spanish race ended. On the day after the Vuelta ended Vankeerberghen examined the injured ankle and proscribed ten days complete rest. The

Giro d'Italia, due to begin four days later, was out of the question. Representatives from Skil went to the Nys house at Vilvoorde and tried to get Kelly to change his mind. They said the injury wasn't that bad, swore that Kelly would survive easily in Italy, implored him to go — they had already spent thousands of dollars advertising in Italy. They needed Kelly there. Kelly trusted his doctor more than his sponsor. He stayed at home.

He rested for ten days and did so with the same discipline that is applied to his training. He couldn't eat because he would increase weight and refused to go for walks because it would put a little pressure on his ankle. Confined to inactivity and the indoor life, Kelly was out of sorts and grumpy. The season didn't look so good. Just Paris-Nice and nothing much afterwards. Now a serious injury threatened to bring about ruin. Dr Vankeerberghen's analysis was, however, totally accurate. Ten days rest did precipitate a complete cure. By the time the Tour of Switzerland came round Kelly was again fit and ready to race seriously. He was fourth in the Swiss race, beaten comprehensively by the very much in-form Anderson. A week later Kelly began his eighth Tour de France. He rode consistently well for fourth overall, his best-ever place in the race. He won the points classification easily but was greatly disappointed by his failure to win a stage. Five times he was second. A tale of maddening misses.

Independent verdicts still held that Kelly lacked something — it was not *le grand Kelly*. At the World Championship Road Race in Italy Kelly rode very well until faltering on the last eighteen laps. A week later he needed a good time trial to win the Tour of Catalonia but failed to produce it, and Scotland's Robert Millar accepted a prize he never expected to receive. The season was slipping away on Kelly. What had the champion won? Not enough. No matter what the rider himself thought, the season moved towards failure.

Towards the very end of the season his luck turned. The

change can be traced to the trip back to Ireland to ride the inaugural Nissan Classic, a five-day race which had replaced the Tour of Ireland. Huge sponsorsship permitted the organizers, Sports Plus, to have some of the best riders in the continental *peloton* at the start of Ireland's first major venture into the glamorous world of professional racing. Irish television broadcast a fifty-minute report on the race each evening and huge crowds turned out to watch at the roadsides. Sports enthusiasts in Ireland had waited for years to record their appreciation of the Kelly and Roche achievements. The warmth of the welcome touched Kelly. Not an occurrence that happens easily. Such good riders as Adri Van der Poel, Teun Van Vliet and Hennie Kuiper were amongst the opposition, but the race seemed to rest between the two Irish stars.

Kelly and Roche are good friends but, on this occasion, they were sharp rivals. Kelly decided he wanted to win the first Nissan Classic. He worked all his life on the continent of Europe, winning races in strange towns, before unfamiliar faces. Noticing the disappointment in the faces because the local favourite had not won. Now Kelly was home. Amongst the people he knew. Winning wasn't just a desire, it was an obsession. On the first day to Wexford a ten-rider break formed. Roche was the notable absentee. Kelly immediately recognized the opportunity to rid himself of his chief rival and so he drove relentlessly at the front of the ten-rider group. Into the town of Wexford he outsprinted Van der Poel to claim the first yellow jersey of the race. Roche finished ten minutes down in the *peloton*. A day later Kelly returned home to Carrick-on-Suir in the leader's jersey of the Nissan Classic. The townspeople crammed into Main Street, where the stage ended, and the welcome for Kelly and the race made an ordinary autumnal afternoon in Carrick quite extraordinary.

A Kelly victory would not have offended anyone's sense of the appropriate but the pattern of the race to Carrick precluded a win for the returned hero. Two breakaways,

Leo Van Vliet and Eric Van Lancker, dominated and had the finish to themselves. Roche broke away from Kelly and Van der Poel to be third and, irony of all ironies, Kelly was outsprinted by Van der Poel for fourth place in his home town. He had, of course, retained his yellow jersey and there was considerable compensation in that. All along Kelly knew that the following morning's time trial from Carrick to Clonmel was the decisive leg in the race. He could lift himself clear of Van der Poel and Teun Van Vliet on the relatively flat road to Clonmel.

This was a time trial that Kelly had to win. The evening before he attended a reception in the magnificent Ormond Castle in Carrick, and it was apparent even then that the time trial absorbed him. After posing for the customary photographs, Kelly was pinned in one corner by a journalist, who started firing questions. He raised his hands, said he would only answer if he could sit down — he had a time trial to ride the next morning and standing now would make it more difficult for him to win. He sat and talked for ten minutes but had disappeared before anybody knew he had left.

The Carrick to Clonmel time trial will remain as one of the finer moments in Kelly's eventful career. Even though the prize at stake was modest, the responsibility on Kelly to win was enormous. He used the burden of others' expectation to intensify his own motivation. Appropriately, the test began in Carrick's *Sean Kelly Square* and, as race leader, Kelly was last to drive down from the starting ramp. All the way to Clonmel he concentrated on getting the pedals around as swiftly as possible. If he maintained concentration, then he could not relax. His head was crouched just above the handlebars; beads of perspiration dripped from his forehead on to his nose and then dropped on to the road. All the time Kelly not allowing himself any respite from the pain. This was Kelly territory and he wanted all to know that, in this part of the world, he reigned.

It was easy to see that he was on to a good performance.
Yet one was not prepared for the sight of both Van der
Poel and Van Vliet within catching distance on the
outskirts of Clonmel. Kelly surged and went past his two
principal rivals. He had taken over two minutes on Van
Vliet and over a minute on Van der Poel. The Nissan
Classic had been decided in Kelly's favour. He beat Roche
by forty-nine seconds. Roche wondered what happened
for he believed his time to be very good. Over the
remaining two days of the race Kelly was happy to let
others help themselves to moments of glory. Roche won
into both Cork and Limerick, Teun Van Vliet escaped for
a stage win in Galway, and Van der Poel was rewarded for
a very good performance throughout the race by victory in
the concluding Dublin stage. From the outset Kelly sought
just one prize and was satisfied that he claimed it with total
authority.

Victory in the Nissan Classic didn't mean much on the
continent of Europe. Kelly's season was still viewed as a
disappointment. Yet it wasn't over. Not for Kelly. The trip
to Ireland provided a refreshing antidote to the list of
failures and near misses he suffered throughout the
season. Boosted by the reception he received at home and
encouraged by his form, Kelly envisaged a way of
salvaging his year. Of turning it around and actually
making it successful. His plan centred on the Super
Prestige Trophy. While Kelly was losing, Phil Anderson
had been winning: entering the final two classics of the
season, the Australian was the clear leader of the season-
long competition. Kelly was second, sixty-nine points
behind. The extent of the deficit should have discouraged
Kelly, but he knew that if he could do well in the Creteil-
Chaville and Tour of Lombardy Classics and Anderson
not be placed, then he would leap-frog over his rival.

Not quite as outrageous as they seemed, Kelly's hopes
depended as much upon Anderson failing as they did
upon Kelly succeeding. But it was known that Phil had lost

form and was unlikely to rediscover it in the last two Prestige events. Kelly was aiming at somebody else; he was again the challenger and much more comfortable in the role. Anderson worried a little but didn't genuinely believe that Kelly could overhaul him. His wife Anne wondered whether it was mandatory to wear a tuxedo at the Super Prestige Award ceremony. It was to be one of the great achievements of Phil's career so far and, on his performance throughout 1985, one to which he was eminently entitled.

16 Survival

Going through the town of Etampes, things began to happen. There was eighty-five kilometres to the finish and suddenly every move was important. Creteil-Chaville, France's final classic of the season, offered interesting possibilities for Kelly. On the climb out of the town he was near the front. The severity of the pace on the hill precipitated a split in the *peloton*. At that moment Phil Anderson was changing a wheel, caught doing the wrong thing at the most inopportune time. About twenty riders were clear after Etampes. Kelly was a member of the leading group. In the group immediately behind, Anderson and his Panasonic team-mates worked furiously. At first the lead was about thirty seconds. It jumped to a minute but then shrunk to just thirty-five seconds. Kelly rode forcefully to distance himself from Anderson. That was the primary consideration. The lead went back up to one minute. There was now forty kilometres remaining and it appeared certain that the Australian was not going to get into the placings in this race.

Satisfied that he had seen off Anderson, Kelly began to think about how he could maximize his chances of gaining the necessary Super Prestige points to overtake his rival. The animal's instinct took charge. The important things flashed instantly before him. Creteil-Chaville and the Tour of Lombardy are first-category classics and points are awarded on the basis of sixty, forty, thirty, twenty down to five points for the tenth place. Kelly needed to win one and finish well up in the other to get the points

necessary to beat Anderson. And even then Anderson had
to finish out of the top six in both races. Thirty-five
kilometres from the finish at Chaville, Kelly assessed the
composition of the leading group. Four riders from the
Kwantum team dominated: Kelly had team-mate Frederic
Vichot at his side, while Moreno Argentin, Jean Luc
Vandenbroucke and Teun Van Vliet were also going well
enough to be classed as dangers.

Kelly didn't like the chemistry of the group. Basically
there were too many riders and the Kwantum representa-
tion was worryingly strong. He reckoned that his chances
of winning were slight although he was convinced that he
should finish in the first three or four. His principal fear
was that Kwantum would use it numerical strength to get
one of its riders clear before the finish. Kelly considered
that it was time to do a deal. He had an offer which he
believed the Kwantum riders could not but accept.
Addressing himself to Van der Poel, Kelly suggested that
if one of the Kwantum riders attacked, he would not
pursue and that rider would win on his own. Kelly would
be happy to sprint for second place. Van der Poel saw the
advantage for his team; if Kelly wasn't going to chase their
breakaway then the most formidable obstacle to a Kwantum victory would be removed.

Although highly interested in Kelly's proposition, Van
der Poel wasn't blind to the obvious: 'But Sean what is in
this deal for you?' Kelly, of course, had a price: 'All I ask is
that in the Tour of Lombardy next week the Kwantum
riders will not work against me at the finish.' Van der Poel
didn't have to contemplate the proposal at any length. He
accepted. The deal almost assured his team of victory in
Creteil-Chaville; and the Tour of Lombardy — well, that
was in the future. On the curiously named Cote de
l'Homme Mort (Dead Man's Hill) six kilometres from the
finish at Chaville, Van der Poel attacked. His move was
countered immediately. As he was caught, his team-mate
Ludo Peeters surged clear. All the time Kelly sat still.

Nobody else had the strength to counter Peeters — the
race was his. All according to Kelly's scheme. At the finish
line in Chaville Ludo Peeters was twenty-one seconds clear
of the six riders fighting for second place.

Kelly's plan involved him winning this sprint but he was
easily beaten by Argentin. Third place still meant thirty
Super Prestige points. He now trailed Anderson by thirty-
nine points with just one race to go. Phil finished thirty-
sixth, four minutes and fifteen seconds down. Rumours of
his poor form had not been exaggerated. Kelly was
pleased by the course of Creteil-Chaville; he knew that he
had a real chance in the Tour of Lombardy. The thing
which continually struck him was the fact that the winner
of the Super Prestige had to be accepted as the most
consistent rider for that season. If he won this award then
who could say he had an indifferent year? Playing for
extremely high stakes again, Kelly was on good terms with
himself and with his cycling life.

Lombardy entailed difficulties. The usual one in the
classics — team support. Kelly's Skil team ranked somewhere in the middle division of professional outfits. It
tended to be good during the early season, reasonably
strong in the Tour de France, but singularly inadequate in
the classics. For a race like the Tour of Lombardy Kelly
could expect little from his team. He spoke with de
Gribaldy about which Skil riders should be brought to
Italy. The *directeur sportif* said he didn't favour paying
expensive air-fares for cyclists whose principal interest in
Italy would be good food. Kelly accepted the point. They
agreed to take just five; Eric Caritoux, Rene Bittinger,
Jorg Muller, Frederic Vichot and Johan Habets. Of the
five Kelly reasoned that only Muller would be capable of
rendering real service over the hilly Lombardy route.

In a very fast Tour of Lombardy the Skil team was
obliterated. Kelly never saw one of them over the final
sixty miles of the race. Muller, unluckily, crashed when
going through an unlit tunnel and the other four simply

did not count when the race reached its decisive stage. As
so often happened in the classics, Kelly was left on his own.
Afterwards the journalists zoomed in on the non-existence
of the team support. Kelly evaluated his team's contribution with grim realism: 'They did their best. I hadn't
expected much. French riders normally don't do very well
outside of France and, anyway, it is the end of the season
and everybody is tired.' One journalist pressed Kelly
further: 'Look my team-mates are not like bad grey-
hounds; I can't take them, stand them up against a wall
and shoot them.' Another suggested Kelly could join a new
team and get better support for himself: 'If I were to leave
there is a good chance that this team would disappear.
That would mean ten, maybe twelve riders without a job. I
would find it very hard to do that.'

Kelly's attitude to his team has always been interesting.
De Gribaldy is not one of the big *directeur sportifs* and his
team tends to be modest. Around Kelly he builds a loyal if
somewhat ordinary team. Each year Kelly vows at some
time that it must improve but that never happens. Mostly
because de Gribaldy is more comfortable dealing with the
less-talented type of rider. In some ways the team
composition suits Kelly. The nature of the back-up means
that Kelly's position as leader is unchallenged and even if
his *domestiques* are not the best, they are at least loyal.
There is also the financial implication. As the giant in a
relatively small team Kelly commands a huge contract.
The team's sponsors don't buy Jean de Gribaldy's team;
they purchase the services of Sean Kelly and are merely
forced to take the rest.

After Creteil-Chaville Kelly chatted with Anderson and
was encouraged. He formed the impression that Phil had
no form and consequently no stomach for Lombardy.
Because of his position at the top of the Super Prestige
table, Anderson and a very strong Panasonic team went to
Italy for the final classic of the season. It was rumoured

that Panasonic tacitly sought support for their man. Kelly felt very relaxed. His form was good. As a twenty-year-old he won the amateur Tour of Lombardy in 1976, and in 1983 he achieved his first professional classic win in the Tour of Lombardy. Now he came to his favourite battleground to save a season and win the Super Prestige series. Anderson wasn't going to get the prize easily.

The 1985 Tour of Lombardy began in Como and finished in Milan's Vigorelli Stadium, a route that was in direct contrast to the normal Milan-Como race. From the very start it was a truly competitive test. After just fifteen of the 158 miles, the Intelvi Pass presented itself. A frenzied charge up that hill scattered the *peloton* into fragments. On the descent fifteen riders had forged a clear advantage. Van der Poel and the talented Canadian, Steve Bauer, were part of that group and so there was consternation in the pack. A vigorous pursuit, lasting almost twenty miles, recaptured thirteen of the breakaways. That left just two others, Giuseppi Saronni and Kim Andersen, who persisted with the attack. The pack was not prepared to relax and continued to chase. This was going to be a real race.

Saronni and Andersen were eaten up on the Esino-Lario climb after sixty-five miles. On that long hill Robert Millar and Silvano Contini set an extremely severe pace. Kelly, Acacio da Silva and the relatively unknown Italians, Giuponni and Calcaterra, were immediately behind. Anderson toiled ineffectively on the Esino-Lario, losing ground all the way to the top. At the summit, Millar, Contini, Kelly, da Silva, Giuponni and Calcaterra led by fifty seconds. Kelly faced a dilemma: 'It was hard on the mountain. Millar and Contini made a very fast tempo. The descent was also difficult. I decided that if there was no reaction from the bunch I would ride all out with the other five. If, on the other hand, the bunch chased then I was going to keep a good bit in reserve. There was still a long

way to the finish and I was not about to gamble everything
with this group.'

The bunch did pursue and the six were caught after
riding for about thirty miles at the head of the race. Kelly
didn't mind, for he had ridden conservatively in that lead
group. It was on the descent into the town of Lecco that
the leaders were enveloped. A new attack formed immediately. Eight riders went clear. Van der Poel, Marc Madiot,
Mario Beccia and Gerard Veldscholten were in that group,
and when it established a two-minute lead it appeared as if
Kelly might have missed the important train to Milan. At
the foot of the Ghisallo climb the eight breakaways had a
two-minute thirty-eight second advantage. On the winding
ascent of the Ghisallo, Kelly led the nine-rider pursuit. At
the front, Madiot and Beccia pedalled clear of the other
six, and crossing the summit the two leaders were one
minute and firty-five seconds up on the Kelly group.
Thirty-five miles of road lay between the riders and the
Vigorelli Stadium.

After the Ghisallo the route to Milan involved mostly
flat terrain and so favoured the pursuit which ate into the
advantage of the two leaders. Kelly's prospects were
greatly assisted by the presence of Claude Criquielion in
the *posse*. He and Kelly had shared many moments
together in the *peloton* and, even though on different
teams, they were mostly on the same side. They got on well
together. As Criquielion liked to say: 'Two boys from the
same rural background.' The Belgian rode very strongly
in pursuit of Madiot and Beccia. So, too, did the Spaniard
Marino Lejarreta. He, Criquielion and Kelly were strongest. Having picked up the stragglers from the original
Madiot/Beccia group, the pursuing party numbered fourteen. Ten miles from Milan it all ended for Marc Madiot
and Mario Beccia. They were swallowed up by the
speeding train behind them. Kelly moved closer to the
great prize.

By this time a defeated Phil Anderson had long pulled

out of the race. Time lost on the Esino-Lario climb could not be regained and Anderson climbed off and returned to Milan in a team car. Having showered, he waited in the Vigorelli Stadium with team-mate Eric Vanderaerden. They heard reports of the race's progress over the public address system. Kelly was in the leading group. Although pessimistic about the outcome, Anderson still hoped for a late attack from one of the other fifteen riders in the group and prayed that Kelly would not finish in the first two. Through the suburbs of Milan Kelly controlled everything. With Criquielion's considerable help he ordained a pace that was fast enough to discourage all aspiring breakaways. Potentially two of the most dangerous members of the group were Kwantum's Adri Van der Poel and world champion Joop Zoetemelk, but Kelly had tied their hand a week earlier in Chaville.

Through Kelly's eyes only the two Renault riders, Madiot and Charly Mottet, represented serious worries: 'Mottet was an experienced track rider and I thought he would be able to sprint well in the stadium.' Five hundred metres before the entrance to the stadium Madiot attacked and Criquielion, faithful to the very end, followed immediately. As the riders entered the stadium Anderson's eyes strained to make out the jerseys. Vanderaerden noticed his nervousness, even thought his team-mate was shaking. Madiot led the string into the Velodrome, then Criquielion, Mottet, Kelly, Van der Poel. Again Kelly let his instinct rule: 'I knew that if I moved up to Mottet's chainring I would encourage him to go for a long sprint, something that would suit me.' As Kelly crept closer, Mottet surged past the two in front. Without apparent effort, Kelly stayed in his slip-stream.

Twice Kelly glanced behind to make sure that Van der Poel was not contemplating a betrayal of the Creteil-Chaville agreement. The Dutch rider was racing for second place. Around the final bend Kelly moved high on to the banking of the track and flew past Mottet. Anderson shrieked *shit*. Kelly won easily. Van der Poel came through late to take second place. It was Kelly's fifth classic success and his second Super Prestige Trophy. At the end of it all he had twenty points to play with. A dejected Anderson returned to Belgium that evening and flew home to Australia immediately afterwards. A year earlier Lombardy was the location as an anguished Kelly tried to protest his innocence of a Paris-Brussels drugs charge. It was ironic that precisely a year later he should be experiencing one of his greatest triumphs in the same region. After the season of sustained excellence in 1984, 1985 had been especially difficult. Kelly fought, often lost, persisted and at the very end emerged gloriously. Survival.

And so a season turned. All through 1985 Kelly retained his No.I position on the computer rankings and the Super Prestige victory emphasized his consistently high level of performance. The events of the season pin-pointed Kelly's chief attribute — his ability to withstand the strain of one of the world's toughest sports. He started the season by winning Paris-Nice, missed narrowly in many big races in between, but finished with an outstanding success in Lombardy. Durable? A major understatement. Easier to think of Kelly as an animal whose natural habitat is harsh and inhospitable. Resilience can be found in every aspect of his life: Curraghduff, his parents' background, his own upbringing, his relationship with de Gribaldy, his own lifestyle as a professional and his performance on the bike. The man was bred to survive.

Being physically equipped to cope with the life is a major component in the survival process, but there is a corresponding need for mental strength. A decade of cycling on the Continent has taught Kelly much. He has fitted into the European way of life easily. When he sought an arrangement with Van der Poel in Creteil-Chaville he was understood. Kelly knew from an early stage in his professional life that without the respect of your fellow-riders it is almost impossible to succeed. Roche says that

Kelly is liked because he is proper: 'The other pros know that if Sean says something he means it. He is straight. If he agrees to ride to some tactical plan with a leader from another team then he will stick to it no matter what happens. Some riders cannot be trusted but Kelly is one who can.'

Coping with Jean de Gribaldy's loose organization demands both patience and resourcefulness. Kelly intended leaving Milan for Paris a few hours after the race ended. He was scheduled to ride the Criterium des As in the French capital on the following day and wanted a night's sleep before the race. But, without mentioning anything to his rider, de Gribaldy accepted an invitation for Kelly to attend a banquet in Milan that night. Organized by a Swiss/Italian cycling body, the banquet was arranged months earlier and the group were honouring Kelly with a special medal to commemorate his 1984 performances. De Gribaldy told the organizers that Kelly would attend. Kelly was told a few hours before he was supposed to leave Milan. He stayed and ended up leaving by car for Geneva at two o'clock in the morning. He arrived into Geneva a few hours before he was to take an early morning flight to Paris.

He landed in Paris around breakfast time on Sunday morning, more tired from the lack of sleep than the physical exertions of the Tour of Lombardy. He had signed a contract to ride the Criterium des As and was going to honour it. Not only that, Kelly won the race. He actually beat Eric Vanderaerden in the sprint for victory. A ninety-nine kilometre motor-paced event, Kelly averaged thirty-two miles an hour in the Criterium des As. You wondered why he had gone to the trouble of winning a race that mattered little? Kelly felt he had two reasons: 'My form was excellent in the Tour of Lombardy and the way I viewed it, I was running out of races. This was my last race of the year. There was also the pleasure. For me it is always a pleasure to beat Eric Vanderaerden.'

Three days later Kelly and Linda went to Spain for two

weeks of sunshine. Two of his closest friends, Ronny
Onghena and Philippe Poissonier, and their wives went
also. It is interesting that Onghena and Poissonier should
be close to Kelly for, even within the modest team of de
Gribaldy, they are two of the lesser figures. Their
closeness to Kelly means that the World No.I is never able
to forget what life is like at the other end of cycling's
spectrum. Pounding out the same effort as the star for
£300 a week. Philippe, 35, has three children; they are old
enough to take an interest in their father's career. They
understand nothing of *patrons* and *domestiques* and continually ask Philippe why Kelly always wins and their Daddy
always loses. Philippe laughs as he tells the story. He says
he doesn't know what he'll do after cycling: 'I prefer not to
worry about the future. I live from day to day.'

During the season Kelly moved into a new home which
he and Linda bought in Vilvoorde. The six years with
Herman and Elise Nys ended very amicably and the Kellys
are now near neighbours to Herman's son, Gustav and his
family. Herman and Elise remain parental in their
devotion to Sean. Linda insists that the Spanish holiday
was the best they ever had. Her husband's pleasure at
winning Lombardy infected the atmosphere in Spain and
Kelly was at his happiest. That meant Ronny and Philippe
spent the two weeks trying to anticipate Kelly's next prank.
Those who know him in Carrick tell that Kelly is a 'terrible
caffler'. Somebody who would do the daftest thing and
find it funny.

He returned to Carrick in early November for his three-
month winter break. Soon he was going through the fields,
rifle slung under his arm, eyes flashing in search of a stray
rabbit. He is an extremely good shot. Ditches, climbing
over gates, looking at cattle, bringing home a dead rabbit
— that's the world in which Kelly appears most comfortable. During the winter he prefers to forget the big
mountains and the small gears of the Tour de France.
According to Linda's brother Gerard (with whom the

Kellys stay during the winter) he will occasionally stay up late and watch videos of some of the major races of the season. But they are the exceptional nights.

From time to time during the winter journalists show up; the off-beat feature, a radio interview, a piece reviewing the season. He rarely turns anybody away. Some want to go to his home place in Curraghduff. Kelly says okay. They meet Jack and Nellie, parents who have steadfastly maintained positions in the background. The farmhouse at Curraghduff hasn't changed over the last fifty years. Just as Jack and Nellie haven't changed. The people and the dwelling, modest and old-fashioned. Kelly introduces the journalist to his parents without any explanations or qualifications. *These are my parents; this is where I came from.* It is not in his nature to make excuses or to play the man that he is not. His faithfulness to his own nature invariably earns admiration. To Jack and Nellie he is the middle son. Only different to Joe and Vincent in that they don't see him so often.

This uncomplicated background has helped Kelly enormously. He was able to get on with his career in his own way. His parents admired what he was attempting but could never interfere. Sean was a man. He would stand or fall by his actions. Such is the tranquility with which the Kelly family accept his greatest achievements that there was never the remotest possibility that the cyclist would get notions of fame or importance. They tell a relevant story in Carrick. It dates back to 16 July 1982. A Friday morning in the town's Main Street. The previous day Kelly won the Pyrenean stage of the Tour de France. Carrick's cycling fraternity was ecstatic. One of its most committed members was walking down the street. Beside himself with happiness, he wanted to find somebody with whom he could relive the story of Sean's wonderful triumph. Eventually he encountered Neddie Kelly, Jack's brother, Sean's uncle.

Our friend had read every morning newspaper and

explained in great detail the merit of Kelly's Pyrenean achievement to Neddie. Nothing was lost in the telling. He wondered what Neddie thought of his nephew now? After this great win? What now Neddie? Neddie Kelly surveyed the cycling enthusiast severely and then pronounced judgement: 'Why wouldn't he win the race; sure he does nothing else except ride that damn bike.' The two parted company. Both, a little wiser.

17 Le Tour

Daniel Mangeas's voice towers over the confusion. Another Tour de France stage has ended and the Tour's official speaker is providing the details. Two columns of solid gents from the Gendarmerie have sealed off a rectangle encompassing the finish line. Riders search for their *soigneurs*, a team leader finds his and wonders why he hasn't brought an over-jersey. Colds can be picked up on the ten-kilometre ride to the team hotel. Journalists knife through the human forest, searching for tomorrow morning's quotes. Ten minutes to speak with six. Above it all Mangeas reigns. This is his world. Regular tourists have heard this voice each day during the month of July and look upon the enthusiasm as they look upon the deep and sometimes violent panting of the riders at the end of a hard day. A part of the Tour scene. Horns hoot as race cars force a passage through the crowds. Once again hundreds have found chinks in the human barriers set up by the Gendarmerie. Sign a postcard, sign a hat, look up for the instant it takes to click the camera. Courtesy is expected. For seven hours prisoners of the road. Now, for a further fifteen minutes, prisoners of the fans.

It might be any day on the Tour. But it is the tenth day of the 1985 race. Epinal, a town in north-eastern France, is the overnight resting place. Thirty-one years previously the Tour had pitched its tent in Epinal. Now, for the second time in the history of France's great race, Epinal reminds the world of its existence. Official information given to the 400 Press tourists states that Epinal is a town 'preoccupied with its future'.

So, too, that evening in Epinal Sean Kelly was preoccupied with his future. His conception of tomorrow's world might not have extended beyond an imminent rendezvous with the peaks of the Alpine region but the preoccupation was still real enough. Kelly had to be pinned into some corner that day in Epinal. Immediate answers were needed to a battalion of questions, a journalist forgetting that the same questions were posed yesterday, would be posed tomorrow. On the Tour the basic survival theme pervades all. Every question could be compressed into one and the answer to that comes on the classification sheet each evening. But such a compression diminishes the Tour, makes great stories irrelevant. Silly questions must be asked for, sometimes, they get lively answers. Animation can emerge from the dullest and most unlikely situations.

Kelly should have been highly pleased in Epinal. But one is never sure with the man whose highs are not very high and whose lows are not very low. Ten days of the race had passed, the first mountains had been climbed that day and Kelly's Tour was progressing nicely. He lay third overall and was holding three of the Tour's six prized jerseys. Green for Points, red for Intermediate Sprints and the combination jersey for doing everything well. That meant three visits to the Tour Podium in Epinal; enough to madden the heart of the weary rider and gladden the heart of his sponsor. As Mangeas packed away his enthusiasm and his voice drifted into silence for another day, Kelly sat on the bonnet of some car and played with the questioner:

'Yeah today went well, got over the two climbs okay. Three jerseys in the Tour is not bad, I'm not complaining. Anderson was the one who struggled today; when the speed went up on the first climb, he simply blew. Came to a standstill. I think he left his best form in the Tour of

Suisse. Yeah, Hinault was strong today, very strong. Just
sat there turning that big gear.' But look hold on. Let's get
back to Anderson. How could he so dominate you in the
Tour of Switzerland three weeks ago and now the
indications are that you will have the better Tour? 'As I
was saying, Phil is not going as well here as he was in
Switzerland.' No, there has to be more to it than that. Your
form, Kelly, is much better in this race?: 'Maybe it is. When
you ride the Tour it is different. You think back on the
races you have ridden earlier in the season and it seems
that in those races you were only riding to 85 per cent of
your limits. You didn't think that at the time, but now you
know it was so. But this, the Tour, this is the 100 per cent
race.'

Sometimes Kelly gave it more than 100 per cent. The little
bit extra that carried him beyond the boundaries drawn by
those concerned with the need for a sporting Tour. Three
times Kelly earned much publicized disqualifications at the
end of Tour de France stages. Not one of his contemporaries can boast such consistency in the misdemeanours
department. In the midst of the greatest controversy of all
in 1980 when Kelly endangered the health, even lives, of
Jan Raas and Jos Jacobs in Nantes, the assistant *directeur
sportif* of his team Splendor, Luc Landuyt, told the world
that Sean 'was the most charming of boys'. It was just this
affair with the Tour de France. It had the capacity of
inciting instincts, otherwise dormant. Kelly might say 100
per cent. Others might deem it a lot more.

There are cyclists who, at the beginning of each year,
will contemplate their programme for the coming season
and grant a special significance to the Tour de France.
Mostly, they are the proven Tour winners and the lightly
built brigade. Hinault could always afford the luxury of
concentrating his mind on the Tour objective. It was a race
he knew he could win. The lightweights like the Tour
because they like racing when the gears are low and the

gradients steep. People like Lucian Van Impe, Pedro
Delgado and Robert Millar. People like Luis Herrera and
his friends in Colombia. For them the Tour is everything.
The world watches while they dance on the pedals. Sean
Kelly feels differently about the Tour. The big mountains
and the intense heat never cheered his summer. His big
bones, broad shoulders and long back were never designed for life at high altitude. But the Tour was *le Tour*
and you had to be there, competing. What would the 15 or
20 million roadside spectators say if you were absent?
When you get there, you give 100 per cent. Or more. A
race that one might be afraid to ride but more afraid not to
ride.

When Kelly finished fourth in the 1985 race he had
achieved his best-ever placing. Encouraging that on the
eighth consecutive attempt the best result was forth-
coming. Proof that the man who is not a natural on the
long Alpine climbs can compete, can apply himself to a
subject which he abhors. Kelly's eight Tours have all had
their moments. The first in 1978 when he was 34th; then
38th in 1979, 29th in 1980, 48th in 1981, 15th in 1982, 7th
in 1983, 5th in 1984 and 4th in 1985. Never has he
abandoned the Tour — to do so would offend his
professional conscience. At the beginning of each Tour
Kelly will say 'I hope to do better than last year'. A modest
ambition but one that satisfies this conservative. He has
never believed himself capable of winning the Tour de
France and his performances in the race should be viewed
in that perspective. When he failed on Alpe d'Huez in
1984 it seemed to Kelly that he had been offered utter
proof of his vulnerability in the Tour. Riding a 2,500-mile
epic demands a certain obstinacy. The will to carry on,
regardless. Kelly has that. Just because one felt incapable
of winning shouldn't halt the pursuit and, anyway, there
were prizes other then the yellow jersey.

Since his entry into the race in 1978 Kelly has won five
stages of the Tour and, far more startling, has finished

second on twenty-two occasions. Twice second place was taken away for what the French quaintly label 'irregularities in the sprint'. He is listed amongst only four men to have claimed the green jersey of points winner on three occasions; Jan Janssen, Eddy Merckx and Freddy Maertens being the other three. A historic fourth green seems well within the scope of Kelly's career. Because he neither had the climbing talent or the spiritual recklessness to try for the heroic, Kelly's deeds in the world's greatest bike race will soon fade into the outer reaches of the memory. Some things are, however, worth hanging on to.

Maybe the most striking memory is of sprinting scrapes. Kelly's disqualification in the 1985 Tour followed cycling's equivalent of the bar room brawl in the finishing straight of Reims. A day later I spent an hour talking with him as the Skil team bus travelled from the finish in Nancy to the Hotel Novotel on the south side of the city. Kelly had both the time and inclination to explore this question of his sprinting and his annual contretemps with the international jury operating on the Tour. Twenty-four hours after a stormy and ill-tempered confrontation with Eric Vanderaerden of Belgium, Kelly's anger had mellowed into philosophical acceptance. Every year there were big sprints in the Tour de France, he reflected; in one of those sprints something dangerous would happen and somebody would get disqualified. Kelly wondered why it was that he was always a central player in the drama. Before the obvious answer could be suggested he had jumped further on in the argument, stating that the controversy did not bother him. 'It is publicity,' he philosophized, 'bad publicity maybe but publicity all the same. Given a choice, I think the sponsor would prefer bad publicity to no publicity at all.'

But what of being the dangerous one in the *peloton*? The one who cares not for others' safety? *L'Equipe's* highly esteemed writer Pierre Chany, reporting on the 1980 Tour from Nantes, wrote: 'There is no doubt that Sean

Kelly exposed himself to the danger of a catastrophic accident yesterday, but in the same incident he also endangered other riders and it is certain that Jos Jacobs was the principal victim.' Few sportsmen can survive without the respect of their peers and Kelly has, generally, worked hard to court that respect. For a few days during the Tour in 1980 he became the unloved desperado. People wanted him to come to his senses. At the end of that infamous Nantes stage, half of Jacobs's Ijsboerke team wanted to forcibly knock sense into Kelly's head.

Disqualification of sprinters in the Tour receives much attention and comment at the time. Then the controversy fades and one waits subconsciously for the next. When it arrives it will invariably seem more dangerous, more contentious than the old ones. For they are a fleeting, spontaneous occurrence. Of major interest today, an irrelevance tomorrow. Yet Kelly's involvement in the three most publicized sprint controversies in recent Tour history suggest something that might not be immediately forth-coming in the after race interview. By tracing those three incidents you learn something about the direction and make-up of the by-roads in his mind. Chronologically the sequence begins on the road to Nantes on the ninth stage of the 1980 Tour.

As the *peloton* sped into the city in the west of France, Peter Post's superb Raleigh team was preparing itself for a seventh stage win in ten days. Road captain and then world champion, Jan Raas, was seeking his third stage win of the race. Part of the Raleigh strategy was to make life difficult for the other sprinters in the race and, as the bunch wriggled through the streets of Nantes, Kelly sensed the presence of Raleigh men near him. Rounding a corner 600 metres from the finish Raleigh's Leo Van Vliet rode directly in front of Kelly. At the appropriate moment Van Vliet slowed; Kelly had little choice but to go for his brakes. Instinct, unfettered by fear, led Kelly to grab Van Vliet and cast him to one side. Three hundred metres from the line Kelly had another Raleigh rider, Johan Van de Velde, in his path. He, too, was pushed to one side. Despite losing momentum clearing a passage for himself Kelly was still in third place with 100 metres to go. In front of him were just two riders, Raas and Belgian Champion Jos Jacobs.

Raas takes up the narrative: 'We were sprinting shoulder to shoulder. Jacobs and I. Then I suddenly looked across and instead of Jacobs's black, yellow and red jersey, there was a blue jersey. I knew that something abnormal had happened and after the line I saw it was Kelly and knew he would be disqualified.' Jacobs and his Ijsboerke team-mates, Rudy Pevenage and Ludo Peeters, wanted punishment meted out immediately and were all volunteering for the role of executioner. Kelly's version of the finish doesn't exactly exonerate him: 'When I finally got into a good position I had Raas and Jacobs in front of me. There was room to go between them at first but as I went for it the gap narrowed. When I got there it had vanished and with their pedals touching my front wheel I could only free-wheel. I could have conceded that I wasn't going to win but I caught Jacobs' jersey and pushed him out to the right and so made enough room to pass.'

Those who saw Kelly surrounded by a would-be murder squad from the Ijsboerke team detected more than a touch of fear in his eyes. Here was an isolated Irishman, operating in the big league and getting caught throwing a low punch. Kelly says he worried not about the Ijsboerkes and their thirst for revenge: 'I was much more afraid of the race jury. They might have thrown me out of the Tour.' Although it had been no ordinary transgression, the jury was lenient with Kelly. He was merely demoted from second place to last in the *peloton*, 108th, fined £100 and penalized fifteen seconds.

Ten days later Kelly won into St Etienne. He could now speak about Nantes. To have done so earlier would have been to invite further criticism. Victory in St Etienne had

come in a way that left no questions: Kelly breaking away
with the Spaniard Ismael Lejarreta and easily outdis-
tancing his rival in the sprint. Everything had been fair.
Speaking to *L'Equipe's* Jean Marie Leblanc, Kelly said the
game he played in the sprints had been ordained by
others. He merely conformed to the rules as laid down by
the sprinters themselves. He accused Raas of being
particularly unfair and added that if he (Kelly) was
dangerous it wasn't for pleasure. Luc Landuyt knew what
he was talking about: 'the most charming of boys'.

Nantes was important for Kelly. Even with his instincts
there was a line beyond which one did not travel in the
sprinting Jungle. Nantes had identified that line. Kelly,
twenty-five, had learned a lesson. At the time he refused to
acknowledge the need to temper his ways but in future his
aggression would be laced with discretion. The mix would,
however, lean more on the side of aggression. If Nantes
1980 had been unholy the Alencon affair in the 1984 Tour
was quite extraordinary. Even confirmed students of
Kelly's behaviour were astounded. The story runs thus.

A long sweeping straight in the city of Alencon, 4 July
1984. A lone Italian Simone Fraccaro dangles thirty
metres ahead of the sweeping *peloton*, frenetically calling
on every ounce of strength. Like a man trying to run away
from a tidal wave. Soon he is engulfed. The multi-
coloured mass is spread across the road, just 200 metres
remaining. Kelly wants this win, badly. Anxiety tempts
him to reach for the pedals too early, the Swiss sprinter
Gilbert Glaus is travelling smoothly in Kelly's slip-stream.
Claus moves to pass through a gap between Kelly and the
right-hand barrier. As Glaus surges there is sufficient
room for him to come through. Kelly senses the danger
and, moving to his right, makes things a little tighter.
Glaus is a sprinter and so he persists. Kelly's right elbow
shifts positions. Where previously it was straight, now it is
pointing wickedly in his rival's direction. Glaus backs off.
Sensibly. As he does so he raises his left hand in protest.

As the sixty kilometres per hour sideshow is being acted
out, Frank Hoste charges on to centre stage to win the
race. The third dog who snatches the bone. Kelly sees
Hoste late and, having dispensed with Glaus, moves to
counter his new rival. Too late. Another Tour second. In
the press room about 200 journalists watched the finish on
closed-circuit television, all concluding that it would be
another 'declassement pour Kelly'. At the finish line third
placed Eddy Planckaert said it was 'a dirty sprint' by Kelly.
Glaus' *directeur sportif* Auguste Girard officially objected to
Kelly's tactics in the sprint 'for the safety of everybody'. In
his defence Kelly said the road narrowed near the finish.
Where there had been room for Glaus with 100 metres to
go, there was no room closer to the line. Most considered
that evaluation implausible. Certainly the race jury was not
enthused. Kelly was disqualified, his second place became
134th, he was docked the customary fifteen seconds and
fined £100.

So far all was par for the Tour course. One reckless
sprint, Kelly the culprit. 'C'est normal'. That evening in
Alencon was splendidly summery and having despatched
damning reports to Ireland, the bizarre notion of visiting
the Tour villain assumed a certain attraction. Along with
John Wilcockson of *The Times* I set off for the St
Marguerite de Navarre school which housed Kelly in
Alencon that evening. *En route* we discovered from the
Tour's lodging list that Glaus's team was also staying at the
school. Driving up the avenue we felt a sense of foreboding about invading Kelly's privacy on this evening. The
extraordinary was about to present itself.

Getting out of the car we could see Kelly in navy
tracksuit talking to a group of riders. They were in red.
Ah, the Cilo Aufina team of Glaus. A little closer and we
could see that Kelly was actually talking to Gilbert Glaus.
Retreating to the car, we waited for Kelly's diplomatic
mission to end. The presumption had been that Kelly was
mending fences, improving Irish/Swiss relations. Five

minutes later Kelly had moved back to his own team-
mates, sitting on the steps at the front entrance to the
school. He didn't appear to mind the unscheduled
journalistic call:
    'Having a little talk with Glaus, Sean?'
    'Ah yeah, nothing much.'
    'Apologizing for what happened today?'
    'Why should I apologize? 'I wasn't wrong!'
    'So what were you just saying to Glaus?'
    'I was telling him that he would be well advised to
withdraw the objection lodged by Girard. That if he didn't
withdraw it he would suffer, maybe not tomorrow but
some day. I have watched the sprint on television this
evening. The road narrowed.'
    As he recounted, Kelly cast pebbles at some unseen
target. But who can say for sure that the target was
unseen? In Kelly's mind's eye it was probably Glaus. The
following day there was a sixty-seven kilometre time trial
to Le Mans. Glaus started at 12.18. Twelve minutes later
Kelly set out. By three-quarters distance Kelly had wiped
out the deficit and on a gentle rise went past Glaus with
ruthless authority. He never even looked to his left in
acknowledgement of Glaus's existence. Sometimes revenge
does not come wrapped in physical force. As Wilcockson
and I drove away fom St Marguerite de Navarre the urge
to re-inspect the finishing straight diverted us. Incredible.
The road did narrow appreciably close to the line. Kelly's
theory had not been as far-fetched as the world had
imagined.
    Two weeks later the entire story was recalled. Kelly
protested his innocence with the usual vehemence. I stuck
to the contention that he had transgressed. All along I had
wondered how Kelly had felt about the fact that my
reports to Ireland, both on radio and in the newspapers,
had accused him of being ruthless and unsporting in
Alencon. At home his family, friends and neighbours
would have heard the accusations: 'The way I see it', he

said as he weighed up the situation confidently, 'is that some people will agree with me, others will agree with you. Either way it should make for good argument in the pubs around Carrick.' Was it Oscar Wilde who claimed that 'there is only one thing worse than people talking about you, that is people not talking about you'.

And so, that was the Alencon affair. The third part in this terrible trilogy of Tour disqualifications was acted out, somewhat indecently, under the gaze of the splendid cathedral in the centre of Reims. The finishing straight travelled along Rue Libergier stopping just under the shadow of the cathedral. For those with an eye for the co-incidental, the Reims controversy happened on 4 July, precisely the same day on which the Alencon affair had occurred a year earlier. Could it be something about the way Kelly interprets the meaning of Independence Day?

Again, disorder came with the arrival of the heaving *peloton*. A day earlier Kelly had won the bunch sprint for second place into Tourcoing; now there was an obvious opportunity for his first stage win since 1982. He opted to track Eric Vanderaerden. Two hundred metres from the line Kelly accelerated to overtake the Belgian. There was maybe ten yards between Vanderaerden's left shoulder and the barrier. Half of the bunch could have streamed through the gap at the same time. As Kelly moved to pass Vanderaerden the passage narrowed. The Belgian wasn't letting Kelly through. No way. To stop the stubborn Irishman, Vanderaerden drifted so far to his left that Kelly found himself sandwiched between a Belgian wall and an aluminium barrier. He pushed Vanderaerden away. Suddenly the Belgian moved sharply to the right and cut off the challenge of Francis Castaing. Kelly pursued, seeking retribution but only earning a disqualification. His own description of the incident lingers: 'Having a boxing match is one thing; having one at sixty kilometres per hour on bicycles is, I suppose, another thing altogether.'

This time Kelly was dropped from fourth to 126th in the stage placings, penalized fifteen seconds and fined £100. The usual stuff. After the finish he was full of fury — for once he had been more sinned against than sinning. Without Vanderaerden's blatant offence Kelly would have won. His transgression had been retaliatory. Sprinter's instinct. Both riders had to fulfil podium duties and that brought them together. Kelly called Vanderaerden a *salaud* (not a polite French term) and the Belgian responded by asking what would have happened if the positions had been reversed. Bernard Hinault was also in close proximity, voicing his disapproval of Vanderaerden's tactics: 'With you Vanderaerden it is always the same — today you get Kelly on the left and then Castaing on the right.' Vanderaerden ignored the intrusion and continued to ask Kelly what he would have done if the positions were the other way around. As Kelly argued the flame of extreme hostility burned itself out. Left with just another defeat he was ready to answer Vanderaerden's question: 'Yeah', he replied, 'I suppose I would have done exactly the same as you did.' For Kelly the sprinting wheel had come full circle. Yesterday the killer, today his victim. He was honest enough to acknowledge that only circumstances altered the roles.

Sprinting blows in the Tour are delivered and absorbed without too much disturbance to the lives of the protagonists. Lose one, win one. Allow one's instinct to have a free reign occasionally. It is all a part of the game. Without the unholy sprint the Tour would be a lesser race. Kelly didn't mark the Reims experience under career catastrophes. He had already won five stages of the race; you win another, you win another two. Nobody will much notice the difference. The sprinters only make up one of the Tour's sub-plots. Greater expectations and longer-term misery ride with the yellow jersey. The magical *maillot jaune*. One day during the Tour of 1983 Kelly got his body into that jersey. Became the focus of the Tour's primary gaze.

He had also realized a career ambition. Wearing the prized yellow in the world's greatest bike-race.

10 July 1983. The ninth stage of the Tour has ended in Pau, has arrived at the edge of the race's first major battleground, the Pyrenees. French rider Philippe Chevallier triumphs on his own, Dutchman Gerard Veldscholten is second and Kelly wins the bunch sprint for third place. Ten seconds for third takes Kelly over Kim Andersen of Denmark and into the leader's jersey. Kelly also has the green, Stephen Roche has the white for best young rider and Ireland has hijacked the Tour de France. Journalists quizzed Kelly — he said he would like to wear it all the way to Paris. That was the public expression. Privately Kelly maintained that to wear the yellow in the Tour was an honour. On the road to Pau an opportunity existed to achieve that honour. He went for it. One never knew if the chance might come again.

Kelly wasn't at all sure of what would unfold in the Pyrenees. A month earlier he had ridden majestically in the Swiss Alps to win that country's National Tour. All of France sat around the table with Kelly and wondered what kind of cards he had in his hand. Deep down Kelly felt they might be duds. All through the 1983 Tour the sun had scorched. Geoff Nicholson of *The Observer* had described it as the hottest Tour since Tommy Simpson had collapsed and died on Mont Ventoux in the 1967 race. Kelly has never liked intense heat. The route from Pau encompassed the Aubisque, Tourmalet, Aspin and Peyresourde mountains before descending to the finish at Luchon. At the foot of the Aubisque the *peloton* exploded. Colombians and other lightweights behaved like starving children at a feast. They went upwards at one speed, a few followed and the majority were shelled out. Kelly was one of those to suffer devastation.

On the third of the four mountains, the Col d'Aspin, lines of people queued to sup at a mountain stream. Waiting was thirsty business. Others were attracted to-

wards the sounds of transistors. Reports of battles on the
Aubisque and Tourmalet enriched the feeling of anticipa-
tion. Kelly had lost six minutes on the Aubisque but there
had been a general regrouping in the valley before the
ascent of the Tourmalet. On that mountain the race
splintered again, this time for good. At the summit of the
Tourmalet the yellow jersey was reported to be fifteen
minutes and eleven seconds down on the leaders. Who
knew for sure? By the time he reached the summit the
leaders would have had further opportunity to increase
their advantage. Flanked by loyal team-mate Joacquim
Agostinho, Kelly climbed the Aspin steadily. Twenty-four
hours earlier the yellow jersey had been a bright new
garment. Resplendent. Now it was heavy with perspiration
and Kelly's feeling of failure. A burden. People at the
roadside tried to encourage. Sympathetic applause. Others,
less sensitive, pointed to the one in yellow, aghast. Then the
stare switched from the jersey to their wrist-watches: *'le
maillot jaune a treize minutes, oh la la!'* At the summit of
the Aspin Kelly had cut his losses to thirteen minutes and
then down to ten minutes and eleven seconds by the time
the brave loser reached Lunchon. It had been a sad day, a
sobering experience. Who wants *le maillot jaune*? Kelly
concentrated on his green and wore it all the way to Paris.

A year later Kelly survived the Pyrenees but floundered
on Alpe d'Huez. But then he had not entertained genuine
hopes of taking the yellow. Just hanging around in the hope
that others would crumble while he survived. Sometimes in
cycling it is enough to merely stand under the tree and wait
for the apple to fall. When Kelly died on Alpe d'Huez in
1984, that was it between the Tour and him. Fini. Try for a
place of respectability in future years. Fourth in 1985 was
especially commendable. On three stages when the race
finished at the summit of a mountain in 1985 Kelly finished
second, third and fourth. Okay, not the original Angel of
the Sky; the man could still grit teeth and fight pain.

'Le Tour' has been good for Kelly and he has, in his

own way, been good for the Tour. One remembers his contribution not in terms of one heroic exploit but for the daily efforts. Lurking near the front of the *peloton* in the final thirty kilometres, preparing for the sprint for first or twenty-first place. Rarely refusing to compete. Then, on other days, trying to stay with the front group in the mountains. Face contorted, digging in.

A similar spirit pervades in the time trials. His performance in the penultimate stage of the 1984 race might serve as an epitaph to Kelly's affair with 'Le Tour'. As a contest the Tour was long dead. Laurent Fignon had the race all to himself for over a week. He led the second-placed Bernard Hinault by almost ten minutes, the fifth-placed Kelly by sixteen-and-a-half minutes. Already a winner of the race's two previous time trials, all the indications were that Fignon would win his third over the rolling and precious countryside between Villie Morgon and Villefranche-en-Beaujolais. Fifty-one kilometres of single combat. Kelly delivered a time of one hour, seven minutes and 19.263 seconds. Barely able to get in one ear, those fractions rushed out the other. With the Tour just one day from completion, and heads almost exploding from the surfeit of figures, we could do without the .263. Or so we imagined. One kilometre to go and Fignon was told that he trailed Kelly's time by two seconds. He surged madly. One hour, seven minutes and 19.215 seconds. What were those Kelly fractions?

Kelly sat by the finish line. He immediately knew the fractions had tipped in Fignon's favour. 'French pigs', was the initial reaction. Unreasonable but understandable. Somebody whisked him away for a television interview. 'Sean, here we are in Villefranche-en-Beaujolais, you have wanted a stage victory all through this race, you have been beaten by .048 of a second. How do you feel about that?' 'It was a fix,' said Kelly. Stumbling silence. Interviewer wonders what next? Kelly leaves it at that. Instinct had again been the guide.

In the press room we sympathized with poor Kelly. Hard to imagine the French race leader losing a race against the clock by .048 of a second in the Tour. But, surely, in these days of electronic timers one can be certain, even down to .048 of a second. A couple of weeks later Jean de Gribaldy told this writer that the Electronic Computer for taking times on the Tour had been out of service that Saturday afternoon in the wine-country of Villefranche. Hand operated chronometres had been used. Suspicious. Kelly has long confined that encounter with Fignon to the dungeons of his memory. A lot of things happen in a decade of riding Tours — why remember the pain? Still, the perceptive one might inscribe on Kelly's headstone:

'Here lies a man who once lost a fifty-one kilometre time trial in 'Le Tour' by .048 of a second. He said it was a fix.'

18 The Afterlife

Linda Kelly couldn't help feeling disappointed. It was late January 1986. In a couple of days her husband was due to leave Carrick for the start of another season. His tenth. Nine months of competition lay before Kelly. His winter at home was relaxing and enjoyable. He should have been feeling a bit down at the prospect of leaving Carrick for the Continent. Should have been but wasn't. That was why Linda felt disappointed. She had noticed Sean's spirits rise during the days immediately before departure. Nothing he did or said, but more his general air. He had been away from the *peloton* for three months. Now he itched to get back. Racing commitments in Spain, France and Italy meant Linda would not see him until the middle of March, six weeks later. Kelly wasn't looking that far ahead. His first race of the season was only one week away. Yes, he was a little excited. He couldn't help it if he liked what he did for a living.

It didn't surprise Linda. Had it not always been thus. This writer recollects a scene in the Dutch town of Meerssen after the 1984 Amstel Gold Classic. Kelly, Linda and the Nyses waited for Stephen Roche to finish with Dope Control. Roche and Kelly were travelling back to Paris together while the others would head back to Vilvoorde. Linda sat on her husband's Citroen. As she moved away from the car, she left a mark where her hand had rested. Fastidious in the extreme, Kelly wiped away the mark. Never said a word, just cleaned the area which had been stained. Mildly annoyed Linda complained that

Sean's priorities were first his car, then his bike and finally
his wife. Kelly heard the accusation, turned and with a
look of deadly seriousness told his wife that she had got
the order wrong: 'The bike comes first'. What could the
chastened lady say?

Through the winter of 1985 Kelly's love for the bike was
at its most obvious. In his scheme of things November is a
month when he purposefully avoids cycling. He will go to
the gym, play some indoor soccer, go for a run but stay
clear of the bike. In November 1985 he found a way
around that. A few afternoons each week he packed a
mountain bike into the boot of his car and drove to the
nearby Curraghmore Estate. There, in the cool quietness
of the tall trees he cycled away to his heart's content.

An hour, maybe an hour and a half; that was enough on
the mountain bike. It wasn't so much the exercise or the
innate thrills of mountain biking but the setting which
pleased Kelly. A man could clear his head in that wood.
Linda says she remarked that when he returned from the
wood at Curraghmore, previously unresolved issues were
sorted out. For Linda, the overwhelming feeling was a
man attached to his bike. The thirteen-year-old who
wriggled a Raleigh All-Steel through a line of churns and
barrels in his father's farmyard was still affected by the
same obsession sixteen years later.

In his early years as a professional Kelly anticipated
earning as much money as he could and retiring when he
was thirty. He didn't realize then that life doesn't work like
that for the professional sportsman. Retirement, for most,
is a course of action precipitated by the decisions of others:
the sponsors who aren't interested any more, the coach
who says he is looking for somebody a little younger, the
doctor who decrees that the body is no longer fit for battle.
At the age of twenty-nine, and at the end of his ninth
season, Kelly signed a two-year contract with the Spanish
firm Kas and so will ride for Kas up to the end of 1987.
Official details of cycling contracts are never disclosed but

it is known that it was the most lucrative deal of Kelly's career.

Money has always been a source of fascination. Primarily because of Kelly's secrecy on the subject and the widespread belief that he has earned huge amounts throughout his career. Kelly's joke is that journalists think of the biggest telephone number they know and work from there. That they are totally unrealistic in assessing his earnings. But the journalists would not have to guess if reliable information were provided. Yet Kelly's secrecy is understandable. He is not any different to most professional sportsmen. For ten years of his life he has done nothing except train, race and rest. Going to bed at nine o'clock, eating special foods and learning to suffer. That's his life. It is a cruel, crude and highly precarious way of earning a living. All it takes is one crash and Kelly, the legend, becomes nothing more than another question set by the Sports Quiz-master.

De Gribaldy insists that Kelly's reputation for being obsessed with money is very unfair: 'I have bargained with Sean for a decade. He is not that concerned about this side of the sport. He earns a lot but it is never a big thing with him.' Calculating the extent of Kelly's earnings is difficult and a task which gets no assistance from the rider himself. For the first five years of his professional career his annual income was not particularly impressive, but from 1982 onwards it grew enormously. Now he is one of the biggest earners. His basic contract for twelve months would be approximately £200,000. Kelly denies it is this high, but the figure, if anything, errs on the side of understatement. After that there are bonuses and endorsements. Kelly's manager and business confidant in Ireland, Frank Quinn, has promoted the rider with some success in his native country.

From the very beginning Kelly appreciated the importance of making his life on the bike pay: 'Professional sportsmen might say different things but they compete, in the first place, for the money. If they claim otherwise they lie.' When Kelly didn't have much money he talked about his hope to accumulate enough to be able to leave the sport and never have to work afterwards. A nice notion but, for Kelly, utterly impractical. What would he do? Put his feet up and read books? Yet Kelly has been careful with his earnings and he may have already realised his ambition to make his life after cycling secure. He will leave the sport a very wealthy man. And why should it not be so? Each penny earned corresponds to a moment of suffering, a bead of sweat, or a chocolate mousse that had to be resisted. Kelly knows he would have been a fool to squander the fruits of his efforts: 'It was hard earned and it will be hard spent.'

Cycling had done more for Kelly than merely provide the financial means to live comfortably ever after. As a teenager he was intensely shy, verging on the mysterious. His inability to communicate with strangers was a problem which surfaced with increasing regularity as Kelly achieved success on the bike. After winning a stage of the Tour of Britain Milk Race as a nineteen-year-old he was interviewed on Irish radio. The interview wasn't an outstanding piece of broadcasting, and it was said after-wards that Kelly was the only man who ever nodded in answer to a question on radio. He lived with his own inhibitions through the early years and eventually he became a more confident and expressive person. He now speaks French fluently, has a reasonable understanding of Flemish and a smattering of both Spanish and Italian.

Even when his answers were curt and monosyllabic, Kelly was an interesting character. Now he can be a truly engaging companion; clever, witty and unqualified in his modesty. Before leaving Ireland for the first races of 1986 he was the guest speaker at a seminar organized by Guinness in Dublin. Kelly was to speak with cyclists in the capital. No speech, said Kelly. Just ask questions. They did, and Kelly's replies fascinated. Somebody asked would Sean train on a really cold day, one of those days when you look out of your window and know it is freezing outside. Kelly had met many people during his career like this questioner. 'The thing', he said, 'about the cold is that you can never tell exactly how cold it is from looking out a kitchen window. You have to dress up, get out training and when you come back, you then know how cold it was.'

An older rider, Tony Allen, who rides in veterans' competitions, seemed a little uneasy as he began his question. He wanted to know about, er, ah, Sean's, er, ah, sex life. Like, in relation to his racing. Before the big races, did Sean engage in, *you know what I mean*, before the classics and the major tours. Many of the younger ones giggled, some blushed. Kelly wasn't in the least put out. Taking the question with total ease, he replied: 'I think it is an understandable question, whether a top rider should have sex before a big race or not. My policy is to abstain for a week before a one-day classic and about six weeks before a major Tour. Usually I am away from home for a long time before a major Tour so there is no problem there.'

The young studs in the audience were visibly taken aback. One of them, Raphael Kimmage, did a little adding up, turned to the lad sitting alongside and said: 'By my reckoning, Linda is still a virgin.' And so Kelly went on amusing, informing and delighting his admirers. The man who nodded on radio. At first he could only express himself in pedal strokes. But he did that so well that he eventually found the confidence to be able to use other methods of expression.

And what of the afterlife? Kelly's early career notion of getting out at thirty has long been dismissed. Such is the excellence of his health that it is easy to imagine him competing for another five years. At the very least. How can the entertainer leave the stage when the crowd is still screaming for an *encore*. A crowd that is willing to pay £200,000 to watch him perform. It takes a bricklayer about twenty years to earn that kind of money. Born in a different Irish town and Kelly's life would probably have been spent on building-sites.

Such is his love for the sport that some of those close to him fear he may be enticed into the management of a team after his own career ends. He is a highly organized person and his attention to the details of the cycling life has become famous. Kelly's bike is always in the best condition, and his devotion to training, diet and rest is beyond the comprehension of most. Yet he is easy to live with, good fun and sympathetic to those whose standards are not like his. Results testify to his competitiveness on the bike. What a *directeur sportif*? Kelly says not likely. 'Sitting behind the wheel of a car driving at thirty miles per hour. That's for others.'

Kelly's life after racing will revolve around Carrick-on-Suir. He wants to spend the 'second part of his life' back in the environment which prepared him for his time on the Continent. There is some good land around Carrick-on-Suir which Kelly wants to farm. Apart from riding the bike, farming is all he knows. Now, it is all he needs to know. He will miss the thrill of a heaving, exhilarating sprint finish and, in a strange way, he will miss the pain which is so much a part of earning a living by the seat of your bike. Nothing can replace the friendship and fun which exists in the *peloton*. The real laws of the *peloton* are made by the riders. Only they know the rules. The bond which links the racers is strong. Men who remain together, defiant. What does the world know about racing up a mountain when the temperature is close to freezing-point, or almost 100 degrees Fahrenheit?

But neither will Kelly get sentimental when it is all about to end. A shrug, a grimace and the reminder that it was bloody hard. What of the good days? Sure there were good days. All the wins. Almost 120 professional victories in nine seasons. And the *fun*. What about the *fun*? Like the day in the Amstel Gold race when Ronny Onghena asked for a drink. Kelly laughs before recounting: 'It was during the early part of the race, not much was happening. I had to pee and, for a laugh, did so into my *bidon*. I knew 'Alex' (i.e., Ronny) was thirsty and asked him did he want a drink. He was very grateful and accepted my *bidon*. He asked me why it was warm, I told him it was hot tea that Herman (Nys) had just given to me. Herman always gave us hot tea. 'Alex' ripped the top of the *bidon* with his teeth and, realizing what was happening, threw it as far away as he could!'

There is more to this man's life than a great sprint.

Epilogue

Seventeenth July 1984. Location, the Tour de France. The day after. Kelly's traumatic defeat on the climb of Alpe d'Huez the previous day had not prevented him from sleeping. He was in reasonable condition for the 185-kilometre race to the mountain finish at La Plagne. It was, probably, the most severe test of the race. At the end of it Kelly had survived.

Leaning against a barrier for support, he was pleased that evening in La Plagne. He said how relieved he was to come through such a hard stage. Particularly after Alpe d'Huez. On Alpe d'Huez Kelly encountered his own limitations every time he turned a corner. On the road to La Plagne he could have taken it easy. He wasn't going to win the Tour anyway. But that was never his way.

Few noticed the merit in Kelly's seventh place at La Plagne. The mob which crushed against the wall of gendarmes sought not to shake the Irishman's hand but to catch sight of Fignon. As always, only one winner. All that didn't inhibit Kelly's feeling of satisfaction. Nine minutes down on yesterday's mountain, a survivor today. The performance jumped Kelly from twelfth to seventh. By the time he began moving towards his team car, the gendarmes had given up the fight to keep the crowd back. Thousands came forward and engaged in an orgy of Fignon-gazing. Kelly was able to leave quietly. He wasn't going to win the Tour but he was going to get on with it. And, he was going to get to Paris as fast as he could.

Kelly's Career Record

Principal Amateur Successes

1972
Junior Champion of Ireland

1973
Junior Champion of Ireland

1974
Shay Elliot Memorial Classic

1975
Three stage wins in the Tour of Ireland
Stage win in the Tour of Britain
Shay Elliot Memorial Classic

1976
Tour of the North Overall
Tour of Majorca Overall
Stage win in Tour of Ireland
Stage win in Tour of Britain
Tour of Lombardy Classic

Complete List of Professional Successes

1977   4 wins
G. P. Lugano
Circuit de l'Indre
1st stage of Tour de Romandie
4th stage of the Etoile Espoirs

1978   4 wins
3rd stage of the Tour de Mediterranean
1st stage Semaine Catalane
6th stage of Tour de France
5th stage of Etoile Espoirs

1979   4 wins
G. P. Cannes
Willebroek Criterium
1st and 5th stages of the Tour of Spain

1980   13 wins
Three days of the Panne Overall
Criterium de Panne

Criterium St Niklaas
2nd stage of 3-Days of the Panne
1st, 2nd, 14th, 17th, 19th, stages of the
   Tour of Spain
3rd stage of Dauphine Libere
19th, 21st, stages of the Tour de France
4th stage of the Tour of Holland

1981   9 wins
St Pieters-Leeuw Criterium
Mellet Criterium
Tienen Criterium
3rd stage of Tour of Belgium
2nd stage of 4-Days of Dunkirk
1st stage of Tour of Luxembourg
15th stage of Tour de France
5th stage of Tour of Holland

1982   15 wins
Tour Haut-Var

3rd, 5th, 7th, 8th stages and Overall
  Paris-Nice
2nd stage Criterium Internationale
2nd stage Midi Libre
1st and 2nd, stages Tour de l'Aude
12th, stage Tour de France
Plessala Criterium
Lannion Criterium
1st and 3rd stages of Etoile Espoirs

1983   16 wins
3rd, 4th, 7th stages and Overall
  Paris-Nice
2nd stage and Overall Criterium
  Internationale
4th stage Tour of Europe
3rd, 5th, stages and Overall Tour of
  Switzerland
Stuttgart Criterium
2nd stage Paris-Bourges
Bellegarde Criterium
G. P. d'Isbergues
4th stage Etoile Espoirs
Tour of Lombardy Classic

1984   33 wins
G. P. Aix-en-Provence
2nd, 7th, stages and Overall Paris-Nice
1st, 2nd, 3rd., stages and Overall
  Criterium Internationale
1st, 3rd, 5th, stages and Overall Tour
  du Pays Basque
Paris-Roubaix Classic

Liège-Bastogne-Liège Classic
Tour of the North West (Swi)
1st stage Tour of Switzerland
Stuttgart Criterium
Bussieres Criterium
Elsloo Criterium
Manchester Criterium
Almelo Criterium
G. P. Plouay
2nd, 4th, stages Tour du Limousin
Paris-Bourges
1st, 4th, (a&b), 7th, stages and Overall
  Tour of Catalonia
Blois Chaville Classic
Criterium des As

1985   19 wins
2nd stage Tour of Valencia
Overall Paris-Nice
1st stage Criterium Internationale
3rd, 7th, stages of Tour du Pays Basque
2nd, 9th, 15th, stages of Tour of Spain
Wielsbeke Criterium
Troyes Criterium
Viane Criterium
Emmen Criterium
3rd stage Tour of Holland
2nd stage Tour of Catalonia
1st, 3rd, stages and Overall Nissan
  Classic Tour of Ireland
Tour of Lombardy Classic
Criterium des As